The Three Worlds
of Leonid

The

THREE WORLDS

OF LEONID

Leonid Berman

WITH A PREFACE BY *Virgil Thomson*

Basic Books, Inc., Publishers   New York

Translated from the French by Olivier Bernier

Library of Congress Cataloging in Publication Data

Leonid, 1896–1976
The three worlds of Leonid.

Includes index.
1. Leonid, 1896–1976 2. Painters—United States—
Biography. I. Title.
ND237.L56L46   759.13 [B]   78–54503
ISBN 0-465-08618-7

To Sylvia

Quand on me demande où je suis né, je réponds tout naturellement : à St-Pétersbourg, oubliant totalement que je vis vis le jour à la campagne, aux environs de la capitale, où mes parents passaient leur été cette année là ; erreur d'autant plus compréhensible que je ne suis jamais retourné au lieu de ma naissance. Et pourtant l'endroit en question était Peterhoff, une des résidences estivales des Tzar, située à une faible distance de la capitale et ressemblant à Tivoli par ses fontaines dont les jets de terrasse en terrasse deversaient leurs eaux dans le Golfe de Finlande. Que moi je commette cette erreur, passe encore, mais que mes papiers d'identité, établis après la revolution en Finlande, la reproduisent est plus sur prenant, car mes parents y contribuèrent. Quant à moi cette erreur du passeport Nansen m'a ravi ; l'introduction de St Petersbourg pour l'étranger était préférable à celle de Peterhoff que peu de Français connaissaient. Pour moi, St-Pétersbourgeois dans l'âme, Peterhoff n'est qu'un accident. Comme tous ses habitants je voue un amour mystique, immodéré et quasi charnel à la capitale. Est-ce les nuits blanches, les brouillards, la course folle des traîneaux l'hiver le long des quais de la Néva, les mirages nordiques, les majestueuses perspectives d'architecture qui ont forgé le type très spécial du Petersbourgeois racé, rêveur, sentimental, élégant, élancé, les cheveux et les yeux noirs, la tête petite et étroite, type auquel je crois avoir l'honneur d'appartenir, sauf, hélas,

Contents

Contents

Preface

BY VIRGIL THOMSON

LEONID read constantly. Pushkin and Proust were his addictions. He loved too the crime stories of Georges Simenon. We shared these regularly, easily 200 of them.

He also wrote regularly, almost every day. Certainly in emergencies, those times in Russia when he was either moving fast to avoid capture or lying doggo somewhere in the Caucasus for the same reason, he kept a diary and wrote in it almost every day. Sometimes it was on scraps of paper that he later managed to preserve during the long trek across defeated France, from extreme northeast to southwest, trying to rejoin his disorganized regiment and to keep ahead of the advancing German armies. Also under the German occupation during his year or more of forced labor in the region near La Rochelle, breaking stones in road work and building the Atlantic Wall. Indeed these passages, liberally quoted in his autobiography, are by far the most vigorous.

After leaving Russia he wrote in French. He even translated into French poems of Pushkin. I have never seen the whole literary output, but I did read some years back a quite wonderful book about the French fishing ports, illustrated with photographs taken by himself of fishermen at work and of the flower-like presentations of fish set out for sale in certain ports. There may also be a book about fishing procedures on different parts of the French coast. I remember something of the sort from the times before 1940, when he would travel from one to another of France's three sea fronts, always painting those

(ix)

seas and their folk as a vast interpenetration of land and water with people working there.

How Leonid came to find his vocation as a painter of such subjects is not approached in this book, nor did he ever at any time essay to explain it. But it had begun, I think, around 1925 or 1926 in the south of France, with painting the Old Port of Marseille from his window at the Hôtel Nautique. And it led him all his life to seek maritime variants in Portugal, in New England, in Indonesia, Egypt, Venice, and the Gaspé Peninsula. Curiously, he never attempted Holland, a seaman's dream. But those landscapes had been so thoroughly painted by the Dutch themselves that they might have been hard to see through a man's own eyes.

A sportsman from his earliest youth, slender, small, a strong one and never ill, Leonid seemed not to be more than briefly inconvenienced by the hardships of war, revolution, exile, and forced labor. No more did a busy love-life wear him down, nor the sedentary practice of literary composition waste his muscles. During several periods his painting was interrupted— during the revolutionary troubles in Russia, during his service time in the French army, his travails in the Todt battalion, and in the amorous servitudes of an exhausting two-year marriage. But each time he came back to real life, which for him was that of a painter, unbroken, unhurt, one might almost say refreshed.

At fifty he moved to America and married, this time for good. And it was from New York that he traveled worldwide, painting other seas and other fishing folk, though save for rice fields in Northern Italy and the terraced paddies of Bali, virtually never waters that were not salt.

Beyond the normal dramas of creation, Leonid's life between fifty and eighty was serene and vastly fruitful. Like many another painter, he kept himself busy, though that busyness often consisted of whole afternoons in movie houses, where he found joyous activity for the eye in that dreamworld of images black, white, and grey. Actually, when films began to take on color Leonid began to give them up. But every day he painted and wrote and read, and summers in the country he played tennis and swam. Even his married life with Sylvia Marlowe, virtuoso of the harpsichord with a professional performer's high temperament and tension, unrolled itself from day to day and year to year as quietly as if it were another film and he no actor in it but merely the unruffled observer of all that action and its courteous helper out front.

His earlier life had been always melodramatic, but by now he had learned repose, and earned it. For the next thirty years he worked quietly and was happy. From birth happiness had been a gift, but during youth and up to full maturity no quietude or calm had ever lasted. America and marriage gave him three decades of an untouchable inner peace. And it was during that time, I think, that with much practice in writing already accomplished, he set out to tell his life story.

That telling was no pouring out of confessions like Rousseau's, though it does possess large fragments of detailed narrative put down like camera shots of reality live and quivering. Neither is it a story aimed at an audience or at any publisher. It actually resembles more than any other writing I know the autobiography that Mark Twain partly wrote and partly dictated over a period of years, knowing that it would not be published entire during his life.

In this way he could tell practically all, and so could Leonid. Not with malice, for there was none in either of them. But in a relaxed frame, with full memory of the delights and horrors and with a narrative view of himself as having passed his childhood and youth and manhood among live people.

That was Leonid's quality as a man. He always spoke of people not as members of any type or group but as characters. And he reproached no one for being as he was. This way of viewing makes for an interesting narrative and for landscape painting of infinite variety.

If this variety turns out in the painting to be mainly variations on a theme, that theme is one compulsively chosen, like

Preface

a vocation, and stubbornly adhered to, like a friendship. With a man so consistent within himself that variations are welcomed and contrasts tolerated, friendship is indeed a privilege. My own with Leonid lasted fifty years. Naturally I was sorry when his life was over. And so it was with this truly told story. I was sorry when it came to an end.

PART I

CHILDHOOD

Chapter 1

Saint Petersburg

WHEN I AM ASKED where I was born, I answer quite easily: in Saint Petersburg, I say, completely forgetting that I first opened my eyes in the country, near the capital, where my parents were spending the summer. My error is all the more natural in that I never returned to the place of my birth. And yet, that place was Peterhof, a small distance from Saint Petersburg, where the Tsars had one of their summer palaces. The water of its fountains, leaping from terrace to terrace all the way to the gulf of Finland, was reminiscent of Tivoli.

Now, that I should repeatedly make this mistake is natural; what is surprising is to find it inscribed on my identity papers, since they were filled out by my parents in Finland after the war. As for me, I was delighted by this mistake in my Nansen passport: abroad, Saint Petersburg was a better introduction than Peterhof, which was largely unknown, especially to the French. Besides, I always felt Peterhof to be a mere accident; like that of all its other residents, my heart always belonged to Saint Petersburg, which inspired in me a mystical, boundless, and almost carnal love. The white nights, the fogs, the mad dash of the sleighs in winter along the banks of the Neva, the northern mirages, the majestic architectural perspectives, all seem to come together to create that very special type of refined Petersburger, dreamy, sentimental, elegant, tall, with black hair and eyes and a small, narrow head—a type to which I feel proud of belonging, except, alas, that I am rather short. When Peter the Great created his capital in the midst of the marshes, he "opened a window onto Europe." The proverb "Scratch a Russian and you'll find a Tartar" may apply to a Muscovite but never to a Petersburger, whose looks and culture are European.

I must return to my 1917 Nansen passport. It carries a second mistake, on account of the difference between the Julian calendar then in use in Russia and the Western, Gregorian calendar. Here again, the mistake pleases me: I was born on June 6, 1896; if you add up all the numbers, 6 plus 6 plus 1 plus 8 plus 9 plus 6, you will get 36, which is divisible by 3, 6, 9, 12, 18, and even 36! I myself don't believe in numbers but I do find it all amusing and am proud that the Allies should have landed in Normandy on my birthday, thus giving me the best birthday present I ever received. The complex lines of my hand, which always delight palm readers, also confirm that I was born under a happy star.

I have inherited my mother's looks and my father's good temper; I am healthy in body and mind, and perfectly happy. I forget all past miseries and live in peace with myself, never wishing I were Rockefeller, Piero della Francesca, the handsomest man in the world, or anyone else. The very existence of our planet and my little spark of life on it both seem to me the miracle of miracles!

Having thus introduced myself, I must confess I find it strange that my parents were not Petersburgers like me. Indeed, they were not even Russian, but Jews from Kovno. Of my father, Gustav Lazarovich Berman, of his origins, of his youth, I know absolutely nothing. Of my mother's family, I know a little more, but, now that it is too late, I'm sorry I did not inform myself better. The few photographs saved from the Russian Revolution show a very beautiful family, united, at ease, and much in demand because of its three handsome sons— Otto, Max, Arthur—and three even prettier daughters— Eugenie, Julie, and Lydia, the youngest, whose son I am. I knew my grandfather, Bernhard or Bernard Manassevich (my mother's already-russianized name was Lydia Borisovna). He was an army contractor (but what did he sell, to which armies and when?). He was a majestically tall old man, handsome, with a military bearing and superb mustachios. His sons, tall and slender like their father (except for Arthur, who was short and fat), always stood in his presence. He died in his nineties when, having grown deaf, he was run over by a tramcar in Berlin. As for my grandmother, Eva, small, meticulously clean, her black hair severely pulled back, both she and her sister Rosa (or Röschen) had been famous beauties in their native city. Eugenie, my mother's eldest sister, owed her attractiveness to her fairness, her creamy complexion, and her almond-shaped eyes, but my mother's beauty was just the opposite: She was slim, very dark and gypsy-looking.

What is the very first memory that I can pull out, today, from the depths of the past? It is definitely that of my nurse holding me tight in her arms and climbing a stile—the gate to our garden. I can see neither the person nor the place, but can still feel the movement and the fear caused by great danger—wild beasts in a dark and sinister forest—and all because of neglect, a gate closed by mistake. My second memory comes a few years later: I am being fished out of my bath. And, still later, I remember a sleigh cut out of a sheet of white paper whose different parts were then glued together by Murinik, my father's best friend. After that come many other memories, as well as those incidents my mother told me about many years later.

Among the photographs I still have are several of myself. In the earliest of these, I am dressed like a little girl, standing on a chair; on my head is a silk hat, long curls go down to my shoulders, and I am wearing a white dress and white suede boots. A few years pass, and here I am, become a "little Lord Fauntleroy." My hair is cut and neatly parted, I have on a dark velvet suit and a huge lace collar adorned with a bow. And finally, I am seven or eight, with my brother Eugene, three and a half years younger than I, in front of a photographer's birch railing: belted suits, knickerbockers, starched collars over the jackets, all the same, even the pose in a twin style that I hated and that shamed me. Other photographs show my aunts, my uncles, my maternal grandparents surrounded by their children and sons-in-law. All these photographs are wonderfully preserved. They were solid, durable work; they are neither faded nor yellowed, and on the back of the thick cardboard you can read the name of Kovno and those of the photographers with their medals and coats of arms.

I spent my childhood at number 13, Great Stables Street, in Saint Petersburg. What a pretty name to a little boy who, like so many other Russian little boys, loved horses. (There were no cars then, except for two belonging to the Grand Dukes.) My entourage consisted of my father, my mother, my brother Eugene (called Genia)—my own nickname was Lioucha— Madi, our Swiss governess, and our cook Agafia, who was present at my mother's birth. There was also a Finnish servant, Ina, but she was not part of the family. These few people, my apartment, my street, and my neighborhood compose the world of my childhood, half real and half imaginary, outside of which I knew almost nothing: all else was terra incognita.

In this little group, the person I saw the least often, so seldom in fact that I do not remember him at all, was my father. He was a banker and usually came home late and rested before dinner. We children were strictly forbidden to go in and bother him. In the summer, he joined us in the country for weekends. But still, even in Saint Petersburg there were Sundays and holidays, and we must surely have been together. How is it then that I cannot remember him, his speech, his gestures? It is a mystery. The few photographs I have confirm that he was kind, considerate—a gentleman, as my mother always said—and small, portly, bald, with a fashionable moustache and extraordinarily frank eyes. In a group photograph, taken in the garden during the summer, he stands beside my mother, dressed in a dark town suit. I am in the foreground, harnessed into the shafts of a child's charabanc, grimacing as always. My mother, seated in a wicker chair, holds my brother, then a fat baby, up to my father; respectfully distant stands the nurse, wearing her *kokochnik*, the old-fashioned cap that looked like a bishop's miter. My father, on the other hand, wears a bowler hat, his hand rests on the pommel of his stick, and a watch chain hangs across his waistcoat. This chain was, according to my mother, one of the appurtenances a gentleman must always have, along with his wallet, change purse, cigarette holder, visiting cards, etc. She would have been terribly pleased if, as an adolescent, I had been willing to burden myself with all this—but I, of course, felt such objects were cumbersome, useless, and bourgeois.

My mother, some ten years younger than my father, still looked very young, very slim, very beautiful. She must have been twenty when I was born. I liked to go out with her: We were often mistaken for brother and sister, so alike were we. With her dark skin, velvety, dreamy black eyes, hair as black as a crow's wing, being elegant and a grande dame, she must have been the spoiled child of the family. One small and rather insignificant physical detail always upset me: her short, thick thumbs (I have always been sensitive to women's hands). I felt far too much admiration and respect for my mother to have a simple, normal relationship with her. She spent much time taking care of us until Mademoiselle Charlotte Wohnlich came from Switzerland. Mademoiselle dedicated herself to us and became our companion. But she completely took over my brother and so turned his head that she "became his mother," and he, her child: It was a form of incest. Since my brother could not pronounce the French word *Mademoiselle*, he shortened it to Madi, a nickname soon picked up by the rest of the family. Everybody loved Madi and, after my brother had grown up, she went on to take care of the house. Madi was small, with a face that seemed flat to me and reminded me of the moon; her speech was Swiss—she would say *plaît-il* instead of *pardon* and pronounced the final *c* in words like *escroc*.

Then there was Agafia, the kind, the devoted Agafia, whom my mother inherited from her family when she was married.

Saint Petersburg

An excellent cook and pastry-maker, with secret jam recipes, Agafia was an old, yellow-skinned spinster who looked like a Mongol. She could neither read nor write, but like Pushkin's *niania* ("nurse"), she spoke an admirable Russian, the dialect of the people, full of old proverbs. She was the typical old *niania* of the fairy tales, the old serf attached to the family, indeed a part of the family, without any private life except for her religion, the Orthodox Church, where again she was a slave, joyously excelling at endless chores—washing floors, for example. She loved God and feared the Devil. In the Church, she found rest, theater, contact with other religious souls, the metropolite, and heaven itself. I don't even think Agafia received any wages from my mother, and anyway, what would she have done with her money? She could only have given it to the Church or the poor. I was often present at Russian Orthodox religious services, even though, like my parents, I was without religion. I liked the Russian Orthodox service, the splendor of the ikons, the smell of incense, the Gregorian chants, and the pope's sermons preached in the old Slavonic language. I also loved to watch my Agafia, transformed now, in her element, slowly with her right hand tracing in a wide gesture the double sign of the Cross, then bending double. It all looked like a wonderful ballet. As for synagogue, I went to one for the first time in Paris, when I was over twenty.

It is hard for me to speak of my brother: Though we loved each other, lived and played together, it was always I who led, who took the initiative, and he who was the imitator. Physically he looked like my father, but he had my mother's character. From the time he was very young, he would often get into a snit and say sharp things, little stings, so he was nicknamed Komar, "Mosquito."

Our apartment's decoration was the epitome of bourgeois bad taste. We had five high-ceilinged rooms, very clean and as silent as the grave. There are three things about the entrance hall that have remained graven in my memory: an enormous stuffed bear serving as an umbrella holder, a large, dark closet in which I was locked up twice for being disobedient—a punishment of which I was utterly terrified; it seemed far worse than the only time I was whipped—and finally a large papier-mâché mechanical toy, a Pierrot sitting on the edge of a well. When wound up Pierrot would sing "Au Clair de la Lune"; while his head and eyes began to move, his hands seemed to pluck at the strings of his mandolin, and the moon's wide face appeared in an opening of a tower.

On the right of the hall, a door opened to my father's study, the first of the three rooms looking onto Great Stables Street. It was sad and dark, and I did not like it; anyway, we children were forbidden to enter. Heavy curtains on the windows cut down the light reaching a large desk placed right across the room; the dark, thick wall-to-wall carpet silenced everything. When my father came home from the bank, he would lie down on the great tufted black leather couch, or else relax with his favorite hobby, an impressive stamp collection. He had all sorts of catalogs and albums, special sheets crisscrossed with black dots, small light blue cardboards to which the stamps were attached before being put on an album sheet. One day my father brought home some twenty sheets that belonged to a series of stamps soon to be published on which were printed the Russian word *obrasetz*, or "sample." I can remember only two of the four different tall stamps, one with the equestrian statue of Peter the Great, the other with the monument to the historical heroes Minin and Pojarsky. I liked old Russian and English stamps although I preferred exotic images of animals and plants. My father often gave me his duplicate stamps; with his encouragement, I soon started my own collection, which grew especially fast when my cousin Gregory, a few years later, passed his collection on to me. But I eventually lost interest. I don't know what happened to my father's collection after he died; it was probably sold. But how good was it really? As for me, I inherited all his editions of the classics, many of which came from the monthly supplements to the famous illustrated paper *Niva* ("meadow"), and were beautifully bound. Many years later, I also inherited my mother's silver, marked with the same initials as mine.

Was it a Courbet or a Boudin that hung on the wall of my father's study? It was, at any rate, our only "good" painting, quite different from those others, in their massive gilt frames, that decorated the living room and were witnesses to the up-to-date taste of my cousin Anatole, who had often criticized the bourgeois bad taste of our furnishings to my mother. To these paintings were added imitation Louis XV furniture, tables, carpets, the traditional spittoons, and, most especially, a grand piano on which my mother would play waltzes—"Daisy, Daisy," for instance, and another one the sound of which still gives me the sensation today it gave me then: of the mystery of a forest at night, with Indians grouped around a campfire. For I was crazy about Indians, American Redskins! Later, I was forced to take piano lessons; being lazy, I was a recalcitrant pupil and would not learn how to read music. At a pupils' concert put on by my piano teacher I played a Mozart sonatina and was then allowed to give it up.

My father's study was dark and sad, the living room banal and formal, but my parents' bedroom was intimate and cozy. This third room looked out on the street, and it was there that my mother spent most of her free time. It had a dressing table; next to that, a smaller table holding a bronze statuette of a nude woman in front of a mirror and two richly bound volumes of *Trilby*, which I detested because of the illustrations; then there was a large double bed and a large closet. One door opened onto a boudoir, which led to the bathroom with its huge (or so I remember) bathtub and several pharmacy chests in which my mother collected empty bottles. A long narrow passage ended in a spacious kitchen, which, like the dining room and the children's room, looked out onto the courtyard. There we heard all the noises from the courtyard: the cooing of pigeons, the guttural cries of a few Tartars who sold Oriental carpets. The entrance to this courtyard was guarded at night by the *dvornik*, the "watchman," who sat on a tall stone and in winter was wrapped in his sheepskin. In the children's room, the *detzkaya*, two small beds were set opposite each other. Above mine on a shelf sat an enormous white-and-red papier-mâché ocean liner. It served as a repository for candy stolen during the day. At nine sharp, after Madi put the lights out and left us in bed, the feast would begin.

Finally, there was a little maid's room near the kitchen that could turn into a torture chamber. I must admit that, being a highly nervous, sensitive, and sensual child, I had early on given in to a bad habit, and since such threats as that it would make me rot had no effect, I was sometimes watched as I went off to sleep. At best, sleep came to me slowly; in that room, it did not come at all. For one thing, I could never get to sleep if there were even one candle burning. But, to end my martyrdom as quickly as possible, I would pretend to drop off. I would snore rhythmically, hoping that my jailer, Madi or Agafia, reading a book by candle- or lamplight near the window, would finally go away, convinced her duty was fulfilled. But as the minutes, quarter hours, half hours passed, with me not daring to scratch or sneeze, I would begin to despair of being free of the odious presence of my bedtime guardian. Today I can still see the half light in that little room and, before the candle, Agafia's face leaning over her big Bible, moving her lips, adding up the syllables, quite unable to read.

In the spring the house's main staircase, built of stone or marble, felt cool. The doorkeeper's lodge, a big wooden cabin, was under the last steps. In it lived a Finnish couple, Ivan and his wife, Clara. Both were very handsome, he tall and dark, she small, fair, and plump, both astonishingly clean. Still, I didn't like Ivan because he scared my little dog Kashtanka ("Little Chestnut") every time we stepped off the staircase. Ivan would clap his hands and pretend to block my dog's way so that he would end up running out between the big man's boots. The dog probably enjoyed it, but I never understood that. I loved my little mutt; he was brown and short-legged; we had found him one night in the street. Our other pet was a parrot in a cage. Only Agafia could take him on her shoulder and, even then, he once bit her ear. All that stupid bird ever said was: "Little parrot wants to eat." I think Nijinsky must have lived a floor below us, for one day as I was coming down the stairs with my mother, a young man passed us, jumping several steps at a time, and my mother whispered to me: "This is the famous Nijinsky."

Great Stables Street, my street, like most others in Saint Petersburg, was lined with two rows of identical stone houses painted wine-red and creating those long, broad perspectives. Near number 13 the street ended in an oval plaza also named after the Imperial stables where the Court carriages were kept. At the other end, our street led to the Nevsky Prospekt, opposite Fabergé's, the jeweler. On the Prospekt, the main and only really lively street of the city, were all the shops and all the banks. Saint Petersburg, a city born out of the marshes as another great city was born out of a *laguna*, still retained its original feeling of unreality. Its vast perspectives shrunk the human silhouette and seemed to isolate the passersby. In 1900, one never saw a crowd. Nor was there life on the canals, which remained empty even in winter for, unlike the Dutch, children did not skate on them. This was a time of horses and carriages, of hooves sounding on asphalt or wooden pavements, of whips cracking, of coachmen shouting *"bereghis, bereghis,"* "careful, watch out." From the Neva came the wail of tugboats. In the evenings, when darkness came down on the city, I liked listening to the silence of my street, interrupted now and again by a passing cab; I would try to guess from the hoofbeats whether the horse was walking or trotting.

Great Stables Street, being residential, had no more than a few shops, all on our side of the street: the shop of the Marceroux porcelains; the Bear, a very elegant restaurant where the most important businessmen would meet for lunch; next door, in contrast, a tiny State liquor store where vodka was sold to workers who would pour it down their throats and munch on salt cucumbers; and finally, at the corner of the Nevsky Prospekt, a tiny stationery store where you had to walk down two or three steps before you could go in and which I knew well. There I would buy large sheets of colored cutouts: medieval castles to assemble, hussars or uhlans with bottoms that folded to make them stand. Opposite the stationery, in a niche, there was some kind of sign or statue, and one day as I looked up at it I could have sworn I saw a motionless nude woman. Another time, on the Prospekt, I saw a bunch of exotic animals, a vision easier to explain: They probably belonged to a passing circus.

Almost opposite my house was a passage leading to a parallel street, Little Stables Street, which was the only avenue with trees in the middle. I went there once a year for the Easter Fair. Here there were none of the picturesque crowds to be seen at a country fair, no jugglers or accordion players, but I would stop in front of all the stalls, buy angel's hair, try my hand at the shooting gallery, and drink up that very Russian atmosphere that I was to find again, years later, in the ballet *Petrouchka*.

My customary walk through the city led me first to the Nevsky Prospekt, and then, turning right, to the Neva. Quite near was the little hunchbacked bridge over the Moika, one of the city's main canals. I have never forgotten the pharmacy on the corner opposite, because of two huge cutout figures making an advertising panel in front of the door: a hefty matron in a bonnet and red bodice frantically soaping the head of a shrieking little boy.

A little beyond the Moika, the main street ended at the Admiralty Garden. There I would watch schoolboys playing soccer, envying the boy, and there was always one, who, refusing to pass the ball to a teammate, would invent tricks to mislead all the others. In the winter, there was skating, and two ice mountains down which children slid, reclining flat on their sleds. The Empire-style Admiralty building nearby was painted yellow and led to the huge square before the Winter Palace and the Hermitage, all in the Louis XV style and painted wine-red.

Then, crossing the square, I would reach the quays, the Field of Mars, and the Summer Garden right near my own street. While the Nevsky Prospekt and the Gardens overflowed with life, the noble perspective of quays and palaces seemed empty, lifeless, almost inhumanly beautiful. But once a year, the huge square in front of the Winter Palace with its Trajan's Column would come to life, fill up, and be a magic spectacle of color and light. Fascinated, I would see the equestrian regiments in the great parade riding by, stopping because of the traffic jams. And then I could admire the hussars, dragoons, uhlans, and cuirassiers, and the Cossacks, those from the Don in blue, those from the Kuban in yellow, those from the Urals in red, and the Tcherkess whose uniforms were my favorites.

Such was the Saint Petersburg of my childhood; I knew almost nothing of the rest of the city.

Now I am amazed at my childhood lack of interest in my native city. I never tried to find out what was happening on the other side of the canal that flowed along the Summer Garden, and while I sometimes went to Gostiniy Dvor, a very long two-storied arcaded building filled with stores, it is only as a young man that I first discovered the *Strelka*, or "Little Arrow": the great park of Saint Petersburg to be found at the end of one of the islands.

It seems to me that when I was a child, the seasons were more timely and their changes more visible than today—or was it simply the Russian climate with its very cold winters and very hot summers? Of the four seasons, it was winter and spring that I liked best. Through the open windows, the sounds and perfumes of the melting snow used to move me. Then would come sinister cracks from the Neva. The ice would split, its chunks bouncing off one another, mounting one on top of the other, all to be swept, in silence now, faster and faster toward the sea.

Saint Petersburg

While the spring was brief and full of these calls to life, the winter was silent and very long. The double windows of our flat were all sealed with putty, not to be opened again until spring. Some moss and a glass filled with water kept them from steaming. To get air, one would open a pane at the top by pulling on a string. Unless I am mistaken, the walls were also double. After taking all sorts of precautions of this kind, we would install ourselves comfortably for the winter. The samovar would then be king; we drank tea out of glasses. Outside, we wore coats lined with otter or Persian lamb, muffs, fur hats, boots. Constantly you heard the sound of shovels cutting the ice and cleaning the sidewalks. We drove everywhere in sleighs. The world was white, soft, silent, enchanting! Everything was white, of a whiteness that hurt your eyes when the sun was shining, of a moonlike white when the grey sky prepared us for more snow.

The beauty of a fine sleigh streaking past one like lightning has always seduced me: A sleigh goes so much faster than a carriage; the Orloff stallion seems to be leaping right off the ground. His neck is arched under the traces, his long mane, his tail wave in the wind, the blue net on his back goes down almost to the ground and catches the ice and dirt thrown up by the hooves. The back legs of the animal seem about to kick in the tiny sleigh with its huge coachman, that monstrous growth looking like a giant larva, so enveloped in coats is he. Motionless, his outstretched arms pull on the reins; his huge mass acts as a windshield for the little lady in back whose wide fur hat almost touches him.

Many Russian children, as I have said, carried a horse in their souls. The first ballet I ever saw was *The Little Hunchback Horse*. It was danced by Pavlova, whom I was never to see again. I wonder if I would have become a painter without those horses, especially the cab horses that fascinated me so on my walks. Much to my companions' annoyance, I would always stop to study them. When I got home, I would ask my mother to draw them for me, but seeing her mistakes, I would snatch the pencil away from her desperately and try to correct them. Sometimes, I drew only the horses' legs, standing or trotting. With my little brother I would play cab: One of us would be the horse, the other the coachman pulling on the reins, and we would dash through the rooms of our apartment. This was brought to an end the day my brother fell and broke a tooth: He always seemed to fall with his arms behind him. Another, calmer game was played with my big papier-mâché horse. We would stand it in front of two chairs and take turns being the coachman. We would invite my mother, Madi, or Agafia for a ride; first, though, we had to haggle over the fare as my mother always did in the street—indeed, as everyone did: "To go to Fontanka number 18, how much?" "*Barynia* ("lady"), for you, only forty kopecks!" "What do you mean, you thief, forty kopecks, you want to strangle me! I'll give you twenty-five and not a kopeck more!" "Come on, little lady, have pity, say thirty-five. . . ." and we'd finally agree on thirty. After all this bargaining, my mother would sit on the back chair, which she was only allowed to leave when the ride was over; sometimes it seemed too long or she might be called away, and then, for the coachman, it was a disaster, the game spoiled, the illusion lost, for one could hardly walk out of a carriage going full speed. In summer, in the country, I would place myself in the traces of a child's cart and run on the sanded alleyways of the garden. I was very anxious to have my wheels follow the curve of the lawn. The wheels seemed a miracle then, and I still feel the same way now when I drive a car.

Another thing I liked to do, of course, was to cut those pictures of uhlans or hussars out of large sheets of paper bought at the little stationery store on the Nevsky Prospekt. They are a special memory because one day, exasperated by my mocking silence as she was scolding me, my mother grabbed these soldiers and threw them into the fire. I said nothing at the moment but the next day, as I went to kiss her good morning, I asked her a question she was never to forget: Would she be sorry if I died in a fire? She, who had quite forgotten her exasperation of the previous day, answered, "Yes, of course. What a stupid question!" "Well," I answered, "that's just what you made me feel yesterday when you burned my soldiers."

Russian holidays were celebrated with splendor, especially Easter and Christmas. At Easter, in the streets, in every house, you saw *verba*, the budding branches of the willows. And, as I have mentioned, there was the street fair in Little Stables Street. In every home, an Agafia would prepare for her *ptentchiki*, her "little birds," the traditional *koulich*, a sort of big brioche, and the *pas-cha*, a sweet cream-cheese-like cake. Nor should I fail to mention the famous painted eggs. Christmas was even better. All night while we children slept, my mother, helped by Agafia and Madi, would prepare a huge Christmas tree, virtually hidden beneath candles, angel's hair, silver garlands, colored balls, and, especially, the papier-mâché toys that I just loved. They could have been Fabergé masterpieces, they seemed so real: small animals or pieces of furniture, a desk, for instance, with its blotter and two candles in their candlesticks. All these marvels came from the Petot stationery.

Aside from drawing, I composed poetry, wrote essays— criticizing, for instance, a children's writer called Tcharskaya —and wrote stories on folded pieces of toilet paper that gave me the illusion of making a real book. I wrote and illustrated the story of Stenka the Pirate.

When I was very young, I believed all the fairy stories I was told. Later, I loved Max and Moritz and a French series called *Bibliothèque Rose*. I wish I still had a few volumes, such as *Les Malheurs de Sophie* and *Un Bon Petit Diable* with the terrible Madame Macmish (what wonderful illustrations!). Later, I went on to Jules Verne, in those big volumes that exist no longer. Longfellow's Hiawatha made me want to learn Indian words. I also devoured the books of James Fenimore Cooper. Wtih Jim Weinberg, my best friend, I would play at Indians, crawling on all fours through the apartment, trying to creep under the dining-room table unseen by grownups.

Saint Petersburg

In the summer, I would collect wild herbs and flowers to dry and classify them in my herbarium. I would also make booklets of transparent sheets of paper and trace the tracks of wild animals, inspired by the work of Ernest Thompson Seton.

In the winter, I would leaf through Braem's three volumes on animals; I liked giraffes, elephants, lions, and camels best. Camels in particular so fascinated me that one day, when I was still very young and would not eat, a verbal misunderstanding gave me the idea that the food I had been refusing was actually camel and I promptly swallowed it with delight.

One winter, my brother's lungs became infected and he hovered between life and death for several months. He was kept wrapped in ice in the living room with the windows wide open. A famous doctor, Dr. Kliatchko, who was short and fat with wild white hair, at last miraculously saved him. When he was finally able to get up, he had been transformed from a round-faced, chubby little child to an extremely thin one. You can imagine how spoiled he became, especially when it came to food. When I was his age it had been very different: My mother brought me up very strictly, and I was forced to eat everything I was given even if I threw up. Nevertheless, I was always a slender child. Also a nervous one. I bit my nails for many years and had migraine headaches so violent that I had to stay in bed for two days with ice on my head. This was probably inherited from my mother, who suffered from migraines all her life. (Later, however, I was completely cured of them, thanks to exercise.) Indigestion, by the way, was constant: We ate too much and too rich food. The *nianias* would stuff their little charges, saying: "One spoon for mother, one for father, one more for your uncle." A pregnant woman, for instance, became a kind of force-fed goose: She would eat twice as much as usual and simply stop moving. As a purgative, we children were given castor oil in beer—so that well into adult life, I could not stand the taste of beer.

We spent our summers either in a dacha in Sestroretsk or in Terioki, Finland, where Aunt Eugenie, my mother's eldest sister, would rent a much larger and less primitive villa than ours. Since both places were only an hour's train ride from Saint Petersburg, my father would join us for weekends, though, again, I have no memory of him. Moving to the country was quite a to-do: For a whole day, beds, chests, kitchen implements, trunks, boxes, etc., would be loaded on four or five *telegi*, those four-wheeled carts pulled by one lone horse. The shaky piles would be tied down, covered with tarpaulins, and then the cortege would start off, the *mujiks* walking next to their horses. It took a day or two for the procession to reach the dacha, which was rented unfurnished for the summer. The one I remember best was the house of Alitowski, the priest, a sort of two-story log cabin, a real *isba*, or "peasant's house," which I loved. It smelled of the country, of wood and resin, and of Agafia's warm baked bread.

Like many schoolboys, I had a tutor, that is, a young live-in student, who helped me with my summer work. I remember only one, called Pchigoda, who was a strapping fellow with a pimply face. I remember him because he had seduced Madi, or had been seduced by her, and my mother was furious. There were scenes which I did not understand. Another thing I remember from that summer was a walk on the beach during which two other boys, one named Persitz, and I discussed the existence of God. When I got home, I gave my mother the great negative news on that subject, and she became angry and told me to stop blaspheming. During that same walk, I also learned a secret that few other people shared: A man just might give birth through the navel. This extraordinary event was called *libadia*.

I liked Terioki more than Sestroretsk: The country was wilder, the house more romantic, and there was the sea, although it was cold. Few people went swimming then, even when the weather was warm. I was very fond of walking barefoot and was always upset when, after the rain, I was forbidden to do so, while all the fishermen's children could still indulge in the privilege. All the houses were in a vast pine forest between marshes and sea. A narrow path, crossing private land, the little "Bruni Road," took us to the sea. I would sometimes pedal on it at top speed on my bicycle, racing with the handsome "Boy," my Aunt Eugenie's Saint Bernard, thinner than a greyhound after having had his hair cut during the summer's excessive heat. The waves would wash small pieces of chopped-up reeds onto the grey sand beach, and the great tides would leave huge puddles on which my brother would sail in a washbucket under the intensive surveillance of Agafia and my mother. When he saw the sea for the first time, he exclaimed, "What a big bathtub!"

It was in Terioki that I saw Uncle Arthur, my mother's brother, for the first and only time. He had come to introduce his future wife to Aunt Eugenie. During a walk, the young lover carried his wife-to-be in his arms across a large puddle; everybody thought this gesture most gallant.

In Sestroretsk we had the famous Dr. Kliatchko for a neighbor; his son Volodia was my friend. He was a well-known daredevil who could go down any staircase on his bicycle and lie down, like Kolia in *The Brothers Karamazov*, under passing trains. Sometimes he would suddenly go off, alone and on foot, to Saint Petersburg. He was tiny, ugly, with bandy legs, a harlequin nose, and freckles on his cheeks; he also lisped. When he found out that I was to go to the same school he attended, the Tenischeff School, he later confessed to me that he had been unable to sleep for a whole night.

It was in Sestroretsk that you would sometimes, in the morning by the garden gate, hear a serenade being played vigorously off-key by a quartet of trumpets paid to perform for a birthday or a Saint's day. It was at the Sestroretsky Club that I first learned to play tennis. I would win cufflinks and other knick-knacks, and make my mother proud. No one taught you, then; each man developed his own style. One boy's movements were so bizarre that he was nicknamed Congo-drive. The best player was Leva Gertzman whose sister, Volia, was awfully pretty. One day a fat girl took me for a walk in the forest;

Saint Petersburg

once there, she lay down on the ground, but I was too shy to do anything more than kiss her a few times.

Sometimes we went abroad—to Karlsbad, for the cure, to Berlin, for a visit to my grandparents, or elsewhere. I have only a few scattered memories of these trips. In Swinemünde, my mother, who was playing the newly published "Merry Widow" four-hands with my cousin Anatole, was stung by a bee; I lost a tennis tournament after having won the first set 6–0 and being so sure of the others that I lost them 6–0, 6–0. In the Tyrol, at Semmering, trains would hug the side of the Dolomites as they passed from one tunnel to the next; I played with a little girl called Babitza; two dragonflies chopped off each other's heads; there was an electric car competition; and a woman balloonist took off, standing in a basket shaped like an eagle with its wings outspread. I do, however, have a fuller memory of Burgenstock, a village above the Lake of the Four Cantons reached by a cable railway. On the terrace of the hotel, my mother, together with my cousin Gregory, would enjoy eating asparagus; while I did not like its taste, its beauty impressed me. There was a walk that led to a small platform, "Ping-Pong Kegel," from which there was a sensational view. I beat up a bigger boy who had pushed me off my swing, and his mother complained to mine, who then unfairly scolded me. I walked into an attic window and remained hanging by my elbows above a maid's room. I got locked up in a toilet, thought I would starve to death, and called for help from a window too high up for anyone to hear me; and finally, I hung a hammock between two walls of the gymnasium so inadequately that, when I climbed up to it on a ladder, the whole contraption fell to the ground and I split my chin.

During the winter of 1905, while revolution raged in Saint Petersburg, my father sent us all to Finland, where we spent several months living in an *isba*. Our only amusements were skiing and sleigh riding. Through the deep winter silence, our magic carpet, the sleigh, carried us into a soft, noiseless, limitless universe where sky and earth came together and the trees, thickly covered with snow, would take on fantastic shapes. Bundled up in furs, sitting on the straw of the wide freight sleigh so tightly wrapped in sheepskins that we couldn't move, we no longer knew whether we were awake or dreaming: Nirvana! Even when I took up the reins and upset the sleigh in a turn, the fall was so slow, so soft that, unable to move, my mother, my brother, and Madi were all convulsed with laughter.

The next incident I created, though, was far from funny. Our *isba* was near a narrow but deep river, frozen over at this time of year. I would often see the village children skating on it during my walks with Madi and my brother. One day, despite Madi's forbidding me to do so, I started across the ice. The weather was much warmer that day, and the ice gave under me. Held up only by my elbows, I was stuck hanging in the middle of the river. My brother and Madi were shouting instructions from the bridge, but each time I tried to get up, the ice would split further. God only knows how I got myself to safety without help, and why I wasn't ill afterward. My mother almost fainted when she heard about the accident. I only truly understood how distressed she was many years later, in Paris: One day I walked into the sitting room while she was telling a friend the story, and I was silly enough to point out to her that she hadn't actually been there to see it. "How dare you contradict me, you wretch," she said angrily, "when I can still see you floundering in that river!"

It was perhaps in 1906—in any case, some time after this stay in Finland—that I entered the Tenischeff School, which was the most exclusive private school in Saint Petersburg. During my stay there, I was popular and enjoyed an undeniable influence over the others. It is not that I was so wonderful at my studies. On the contrary, I might not even have risen to the next grade. But I was the best athlete, the best draftsman, I contributed heavily to our artistic papers and my pranks were successful. My handicap as a student was not so much laziness as distraction. "Your son, Madame," a teacher once said to my mother, "your son writes charades." Years later in Paris, coming home to my bachelor's flat, I was to go out onto the balcony, throw my keys off it and put my lit cigarette in my pocket. And recently, a check I wrote was sent back to me because I had made *three* errors. Even today, I forget to put an "s" on plurals. My brother, on the other hand, never in his life made a spelling mistake though he writes five languages. Still, in spite of all my faults—perhaps through the offices of my parents—I managed to stay in the director's good graces and went to his house every Sunday to take dancing lessons with a very exclusive little group consisting of a few students of the Tenischeff School and an equal number of little girls. Among these were the two Zaharoff sisters, whose parents were friends of my parents. A French dancing master taught us how to dance polkas, mazurkas, waltzes, and the Spanish step.

The next year, away in Sestroretsk, my father died. His lungs had become inflamed; this was then a very dangerous illness. Our friend and neighbor Dr. Kliatchko was not able to repeat his earlier miracle with my brother. For weeks, my mother stayed at my father's bedside. Finally, wracked with fatigue and grief, she followed medical and family advice and indulged in a few innocent pasttimes, like walking, and a little tennis. It was during a tennis match that she was called away urgently, and I was not to see her again for months.

All through her life, my mother had feared the number 13. She had been married for thirteen years; she lived at number 13, Great Stables Street; finally, my father died on July 13. As for us children back in Saint Petersburg, we were not told the truth. I thought my father must have died but, to my shame, did not feel at all grieved. My life continued festive; instead of being sent to the country, I went to live with my friend Jim Weinberg. I have no idea what happened to my brother. At Jim's, in the evenings when his parents were out, we would play at being Indians and run around the apartment in the nude.

Saint Petersburg

It was while watching Jim's three- or four-year-old sister being bathed that I saw my first naked female. We dared to ask the maid to show us her naked thigh and, laughing, she did.

One morning, while riding with Mrs. Weinberg in her open carriage, I saw my little dog Kashtanka, who had vanished at my father's death, in the middle of a dog fight. Madly excited, I leaped out of the moving barouche, hugged the dog to my chest, and begged Mrs. Weinberg to take me to my Aunt Eugenie's where my mother, in her extreme grief, had found refuge. It was a miracle for me that my little dog could have been found so far away from home. The only thing that frightened me about seeing my mother again was that I had disobeyed her by not wearing my long underwear. As soon as the entrance door opened, I rushed into the living room, shouting: "Kashtanka is found, Kashtanka is found!" Another door opened, and someone started scolding me, telling me not to be so noisy; my aunt was asleep and my mother was very ill. Leaving the dog, I walked out angrily. It was full day, noon in fact, but the apartment was dark, lifeless, and no one paid any attention to me and my Kashtanka.

My mother loved and spoiled us, gave us a happy childhood, but hers was a cold personality—either because it was her nature or because she was shy—and so we children never saw any expression of emotion. Effusiveness was ridiculed by us as *teliachi nejnosti*—"calf's tenderness." My brother and I were never coaxed, cuddled, confided in; our only kisses came with good mornings and good nights. Today's friendship between parents and children would have been inconceivable; age was an impassable barrier (that was not without its charms). Children had to obey without asking questions and without discussion; they were silent when grownups spoke, were not allowed into the kitchen, and so on. This lack of any physical contact between parents and children was common in my whole family. My uncle and future stepfather, on his deathbed, could not ask his sons to come to him for a last kiss. When, later, my mother died before me, I felt much more sorrow than I showed. She would have told me that I was a good son. In her lifetime, for instance, I could never take my mother into my arms to console her. She was so fanatically clean, so mad about hygiene, so fearful of dust and microbes, that, whenever I came back from a trip, she would make me wash my face before allowing me to kiss her, which offended me and killed my impulse. I had never seen the smallest inch of her body, not even her ankle! My mother was never a woman for me, but a virgin. And I have always wished I had had a sister. . . .

I also inherited this paralysis, but only partially; with me, it is not physical, but verbal. I am incapable of saying to the people I love those little words that mean so much to them, even that capital sentence: "I love you." The word "darling" seems conventional to me, and I hate listening to people use it. The names or nicknames of those we love seem to me so much more beautiful, tender, and even intimate.

After my mother's death, I began to wish that I had known more about her youth. Did she marry for love or convenience? Could she, so beautiful, have loved my father, an aging man, a conventional gentleman? Did she simply obey her parents? That postcard from the Blue Grotto in Naples, which I still have, is it witness to a honeymoon?

My father's death left my mother without money. Once she recovered from that new widow's bout of illness, it must have been Efim Schaikevich, Aunt Eugenie's husband, and her elder brother Otto who decided to provide for us by sending us all to Germany where life was cheaper and schools were excellent.

In any case, early in 1907, my mother, brother, Madi, and I left Russia for Germany.

Chapter 2

Germany

1907–1911

MY STAY IN GERMANY lasted for three and a half years, one in Wiesbaden, one in Munich, the rest in Berlin. I suppose my mother chose Wiesbaden so as to be close to my recently widowed grandmother, who had left Berlin and moved into one of the numerous "pensions" lining the promenade that gave onto the town's main street. Wiesbaden was the ideal place for elderly people of independent means. They enjoyed all the benefits of a quiet life: clean air, absolute calm, walks shaded by the branches of beautiful trees, the closeness of the town, and even a casino with its park. It was in this casino that I enjoyed my first play, Shakespeare's *Julius Caesar* with the famous Basserman, and my first operetta, Franz Lehar's *Eva*; one of its waltzes haunted me for a long time afterward.

My grandmother had settled quite near her younger sister, Rosa Gabrilovich, who lived with her husband and two of her children, unmarried but of mature age: Arthur and Pauline. Her youngest son, Ossip, the well-known pianist and conductor, had married Mark Twain's daughter and was pursuing a brilliant career in the United States. While "Aunt Röschen," as everyone called her though she was over eighty, was youthful looking, elegant, and even coquettish, her husband was a senile old man, unpleasant to behold with his shaking body, peeling face, and teary eyes.

Around the Gabrilovich household gathered some of Ossip's friends, famous musicians like Isaie, the violinist, Thalberg, the pianist, who came from the Swiss branch of the Schaikevich family, and Elley Ney, who would later give piano recitals in

Saint Petersburg. This musical atmosphere dated back to my mother and aunts' childhood in Kovno. Even now in Wiesbaden my mother from time to time would play a few waltzes; her sister, Julie, interpreted Chopin with ease and brio while smilingly looking you in the eye; and Aunt Eugenie, favorite pupil of the great Anton Rubinstein, had given up a brilliant professional career to marry and bear children. Of her three sons, the eldest, Anatole, played the cello and Gregory, the youngest, the violin. As for me, gifted but lazy, I refused to go on with my piano lessons; my brother was never forced by my parents to take any.

We moved into one of those excellent, clean, but terribly sad pensions filled with old people. The apparition of a couple of newlywed Swedes, as beautiful as young gods, thus seemed like a real ray of sunshine. I had been sensitive to feminine beauty since my earliest childhood—my mother had had many an occasion to notice it—and so could not resist the new bride's charm. Since I was unable to imagine her apart from her cumbersome spouse, I would dream of sleeping under the blankets in their big bed, at the feet of my idol, all curled up like a little lap dog; neither her husband nor I might touch her, for only thus were we equals. When the couple left, I quickly forgot about them, but women's bodies, which I had still never seen, continued to haunt me. So I bought several postcards at a newsstand and kept them hidden. They showed a man's head— or was it a skull?—but when you looked closely, it would change to nude women holding one another in the manner of Arcimboldo, the *trompe-l'oeil* painter of heads made of vegetables, flowers, fish, etc. How surprised I was, fifty years later, when I saw one of my postcards reproduced in a surrealist book about Dali.

For Christmas that year, my mother gave me the prettiest watch to be seen in the window of one of the town's jewelers. She had always been anxious to have me carry a watch, a pocketknife, a wallet, and a change purse, all objects that she thought elegant and fashionable. This watch was to seduce three generations. It was very thin, with platinum and copper stripes, and was designed to be worn in the little outside pocket of one's jacket with a chain through the buttonhole. It was the fashion at that time. When my grandmother saw this wonder, she promptly confiscated it, made me give it to her every evening so that she could put it away in a locked drawer. Was she really jealous of my having the watch, was she in fact afraid that it would be stolen, or was it just an old woman's ruse to make sure her grandson would come and kiss her every morning and night?

My receipt of the watch was followed by another significant event, my grandmother's birthday. As a celebration, and also as a distraction from the monotony of life in Wiesbaden, my mother decided to surprise my grandmother by getting me up in a disguise. I was bundled into one of her pretty white lace dresses and given a big, beribboned hat with false hair hanging from it. My feet, though they were too wide, were forced into a pair of Madi's narrow shoes and, so attired, I was given a suitcase and put into a cab bound for my grandmother's pension. Once there, in the entrance hall, in full view of my accomplices, trying desperately not to laugh, I rented a room, signed myself Fraulein Kissmich, just arrived from the country, and had my grandmother sent for. Our little act was a complete success. My grandmother and the various members of the Gabrilovich family, although intrigued by my extraordinary resemblance to my mother, were quite unable to recognize me or figure out who I might be. An Austrian officer started to flirt with me, and the pension's eccentric young intellectual who took a bath every morning (at a time when private bathrooms did not exist) began to shout his favorite phrase: *"lecka-popo,"* which caused the old ladies to giggle. The comedy ended when, to the amazement of all present, I flung up my skirts and took off my hat. The next day, I went to a photographer who did a photo of me in that disguise, which I still have.

During this time, a young student named Philip Hahn came

to give my brother and me lessons. Sometimes, though, I had to go to his house, and since he lived next to the slaughter-house, curiosity made me to go inside this sinister establish-ment. I also told myself that a man should see and know everything in life. The huge hall resounded with the shrieks of the poor animals being slaughtered. Pigs had a knife thrust under a leg, which was then pumped up and down so as to get out all the blood, which would go into making blood sausage. Sheep had their necks slashed, and as for oxen, their heads were simply chopped off, though sometimes a hammer would push a nail right into the brain, thus causing instantaneous death; I was never able to find the reason for this relatively merciful treat-ment. What I saw that day was horrible beyond belief. When, before my unbelieving stare and despite all laws of gravity and balance, a cut-off cow's head, held to the neck by a thread only, came up and looked me directly in the eye, I found myself unable to stand the scene. My legs trembled, nausea rose in me, and, sick and shaking, I fled, swearing I would never want to know everything in life.

In Munich, the second stop of our German interlude, we stayed again in a pension situated near a park. It belonged to the widow Richter with whose daughter Lotte I had my first romance—which went no further than kisses. As is often the case with deformed people, Lotte, though a hunchback, had a pretty face and did not lack for followers among the pension's inmates; there was even a Hungarian count who was desperate to marry her. But I was the one she favored, and we spent all our time thereafter smooching and hugging on her divan-bed. Madi saw us one day, so we had to meet in the park after that. It was in that same park that I began to draw one of the oldest oak trees—in such detail that I was not likely ever to be finished.

Our life in Munich was so much more varied and so much more fun than in that hole of a city, Wiesbaden. Still, my brother and I were very happy finally to be entered into a private school—and it was high time. There were two outstanding boys in my class, and they could hardly have been more different from each other. The first, Percy Pennibacker, a flaxen-haired, freckle-faced American, was the best *Schlagbal* player; this baseball-like game was very popular in German schools. During the intervals between classes, Percy would stand in a corner of the common hall without speaking to anyone. He would stay there, hands clasped behind his back, and fill his chest with air which he would keep in as long as possible until finally his face turned crimson. As strange and as shy as this boy was, so the other, Peilbach, was common and corrupt. He had every vice, would bite his nails to the bone, was a secret smoker, and would jerk off in front of his friends, telling them to do the same. He managed completely to ruin a big, naive boy, barely weaned from his mother and whose flesh was as pink as a suckling pig's.

Sports, very popular in Germany, were new to me, and I loved them more and more. I did have to give up soccer, however, after I almost broke a shoulder bone being tackled by a giant. When I recovered from this injury, I started training with more zeal for track and high jump, for which I was particularly gifted. In winter, on the other hand, when it was raining or freezing, there was no greater pleasure than to go to the wonderful new swimming pool on the Isar in which one felt as if one were in a huge crystal ball. The water was so green, with a tropical clearness, that one never wanted to get out of it. In this pool, I watched swimming meets and was taught the breaststroke hanging from a rod like a fish caught on a hook. In the dressing room, the schoolboys would split into two groups: the model students and the bad boys, with whom I belonged. And while I and two or three others would avoid all group contact and prefer to find satisfaction alone, the others, and there must have been a good dozen of them— lively and noisy, naked as the day they were born and glistening like frogs—would try to satisfy themselves together, which they had trouble doing since they were too young to have proper erections. I don't know whether the games of these future Spartans were full of vice or innocence but I do not think, at any rate, that they should be taken seriously. After a long evening spent in the water, we would leave the pool under the stars, nibbling at hot chestnuts (their smell has always reminded me of that pool) and listening to the Isar flow by.

Unlike me, my brother never took an active part in any of the sports meets; but he knew more about sports than anyone else—the names, the matches, the records, so that my mother nicknamed him Sport im bild ("Sports Illustrated") after an elegant magazine of that name. Not being a practicing athlete, Eugene never came with me to the *Wanderen*, a scoutlike organization that arranged walking tours through the countryside for groups of several boys with one or two leaders. We would walk in step, a rucksack on the back, and sing *lieder*. At the end of the first day, we would be overcome with fatigue, but by the next morning we would have our energy back. We would have picnics by the side of a stream and walk into the heart of medieval villages. I was thus lucky enough to walk through the Hartz, the Schwartzwald, and the Alps near Kufstein where I saw the famous *Alpenblühen* (mountaintops lit by sunrise or sunset), and was caught by the leader smoking my first cigarettes, which scared me because I was afraid he would tell my mother.

In Munich, and later in Berlin, I lived surrounded by young Spartans in an atmosphere of sentimental friendship: *Brüder-schaft*, from which women were banned. It was flattering, I must admit, to be popular, admired, even desired! The gym teacher called me Bährochen, "Little Bear." But as much as the female body excited me, the male body left me cold. "The water runs off a goose's back," says a Russian proverb, so my mother should not have worried when she found in the toilet a torn letter from Carl Preuss, who was handsome and an athlete. That Carl Preuss and his friend Curt Pahl, both older and more sophisticated than I, had always treated me with respect—except for the one incident at the pool: I was in the shower and did not see Carl Preuss coming in to my cabin, but felt a hand taking my chin and turning it. He gave me a big kiss on the lips and then disappeared. I had barely been alone for a moment when the same scene was repeated, this time with Curt Pahl. Amazed, I exclaimed: "What! One after the other!" Nowhere outside of Germany have I known this atmosphere of sentimental and sexual close masculine friendship.

I had, as I said, been a nervous child who bit his nails, had headaches, and even wet his bed; now I became an athlete. Sports and outdoor life, *wanderen* and swimming, all hardened my body and gave me lifelong health. The more my body grew, the more my mind became atrophied for lack of mental exercise. We were interested in nothing but sports and operettas. When our Schaikevich cousins, Anatole and Gregory, came to see us, they were quite alarmed—but I'm anticipating. Let us first leave Munich and go to Berlin.

As soon as we arrived in the capital, we were entered in the Siementz Oberrealschule in Charlottenburg, on the Kurfürstendamm, and we moved into the neighborhood near Lake Lietzensee in one of those modern barracks that had sprouted in a sort of no man's land. My brother ranked second in his class and even I, miracle of miracles, was among the first. It wasn't difficult since the work was mere child's play compared to what we would have to do later in Russia. It took just a half hour to complete the day's assignments and one could go off to the sports ground with a light heart, safe in the knowledge that the master would never ask you about yesterday's lesson. Besides that, I came upon a very simple little trick that kept me ahead of the master's questions. Since he would invariably call on us in alphabetical order, I could just stay slightly ahead by having one extra mark and thus being ignored when my turn came. This could easily be achieved by answering for another pupil who did not know his assignment.

I started to learn English from a fat, red-faced German with a teutonic accent. "Hello, Bob, get up, don't you hear the bell ring loud enough?" Each assignment consisted of a chapter of this Bob's life in school: his rising, breakfast, sports, studies, and holidays. I was the most popular student in my class, first in sports, French, and drawing, and thus first also in geography since I was better than anyone else at copying the required maps from the atlas. After painting the valleys green, the mountains brown, and the ocean blue in shades that varied according to the different heights and depths, I would even varnish the maps. Once I did better than that, sculpting the Australian continent and surrounding it with water. The idea had come to me of asking an old carpenter of my acquaintance, not too burdened with work, to cut out several contours of the continent of various dimensions, which I had drawn on plywood; I then nailed them one on top of the other in an aquarium. I modeled the relief with clay and, once dry, painted it like the maps. This masterpiece completed, I brought it to school where, before the geography teacher, surrounded by the other students, I filled it with water. My success was, as you can imagine, immense, all the more that I gave this cumbersome object to the school. After this gesture, how could I not be *persona grata* in geography!

Certain pranks also helped to make me popular. During one whole period, for instance, I stayed in a closet lying between two shelves without daring to move or sneeze. Some of my exploits outside of school were not so funny. My friend, the son of the old carpenter, and I would imitate Busch's Max and Moritz. From a window above his father's workshop, we would have fun pouring water on those of the passersby whose faces we did not like, until one day an enraged couple began to bang on the door, refusing to go away. Fearing the worst, I went down to the street and, pretending to be the absent landlord's son, promised the plaintiffs that the culprits would be duly punished.

As a child, I had dreamed of being a coachman; now my ambition was to be a winner in the Olympic Games. My most glorious moment came during an interschool competition when I won the high-jump contest with a leap I never afterward equaled. I was carried off in triumph on my friends' shoulders, the bandage I wore on a wounded foot was shared as a souvenir, even my brother was honored. My track hero was Richard Rau: I collected and pasted in albums all the reproductions, all the photographs I could find. I even went so far as to write a naive little sports story, which I had the audacity to send to a newspaper; of course, it was returned to me. In it the hero, the greatest fifteen-hundred-meter runner, about to win his most important race ever, deliberately allows his best friend to pass him. What a sublime sacrifice, what a noble friendship! You can really see how deeply I was influenced by the German notion of camaraderie.

All the sports and practical jokes in the world, however, could not free me from my obsession for women. When alone at home, I would feel sad and want to cry, for no reason. I, who lauded stoicism and hated to reveal my emotions, burst into sobs when Madi accused me one day of making agreed-upon signs to a woman at her window across the street. Alas, she was signaling someone else in our building! On the other hand, Madi never suspected me of looking through the keyhole at our maid Emma when she undressed; and I never managed to see any of Emma's flesh. How was it possible that, instead of living a gilded life, this Cinderella spent her time dusting and cleaning? For she was incredibly beautiful, that girl, beautiful as only a German woman can sometimes be. Very fair and golden, Emma had cascades of hair that shone like golden rain. Her skin was moist, so were her darkly shaded eyelids; an irresistible sensuality emanated from her entire being. At this point, Lotte came from Munich to pay me a short visit, but I was cold and distracted and could find nothing to say to her during the walk we took around the Lietzensee.

It is also in Berlin that my brother and I were both circumcised and baptized. When I was still a small child, my mother had been advised to have me circumcised for reasons of hygiene. I cannot think why my brother had also to endure it. We spent two days at the hospital in delirium. As for the baptism and Bible course that went with it, that was to make our life and choice of career easier in a Russia of pogroms and anti-Semitic persecutions. I cannot remember today whether I became a Lutheran or a Reformed Protestant. My parents were atheists; they had left me completely ignorant of the Jewish religion. I had never yet been inside a synagogue, but had frequently been taken to Russian Orthodox services by Agafia. My Schaikevich cousins, my English cousins, the Mayers, were all baptized. Theodore, along with the son of old Baron de Guinzbourg, was an officer in an Infantry regiment and similarly. I later became a cadet of the Constantine Artillery School. When my future stepfather, then my mother, were to die in Paris, their funeral services would be held at the Orthodox Church on the rue Daru. Thus, while I could not love the Jewish religion, there was nothing to attract me to Protestantism: I found it too cold and formal, and always preferred the Orthodox Church. And now a question must be answered: Did I believe? It is difficult to say. I certainly did not have the faith of an Agafia; I probably had no faith at all. Did I merely love the Church the way an esthete loves a work of art or a landscape? No, it was more than that since, once inside a church, I felt the need to meditate, to purify myself, to rise beyond the petty occupations of the day, to free myself from earthly matters. I believed there was spirit infusing matter, I believed in the miracle of creation, in the balance of the universe, in the mysteries of life and death. Even as a child, I loved ikons, candles, incense, Gregorian chants, Slavonic sermons, and Agafia's slow, halting gestures when, with the sign of the Cross, she bent almost double or kneeled in spite of her almost paralyzing rheumatism. Agafia, Holy Russia, a white monastery mirrored in a lake, churches rearing their Byzantine cupolas over birch forests, all these went into my love for the Russian religion. When later, for almost thirty years, my life became linked to another country I loved and of which I became part—France—then I grew to love Catholicism with its cathedrals, its golds and purples, its cardinals, its organ music, its sculpture, and its little village churches through which, during the Mass, wafted all the country's sounds and smells.

Toward the end of our stay in Berlin, my mother went more and more often to Saint Petersburg, prolonging her stays there at the invitation of our Uncle Efim, whose wife, Aunt Eugenie, had died shortly after my father's death. Uncle Efim more and more felt the need to have someone to run his house, organize important business dinners, and preside over his parties. That someone was my mother. Thus on returning from one of these trips, she told my brother and me the great news that she was going to marry Uncle Efim, whom we knew well and loved. Our reaction was completely unexpected, both for her and for ourselves. Faced with this incredible betrayal of our father's sacred memory, this father whom we had known so very little, we burst into sobs and hid in our rooms. And when, a little later, we came back to the dining room, calmer now, she warned us: "Above all, children, don't imitate your cousins, those gilded youths who do nothing but party, make debts, and sleep all day; anyway, you won't have their money!"

Despite our upset, this was all very good news. The orphans were to have a family, to recreate, really, their old family. There had always been a close tie between our family and Aunt Eugenie's. My mother had known Efim Schaikevich since, still a child in Kovno, she had seen him court and marry her eldest sister. Married in her turn and living in Saint Petersburg, my mother must have followed with interest her brother-in-law's brilliant career, first as the most eminent business lawyer in Russia, then as one of the most important bankers. One thing seems curious to me: This man, known and admired for his proverbial integrity in business, would when he played croquet with my mother, then a little girl, cheat. "You know," my mother would tell me, "each time I turned my head, his ball, which he could not get through the hoop, would suddenly be in front of it, as if by magic, and the monster, laughing, would win the game."

It was high time for my brother and me to be getting back

to Saint Petersburg. Our mother was away more and more; school was too easy, too much time was spent on sports, playing with marbles, or doing nothing at all. We were sliding down a slippery slope. As I have already mentioned, our cousins Anatole and Gregory were appalled when they visited us. We spoke to them only of sports and operettas.

I should have been pleased to go home to Russia, but instead I felt unhappy. It meant the end of everything I enjoyed most, especially my sports career. Except for soccer, almost no sports were played at home. Since you cannot well refuse the last request of a man condemned to die, my mother allowed me to go to the Stockholm Olympic Games. The year was 1912.

I left accompanied by my tutor, Carl Haas; he was a young, handsome student whose face was covered with the scars of his recent duels (but why did I need a tutor when I was such a good student?) and came back with my old Wiesbaden friend, Philip Hahn, who had come to replace Haas. I drank punch in Stockholm, walked around the city during the white nights, kissed girls in the dark during games I did not understand. In Norway, I spent a few days in Christiania [Oslo], the capital, took a dip in the freezing waters of the Hardanger Fjord, fished near William II's yacht. In Copenhagen, I admired the City Hall elevator, which never stopped, and in Hamburg, the tunnel under the Elbe.

My mother was now remarried and ordered us back to Saint Petersburg.

Chapter 3

Return to
Saint Petersburg

1912–1914

THE BELL RANG ONCE to alert the travelers, twice to get them into the carriages; when it rang three times, the train started. We were in Russia and had crossed the border without any trouble, small fry with little to offer the customs inspectors. For Virchbalovo (my stepfather told me) was not an ordinary border. A modus vivendi had been established between those Petersburgers who preferred not to have their luggage searched and the Chief of Customs, a well-known character, highly regarded in the capital and always ready to help everyone out. The traveler would be asked into his office; once seated in front of the Chief's desk, he would suddenly feel a low blow to the stomach: A small drawer, responding to an invisible spring, had been catapulted out. In this drawer the hand of the sophisticated traveler would deposit a bribe, after which the open sesame would close as if by magic; through it all, the two actors of the little drama never interrupted their pleasant conversation.

At the railway station we found a sumptuous chauffeur-driven limousine waiting for us. How sad, ugly, and repulsive the station square seemed to me, with its leprous buildings, muddy pavements, and broken-down cabs pulled by starveling horses; and in contrast, what a pleasant surprise, a little later, to come to my parents' apartment, spacious, light, and so welcoming. While a clock somewhere chimed noon, a gentleman wearing white tie and tails came into the sitting room. Surprised, I bowed respectfully to him: He was one of the servants. "Here you are at last, my dear children," said my mother, as she kissed us. "You are welcome but, and I don't want to have to say it again, do not imitate your cousins— *Abschrekendes Beispiel* ("disgusting example")."

Thus a whole new life in the midst of a large family started for Eugene and me, a life that soon had me forgetting Germany and my sports ambitions. Around Efim Grigorievich Schaikevich, the patriarch, now my stepfather but whom, by force of habit, I continued to call *Diadia* ("Uncle"), gravitated his three sons, Anatole, Theodore, and Gregory—or Tolia, Fedia and Grisha—several uncles and aunts, and some distant poor relations such as the Silbermans. All would appear at mealtime: My stepfather's board was open to all in the old Russian tradition of hospitality, which stipulated that the men must kiss the hand of their hostess before they left the table.

Dear, dear Uncle Efim, so kind, so generous, so simple, so willing to give everyone his freedom. I loved him; he not only liked me, he respected me as well—and this was quite unique— for I was the only one who ever repaid the money borrowed from him. I would regularly return the loans that helped me get through the end of the month, as I received a very small allowance. Slipping me a few rubles was one thing, but a loan was sacred, and since I always paid him back when I said I would, I had an open line of credit. As you can see, I was in no way influenced by my cousins' behavior, especially not by Theodore's principle of borrowing and borrowing more and more so as to die with enormous debts.

My stepfather was barely taller than I. He was neither fat nor thin, and had truthful eyes, a small drooping moustache, and a bald head—the idea that his barber, who shaved him every morning, had to cut his hair now and again always seemed funny to me. My stepfather always looked very Mongol. This may not have been surprising after all since, according to one version of the family's origin, they had converted to Judaism to avoid or protest certain of the Tsar's decrees. His name could hardly have sounded more Russian: Schaikevich means "he of the robbers' troupe."

Return to Saint Petersburg · 1912–1914

Happy, cozy, enchanting, our days glided past like a sail on the surface of a peaceful sea. Eugene and I were now the youngest members of the clan. I did not dislike my transformation from the oldest brother of a small family into the younger of a large one. My cousins liked us and took us under their wings: my uncles and aunts were pleased to find their long-lost nephews again. We all got along together perfectly well and I simply could not tell which of my cousins I liked best, Anatole the brilliant esthete, Theodore the materialist, the fusspot, or Gregory the poet-dreamer.

In addition to my three cousins, I must now introduce Uncle Otto, my mother's eldest brother; Uncle Paul, my stepfather's younger brother, and his wife, Aunt Mania, who were both friends—which is more than I can say of my stepfather's elder sister, Liubov Grigorievna Segal, a little old woman, a widow with whom I did not have much in common, and of her son Jules, a lawyer, fat, bald, flabby, always sweating. I frankly couldn't stand Jules or his wife, an M.D. who would punch me in the nose everytime I bent forward to kiss her hand.

I don't really know why, perhaps because of his magnificent upswept moustaches, as white as his hair, but Uncle Otto always put me in mind of a handsome cat, the one with nine-league boots, the Marquis de Carabas of the fairy story. This Manassevich, so neat and tidy, looked like a great European noble, totally at ease in his Knabe suits, cut to perfection from those wonderful London materials. He was fifty, about the same age as my stepfather. This epicurean really knew how to live: Always and everywhere, he would give royal tips (my stepfather was always afraid of corrupting people), and thus would get the best table, the best place, the best room, and the promptest service. Financially comfortable —he was in insurance—he was even said to be rich through owning gold (in bars or coins?). Divorced, childless, he was considered an inveterate bachelor. I never went to his apartment; I did not even know where he lived. He had horses and a coachman, and an old peasant woman, Matriocha, took as good care of him as if he had been her own child; years later, I learned that she had borne him an illegitimate daughter of whom Aunt Julie took care.

All the men in the family, except for my stepfather, smoked cigarettes; and since the smoke upset my mother, they would generally retire to one end of the room or even next door. They always went to Bagdanof's and bought two boxes: One was full of Turkish tobacco, light, fine, and perfumed, the other of rice-paper tubes with long cardboard holders. Each smoker would prepare for himself his day's ration in a little metal machine that opened in the middle and was no wider than a pencil. Uncle Otto's waistcoat looked like the chest of a Georgian warrior, bearing, however, instead of cartridges, many long amber cigarette holders, all alike and containing a piece of cotton that served as a filter. In his left pocket were ranged those he had already used and in his right were the new ones. Uncle Otto, as you see, liked order, hygiene, and care. All the smokers would continually spit into spittoons, which was then considered elegant. Instead of the click of the lighter one hears today (matches and touchwood were used then), there was that of the many cigarette boxes: flat, tall, made of gold or silver with a picture engraved on the cover: a troika, the two-headed eagle, the Peter and Paul fortress. . . .

While Uncle Otto reminded me of a magnificent cat, Uncle Paul, short and stocky, with his big, droopy moustache, his uncontrollable mane, and his bushy eyebrows, could be compared to a large seal. Still, he was not scary for he was smiling and kind. Smaller than Uncle Otto, about the same height as his brother, my stepfather, he was as strong as Hercules and I feared his handshake. Aunt Mania, his wife, née Maria Effron, came from a large family of half-brothers and sisters whose patriarch was as well-known as Webster for his publication of the Brockhaus and Effron Encyclopedia. They were a perfect couple, compatible even in their politics since they both belonged to the Cadet party. Everyone, myself included, admired Aunt Mania's mind: open, logical, cool, masculine. And while I liked her, I must say that her physical appearance was unpleasant to me. I never saw her dressed in anything but black; I thought that her body looked like a tower; her hands were too short and doll-like; her fingers ended in almost non-existent nails. She had a yellow complexion, a large pimple on one cheek, and a red mark on the bridge of her nose left by the pince-nez she wore to remedy her short-sightedness.

Uncle Paul and his brother were both masters at bridge, a game that was beginning to replace whist. But while my uncle took chances, seemed to see through the cards, and would make sensational grand slams, my stepfather, as was his custom, was prudent and solid. A Sunday rarely went by but those two had a game with Theodore, a good player, Anatole, very wild, and Uncle Otto, frankly bad. Now and again, passions would rise, with the parents scolding the children and the children quarreling among themselves. Words like idiot, moron, horse (which is used in Russian for ass) would fly through the air. Sometimes even swearwords were used, which my mother, who was innocence itself, would not understand, though she resented the "behavior of these *mujiks* who think they're in a tavern." Besides, this was Russia, not England, the land of gentlemen. In the evenings, when they were alone, my parents would play Coon-can, a Russian gin rummy, or solitaire, and often my stepfather would change the order of the cards to make the game come out, while talking to my mother but thinking about business.

Bridge, however, was played only on Sunday and was not in any case the family's main pastime. It was billiards that occupied the place of honor. We spent most of our time in the billiard room, which was the pleasantest of the whole apartment. Copied from a Scottish castle, it was lined with green cloth between oak panels. A thick wall-to-wall carpet silenced all footsteps. A window of thick, green bottle glass made into small panes let through a watery light, and big logs burned in the fireplace.

On our arrival in Saint Petersburg, Eugene and I discovered

that our uncles and cousins were accomplished billiards players, and this stimulated us to catch up with them. Thus billiards became a favorite pastime of ours as well. On his return home from the bank in the evening, my stepfather liked to relax by playing a game with Eugene or me. This would often go on forever since my stepfather's strategy was defensive, watching for his opponent's mistake, implacably placing the ball on the stripe, thus making the game extremely difficult. Neglecting the Kiel variety, we would favor the Pyramid, which demanded an absolutely precise handling of the cue since the balls would barely go into the pockets. On a table built to French specifications, we had to get sixty-one in order to win with balls numbered from one to twelve. When Eugene and I lost the game, as we did often in the beginning, our elders, for fun and to follow an old tradition, had us crawl under the table—a much kinder forfeit than the old standby of having us swallow as many brioches in a row as the four stripes could hold.

Frivolous as this may seem, I must now go on to the food, the servants, and the apartment, since they were the backdrop of our daily lives.

Two cuisines alternating and complementing each other, the Russian and the French, made for an incredibly rich gastronomical climate. How well, how excessively much, we ate! There were no Sundays or holidays without guests. We would start with appetizers—caviar, fresh and pressed, both served in little pails and eaten by the spoonful—chased by little glasses of vodka poured down one's throat. An exquisite smoked white fish, the Sig, preferred to sturgeon or salmon; then a huge assortment of soups, cold and hot, accompanied by a no less huge assortment of *pirojki* or *kulebiaka*, pastries filled with minced meat or fish, cabbage or kasha. After some Westphalian ham, meat would make its appearance: minced veal or chicken cutlets, tender-boned chicks, white-meat game in winter. I pass over the cheeses and desserts. As for the wines, my stepfather had chosen them himself while in France, in restaurants and hotels.

Return to Saint Petersburg · 1912–1914

It was not only because he loved good food that my step-father had to keep a chef; business dinners to be given and returned, and his position in the world of high finance made it imperative. Our master of the cordon bleu was always someone internationally known—who came from a foreign embassy, a famous restaurant, or the service of a prince—and seduced to our house by his weight in gold. Among the three or four chefs we had in succession, one was so great a master that he spoiled us not just with his complicated dishes but with the simplest ones as well, like *oeufs en gelée*, so delicious as to be unforgettable. Alas, he had to be dismissed because he broke a plate over the butler's head. He was not only a regular cook but a pastry chef as well, constantly surprising us with monumental, tastefully decorated cakes. In his free time, this extraordinary man painted watercolors, wrote verse, and read Russian literature. He had traveled a great deal and spoke several languages. I knew all this, ate his cuisine every day, and, still, I never met him and am surprised today at my indifference to this, to me ghostlike, master. I don't think that I ever stepped across the kitchen threshold or that he ever ventured into the dining room to be complimented or even to discuss a menu—for they must have been made up daily by my mother, or, rather, Madi, before being taken to the staff. We did once, by the purest chance, happen on our famous chef who was soon to be dismissed for his conduct with the plate. One day as Theodore was returning from the Tsarskoie-Selo (Pushkino) station, he became curious about a very elegant stranger who, having shared his first-class compartment, was now walking down the boulevard in front of him. When he reached our villa, this gentleman opened the garden door but, instead of going up the steps to the main door, entered the basement.

Everyone in the family ate too much, but it was really Gregory and I who were the true gluttons, downing first five large slices of ham, for instance, then continuing unhesitatingly with two partridges. One day in Finland, I even swallowed seventy-five large sprats, *koriushki*. On the other hand, *blinis* ("pancakes") were not my strong suit: I could never go beyond twelve—while the real Russians, it seems, like Leonid Andreyev, the writer, would measure them by the foot. During my stepfather's great business dinners, Eugene and I, exiled to the small dining room, would be given all the dishes that the servants had put down on the marble-topped sideboard. And so while I had eaten many French dishes, I knew very few of their names. Once when I was just beginning to go out, I read a menu and, consulting my guest, ordered two consommés followed by a parfait.

We must have had a dozen servants, including the helpers. Aside from the chef, there were two or three servants in white tie; Madi, perfect in her new role as housekeeper, greatly admired and complimented by all (my mother was always a bad housewife); Annouchka, who had been housekeeper under Aunt Eugenie, was now my mother's personal maid and accompanied her abroad; the indefatigable Agafia, baking brioches for tea (which mostly ended up in the muzzle of my dog Boy; not that he begged, but anyone crossing the dining room thought it a duty to throw him one or two); a seamstress (in a little back room near the kitchen) who retouched and naturally spoiled the dresses my mother had bought in Paris at Vionnet's and Doucet's; Ilia, the imposingly large coachman; the stableman, a square-bearded giant who wore boots and a caftan; Antoine, the thin chauffeur with his English cap, a flower in his buttonhole (who, I later learned, was another of the servants who either seduced Madi or was seduced by her); the chauffeur's helper; and finally the pink-cheeked Matriocha, the new maid freshly arrived from the country and assigned to clean our rooms in the upstairs apartment.

We lived at number 35, Nikolaevskaya, a dull street like many others, paved with stone, very quiet, and lined with two rows of houses covered in peeling paint. Why did I never venture in the direction opposite from the Nevsky Prospekt and diverge even a little from my usual daily route? This lack of curiosity in myself I find very surprising today, when I am so full of curiosity about other cities. Then there were two worlds living side by side, inextricably bound and yet divided by impenetrable though invisible borders, two worlds that might have been more distant from one another than continents. On the one hand, there was the city I had known from birth, where I lived and grew up, and on the other hand there was *terra incognita*, with its suburbs, its canals, its little bridges, even its summer residences—of which I did not even know Peterhof, where I was born. While I regret it, I do not think my ignorance was exceptional: Few people come really to know their own city.

The severe and majestic perspectives of Saint Petersburg did not house any wonder in the passerby. There was nothing gay or intimate about its beautiful architecture. In fact, a certain feeling of anemia gripped the city. Everything was solid, yet it seemed unreal.

The downstairs of our house, on the other hand, was to me like paradise. Three large rooms looked out onto the Nikolaevskaya: the dining room, a bedroom, and, between the two, a living room where five French windows opened onto a narrow iron balcony. From the dining room, going toward the back, one reached first the billiard room with a small dining room next to it; then, up two or three steps, a passage led to the kitchen. In the apartment's other wing, the same arrangement prevailed: first my parents' bedroom, then my mother's future bedroom, a boudoir, a bathroom, and finally a linen room. Anatole, who years before had criticized my mother's modest apartment, now did the same to his father's, so far forgetting himself one day that he declared all bankers to be cretins. He had not approved of the arranging of the new apartment by a pompous gentleman, an internationally known architect, probably the first interior decorator of the time. I must admit the billiard room was a masterpiece, but you could not say the same for the Steinway that, covered in mahogany laden with bronze ornaments, had been transformed into a pretentious "piece" in the Riesener style. And God knows what would have become of my mother's bedroom if it had been completed as planned, with its silk hangings and its big Pompadour bed crowned with a canopy!

What one first noticed in the living room was that it contained three pianos: the Steinway grand, a Bechstein grand that had belonged to Aunt Eugenie and was now against the wall under a big portrait of her by Sorin, and a Steinway upright that would electrically play rolls recorded by various great pianists: Paderewski, Busoni, Hofmann. I spent many lonely winter evenings while my parents were in Monte Carlo listening to great performances of Scriabin Etudes, Chopin Preludes, Wagner's *Feuerzauber*, etc.

I don't know whether my stepfather was poor when he was just a law student. But after his marriage, with the help of relentless work and a photographic memory, he quickly became the best-known business lawyer in the country—while Grusenberg, who defended Beilis of the famous blood-libel, was known as the best criminal lawyer. Later, it was as an authority on the law that he, together with Wishnegradsky, was called upon to head the International Bank of Commerce of Saint Petersburg. The bank had branches everywhere in Russia as well as in Paris, Brussels, and Geneva; it was shortly to open a branch in New York. The financial press always cited my stepfather's fortune as one of the greatest in the capital, and this at a time when the stock market was going up, life was relatively inexpensive, and there were practically no taxes. As a financial expert, my stepfather was sometimes invited to attend cabinet meetings; the family always said he would have surely become a Minister if it had not been for his Jewish origins. He was linked to other businesses also and, after marrying my mother, he began to set up a separate estate for her. My mother now bought her dresses from Parisian couturiers and had a Parisian apartment. She went to Monte Carlo with my stepfather, wore beautiful jewelry and an unrivaled ermine coat worth twelve thousand rubles! Since he disliked nepotism and was aware of his sons' dreadful reputations, my stepfather had always kept them out of his business, at least until my mother insisted he give them jobs. He finally agreed to take Gregory into the legal department of his bank, and Gregory did extremely well there. He also placed Theodore at the head of a new small business, Yuravetta, which he had created with a certain Wurgaft. When the war began to go badly, his colleagues tried to save their money by illegally transferring it abroad, thereby weakening the ruble, but my stepfather, a patriot and man of legendary integrity, refused to follow their example. He lost all he had during the Revolution. Thanks to the bank's foreign branches, now united under the new title International Commerce Bank of Paris at 26, rue Lafitte, and of which he was to become the Director, he was saved and able to support lavishly the dozen family members who depended on him. After his death came the deluge.

My stepfather had always loved his relatives, but he loved his bank still more, so we sometimes teased him about how he was really married to the bank; and gossip, at the time of Aunt Eugenie's death, charged him with having returned to the bank, which was his mistress, much too soon. In the evenings, after a day's work, he would be with us physically, but his mind would be elsewhere. Whether we played solitaire or billiards, or even conversed, we could feel his inattention. He had been just the same when his sons were growing up: He loved them, provided for all their needs, even spoiled them, but he had never had the time or the inclination to care for them, get close to them, become their friend, their advisor, their guide. It had been the same with their mother who at first had been terribly spoiled, and had then become ill and left her children in the hands of nannies and tutors. Father and sons did love one another, but their shyness would prevail and keep them from intimacy of any kind. My cousins went on being unable to express their feelings until their father's very end, and on his deathbed, he was unable to ask his sons to come close and kiss him. Thus my cousins grew up into young men, who, though kind and charming, had no discipline, no taste for work, nor any serious occupation in life. Yet, a wonderful feeling of strength and security was given to everyone by my stepfather. Life was an enchantment, they felt, and nothing bad could happen.

At first, I had no favorite among my cousins; I liked them all. Curiously, the one I saw the least often was the youngest, Gregory, who still lived at home upstairs with us, for by the time I got back at night, he had already gone to see his mistress (a lush-looking officer's wife who was older than he), and when I went down in the morning, he was sound asleep, having come home in the small hours. I saw more of Anatole and Theodore, though they lived elsewhere, for they often came to lunch or dinner.

Gregory had curly black hair, a young girl's curving eyelashes, heavy eyelids swollen with sleep, and looked like a dreamy adolescent. This *wunderkind* had learned how to read at the age of three. He it was who, when he finished school, gave me his stamp collection. Like many Russian students, who learned fast and forgot even faster, he managed (a miracle that others would also perform) to take and pass all his exams at the Polytechnic Institute in one month, staying awake at night by drinking oceans of tea and going from one exam to the next every two or three days. Needless to say, he had not attended any of his college classes or opened a book before that month.

Gregory the poet wrote verse, but was a highly organized man. Each day he wrote down his expenses, which happened to be minute because he did not imitate his brothers who wasted money. He even wrote in his calendar, day by day, what he intended to do throughout the year. For instance: "On April 5, I will get up at eight o'clock, but on the 6th at nine, after which I'll go and see such and such a friend, will have lunch in such and such a restaurant, will visit the Hermitage but only look at the Rembrandts, will read such and such a book in the evening and go to bed at. . . ." His whole life was laid out to perfection in advance, but not one of these noble plans, alas, was ever carried out. Even his way of sleeping looked like no one else's: Curled up in a ball with his sheets and blankets completely covering him, he would make a mound in one corner of his double bed, which then looked empty, and more than once the maid Matriocha shrieked when, making up the bed, she touched her master, a flesh-and-blood ghost.

Theodore the smart aleck would listen to you ironically, cynically, one eyebrow always raised. But this clever man, this believer in the material world somehow never managed to become practical. What he liked to do was tease, teasing all those he loved. No one was better than he at helping out a friend, pushing through a project, obtaining a difficult document, or pleading your cause. The more difficult the case, the more he was in his element. I never saw him fail; always one would go to him for help. And then he teased you some more by keeping you in suspense, telling you he hadn't had time, or that he had forgotten about you, or that he had failed, while, all the time, he had the needed paper right in his pocket and would finally give it to you. And woe to the friend who began to get annoyed or angry with him, for then my cousin would become sadistic and cruel. Whenever he saw in an official building a door saying Do Not Enter, he would head straight for it. "Are you sleeping?" he once asked Tupsik, his mistress, waking her in the middle of the night, and on being answered yes, would say: "Well, go ahead and sleep then. I'd be the last to wake you." Better than anyone else I have met, this attractive eccentric knew human nature, how to be a diplomat, how to seduce women. I have seen people who were actually hostile and did not want to pay any attention be unable not to listen to him, then start to smile, laugh, then answer, get intrigued, and finally end by becoming his friends. He was certainly not handsome, but he was neat, pleasant, elegant, aristocratic looking. And he might have been quite perfect were it not for two great faults: a total neglect of time and an obsession with the part in his hair. I don't think there ever was one time in his entire life when he arrived at a dinner party on time or was present for the overture and first act of an opera. Thinking his father's position allowed him to do anything, he would appear halfway through the most elegant dinner and, in the midst of an icy silence, take his seat with phony humility and start to say amusing things to the other guests who would, little by little, lose their frowns and forgive his rudeness, saying: "Well, after all, let the devil take you!"

When my stepfather had finally put him at the head of Yuravetta, he was supposed to arrive at his new business around ten A.M. each day, a thing that practically never happened. He appeared to have a feeling for business but was quite unable to discipline himself. What his mood was would depend on how he got up that morning but, above all, on the part in his hair. How often I witnessed the comedy of that part!

Starting with his difficulty at waking up, Theodore would manage to get out of bed, have breakfast with his German shepherd, shave, and take a bath—in which he liked to spend an eternity; then would come his greatest trial, the part, which might take from a minimum of ten minutes to well over an hour. Throughout this time, his office would be ringing him on the phone. His valet would answer that his master would be there in ten minutes, five minutes, that he had already left— all this while our man was still battling his part! Sometimes it would seem perfect to me and I would breathe a sigh of relief when suddenly Theodore would unmake it. He would comb and comb again, wrinkling his brow so that the hair would part naturally, copiously sprinkling it with cologne and overseeing this difficult operation with a second, hand-held, mirror placed behind the head and reflected in the front. This style of parting had come from Germany at a time when monocles and smartly turned up moustaches were the fashion; it was called *poposcheitel*, or "parting of the arse," and had to go straight over the head right down to the neck. Theodore would make it and unmake it so often that his forehead was sometimes red from rubbing. The whole thing was worthy to be a story by Gogol—a story in which the part would take revenge on its wearer.

But if parting his hair ruled Theodore, Theodore ruled poor Matriocha during the period when he slept in my room while his own apartment was being repainted. "Matriocha," he would say in the evening, "tomorrow I must be at the office at ten without fail. It's very important, so start waking me at eight, keep insisting, and pay no attention to anything I say. This is an order." And the next morning, when poor Matriocha would try to rouse him: "Leave me alone. Anything I said yesterday doesn't count, stop bothering me; if you don't obey right now, I'll have you fired!" And Matriocha would stand in front of the bed, in tears, not knowing what to do.

I must recall two incidents connected with Theodore that occurred during family luncheons in the summer, one years before the other. The first took place when I was a child and Aunt Eugenie was alive. A large group was gathered over lunch. Since it was impossible to get Theodore out of bed, someone pretended to him he was being called on the phone by his mistress. He immediately rushed through the dining room in a long nightgown, barefoot, his hair straight up, to the accompaniment of much laughter. The second incident took place in Tsarskoie-Selo just before the war. Theodore suddenly, in front of everyone, slapped our servant Andrey in the face. He froze to the spot—we actually all froze with horror. He immediately repented. I do not know if I would have remembered poor Andrey without this ugly incident, for he was soon after killed in the war.

But of my three cousins, it was certainly Anatole who was the most interesting. Here he is, the brilliant Anatole, the aristocrat, the esthete, the art collector, the rebel of the family, the self-made man who exerted such a great influence on my brother and me. He opened our eyes to a new world, very different from what we saw every day, from middle-class routine, from thoughts of money. He encouraged us to become painters and convinced our parents to let us choose our own careers. We were enormously lucky to have found both a friend and a stimulator in him and to have had our parents as allies who helped us all our lives. Still, with the passing of years, my feelings toward Anatole have changed. In the beginning, I admired him totally, drinking in his words when he talked about painting, about his travels in Italy, about his thoughts on Russian literature. I listened rapt when he played Viennese waltzes on the piano. Then gradually the scales began to tip the other way. He began to seem too brilliant, too dilettantish, sometimes lacking in solidity. Besides, I more and more began to resent his powerful and irresistible influence over my adolescent brother—at a time when Anatole himself had a son, Andrey, three years younger than my brother, who lived with his divorced mother and was never brought to see us. Anatole ignored his son but considered Eugene to be his disciple, his spiritual heir. Eugene became his shadow! But anyway, it is all so far away now; more than fifty years have passed, Anatole is dead, Eugene and I, separated by an ocean, lead very different lives. Peace be to the passions, the years, and the ashes.

Thanks to his father's position, to his charm, to his art collection, to his wide acquaintance as a journalist—his supposed profession—Anatole occupied a unique place in the life of Saint Petersburg. He knew the whole city and everyone knew him. It was the time of the Shchukin-Morosoff phenomenon in Moscow. These two unlettered merchants, multimillionaires, living in the complete artistic vacuum of their city, suddenly heard, like Saint Peter in the desert, a divine voice ordering them to buy paintings by Renoir, Cézanne, and Van Gogh. And with the help of clever dealers, at a time when almost no one was interested in impressionism, they collected such a tremendous quantity of those painters' best canvases, along with Matisses and Picassos, that, after having covered the walls of their huge and probably dark houses, they pushed them into remote corners and under their children's beds. While this phenomenon was taking place in Moscow, that of Anatole Schaikevich, on a smaller scale, was happening in Saint Petersburg.

The Anatole phenomenon was quite different from the Shchukin-Morosoff but just as amazing. What miracle had converted that pagan, that lover of enjoyment, to art? Who had made him give up the bourgeois existence he shared with his entourage, leave the fashionable spas of Karlsbad and Marienbad and wander off to Venice, visit the Rijksmuseum or the Prado, go to Versailles or Chartres? Anatole was ahead of his time, creating interior ensembles composed of art objects where porcelains, sculptures, paintings, and furniture complemented and displayed one another. These arrangements had for their background—and this had never yet been seen—rooms painted in one color and each one different; my brother was to copy this some fifteen years later.

The room in his apartment I remember best was the dining room. It was painted a handsome cobalt-blue, with dishes and porcelains hanging on the walls, vitrines with Sèvres and Meissen figurines and chests filled with *sarafans* (antique women's costumes); the furniture was of light Karelian birch. In the sitting room, of which I have forgotten the wall color, there were shell-shaped Venetian furniture, baroque mirrors, a big gondola-shaped chandelier, one or two Guardis or Canalettos, real or fake, next to a big Dosso Dossi—which some experts (among them Bode of the Kaiser Friedrich Museum in Berlin) thought attributable to Giorgione—a Poussin, and some other paintings. But the real pride of Anatole's collection was his group of some thirty Dutch still-lifes, and he transmitted his passion for them to us. While these jewels, set in massive, finely sculpted black frames, awakened my admiration and desire to know a Van Heusum from a De Heem, to my brother they became a source of inspiration and imitation for the paintings he was to do. I instinctively felt this was an error and, in fact, it took him two years to free himself from such mistaken ideas. Very quickly he became a still-life virtuoso, using sometimes the light of a single candle.

The Moscow merchants Shchukin and Morosoff had all their treasures nationalized—which is to say, stolen—by the Soviets. The fate of Anatole's apartment was hardly better. First he lost some of his Dutch paintings when a smuggler who was supposed to bring him the rolled canvases in Finland absconded with them. For two or three years, friends of his who were Bolshevist sympathizers were able to protect his empty apartment from being despoiled. Around 1922, a Swedish diplomat wrote him in Paris offering twelve million krone for the apartment and all its contents. The idiot refused the offer and thus lost his last chance of recovering anything at all. After that he had to be supported, first by his father, then by my brother.

I know few details of my cousin's childhood. Upon graduating from the University, still very young, he married a *demoiselle bleue*, a very beautiful young girl, very popular, belonging to an excellent Russian Orthodox family: my Aunt Varia. She had dark blue eyes, finely chiseled features, and her skin was so white and so transparent that one could see all her veins. But a middle-class life and the birth of a son must have quickly wearied Anatole, for he divorced and took to debauchery and travel. A bottle of champagne waited for him every night in his favorite nightclub. He visited Europe, Morocco, Tunisia, where he caught syphilis. He became interested in occult matters, went in for turning tables with Ouspensky, smoked opium with Gurdjieff, buried his most beautiful mistress in Venice, lost fortunes at cards, which were paid by his father, discussed painting with Bode, literature with Andreyev and Gorky, like Proust's Swann, began an essay on Vermeer, wrote stories, dabbled in journalism, and finally began to collect his art objects.

Anatole looked like his mother: Always remarkably handsome, he was even more so at twenty because of his perfectly white hair (his son Andrey, the very picture of his father, also went white early). A photograph of him I still have taken at that time for a fancy-dress ball proves it. In contrast to his white hair, his eyes were black, languorous, and velvety, as shiny as plums, and his whole delicately chiseled face was worthy of a master's hand: a thin-bridged nose, voluptuous, trembling nostrils, and a slightly heavy, sensual bottom lip. As for the rest of him, Anatole was very neglectful. He was quite untidy, not even very clean; his nails were sometimes dirty and broken, his clothes rumpled. He was like those Parisians of the turn of the century whose reputation for elegance and good taste was based on the look of their wives or mistresses. This penniless millionaire—thanks to his father and to dinners where dishes and guests were sedulously selected, to his collection and his mistresses—could afford not to bother with his appearance. He was a little nearsighted, and his one affectation was to wear a pince-nez hanging from a very long gold chain around his neck.

Eugene and I knew only Anatole's last mistress, Claudia Pavlova, whom he later married in Finland at his father's insistence. She then became his "Fair Lady," and he believed in her genius forever after. For, unlike Pygmalion, who made the mistake of giving life to his statue, Anatole the visionary tried to turn human beings into masterpieces. Eugene remained his spiritual creation for a long time, Claudia for his entire life. And my brother always retained his taste for luxury, for theater sets and ballets, a love of detail and a passion for collecting art.

Our prize Saint Bernard, Boy, had been bought by Anatole at a dog show, who then passed the dog on to his father to avoid having to take care of him. Later, at an international automobile show in Berlin, Anatole was seduced by an ultra-modern automobile, an Opel, which he also passed on to his father because it cost too much to keep. He had started by buying and being unable to keep; now he kept everything and his father had to pay for his living, his collection, and his new apartment on Kamenyi Ostrof (Stone Island), next to Kchessinskaia's house.

Eugene and I, once wild boys fresh from Berlin, had adapted quickly to our new life in our old city, and become serious, studious, focused adolescents interested in art and literature. I remember that when, as a child, I was shown reproductions of da Vinci, Titian, and other giants of painting by my mother, I found them dull and could not understand why I was supposed to admire them. Now I forgot about sports. When I heard Anatole and Andreyev talking about art, I would dream more and more of a trip to Italy, while wondering if what I imagined about it did not go beyond the reality. Anatole preferred Venice—light, charm, and the baroque— and Andreyev, Rome, the eternal city, cradle of history. And could one forget Florence, could one not love its harmony, its balance, its spirit, and love Rome as well?

Then there were the women. The pre-war period was still the time of *Camille*. There were three kinds of women: ladies, kept women, and prostitutes. Young men of good family would avoid marriageable girls and their mothers, whom they regarded as even more dangerous than the then-current venereal diseases. When Theodore went on a business trip to Moscow or Tula, I would overhear him and Uncle Otto talking in hints and stifling their laughter: That probably meant he was taking a companion with him in the sleeping car. Equally mysterious whispers were exchanged by Anatole and my parents, but it was quite a while before they decided it was proper to visit him and meet his new mistress. When finally, hoping to meet her myself, I was allowed to accompany my mother to my cousin's apartment, I not only did not see her, for she had been asked to go out, but I could not even discover any trace of her existence: a dressing table, a bottle of perfume, a few hairpins fallen on the floor—there was nothing; she had vanished into thin air. And when I finally did meet her, later, I was almost disappointed. What, this was the vamp, the *kept woman*, this simple young girl, fresh and pretty, very much of the people, without much culture, barely older than I and with whom I immediately became friends? Claudia Pavlova had a typically Russian kind of beauty, with a pure, rounded oval face, magnificent eyes, an upturned nose, the torso of a professional dancer, which she was, with arms I later found a little too sharp-angled, and overdeveloped leg muscles. It was in a nightclub that Anatole had discovered his muse, who was then doing a turn in which her partner finally carried her through the air at the end of his extended arm. For the rest of his life, Anatole believed in her genius and tried to make her into a second Anna Pavlova. Claudia was the only person in my family whom I ever saw in a tutu, that is, half-undressed, and I found her shaven armpits ugly, which led to my being called primitive and even innocent. As for Eugene, he had such a crush on Claudia that he did not look at another woman for many years. He became her page, which pleased her and flattered Anatole, who was not jealous. This type of *cavaliere servante* was then quite common in Russia, as one can see in Turgenev and Chekhov. But while Eugene loved Claudia and worshiped Anatole, Anatole for his part considered both Claudia and Eugene as his creations, and Claudia, who was never unfaithful to Anatole, always retained her very deep friendship for Eugene.

It was shortly after my return from Germany that I had finally lost my virginity. Thank God! I was finally free. I had become a man and like unto other mortals. It seemed to me that only one great obstacle remained before I could leave adolescence behind and become independent: That was finishing, at any cost, the school that haunted and frightened me. My fall, or my deliverance as I called it, took place, of course, with a streetwalker. While I vaguely remember the room and even the neighborhood, I have quite forgotten the girl. Is this a clue to my future vocation as a landscape rather than a portrait painter? I have always had a perfect memory for places. I remember the café where, with a few friends, I met these ladies of love. I can still see myself with a friend and two girls we picked up in a dirty, empty room with tables along the walls; we drank some liqueur or other. Is it a café or a brothel? We are on the third floor. Downstairs, in the entrance, there is a little baroque grotto, a fountain, goldfish in the pond, and colored electric bulbs. My friend and I talk incredible clichés to the two prostitutes, who are making us feel shy. The window opens onto a little square plaza at the edge of a lifeless canal with a little Van Gogh–like bridge crossing over it. It is empty, run-down, and as sad as the atmosphere inside the room. I seem to have already seen this bridge, or is it another, similar one? I crossed it as a child, many years before, on my way to see Anatole, still married then to Aunt Varia, celebrating the third or fourth birthday of their son, Andrey.

Later—I must now be sixteen or seventeen—I am invited, without Eugene, to a big artists' party at Anatole's. There are at least fifty guests having supper at little round tables. All the Petersburg celebrities are present: writers, painters, journalists, artists from the Maryinsky Theatre, classical dancers like Obuchoff, Romanoff, Smirnova, and Lukum, known for her role as a cat; clowns and acrobats from the Winter Circus including Rastelli, the celebrated juggler, the inventor of all modern tricks including his famous act with flaming torches. The party is in full swing; toasts come in series, we drink, we laugh . . . when suddenly Uncle Otto at my table notices that my glass is empty and asks me why. Embarrassed, I whisper that I have "a disease." His face lights up; he stands up, clinking his fork on his champagne glass, asks everyone to be silent and declares: "Ladies and gentlemen, I propose a toast to my dear nephew here who is himself unable to drink because he's caught a certain disease." Everybody stands up and drinks to my health, then Uncle Otto embraces me as he would a soldier who has seen fire for the first time; I am horribly embarrassed.

When my father died, I had inherited his chest filled with Russian classics. I loved books and now started to buy the new scholarly editions of Pushkin and Lermontov as soon as they came out. I read with passion and preferred spending my money on books rather than on girls, though I could not do without them either. Knut Hamsun, Selma Lagerlöf, Rodenbach, Oscar Wilde, Eugène Sue, Paul de Kock, Remy de Gourmont, Henri de Régnier, Pierre Louÿs, among others, were then in fashion. I was continually dropping into the French bookstore on the Nevsky Prospekt to buy its yellow, paper-covered novels, all the same size, and with pages you had to cut. A taste for the French classics was probably transmitted to me by a young Frenchman who came to our house and read to us; he introduced me to Maupassant, whom I have loved ever since. Anyway, everything French was in fashion, culture, clothes, cuisine. Plays, always with Francen and Dermos, were all the rage: They were light works showing lovers discussing life in bed. Our first films were French and starred Max Linder and Prince; I would invariably come away from them with a terrible headache.

It is during one of my visits to the French bookstore that, purely by chance, I saw the Piper Verlag illustrated books on Cézanne, Van Gogh, and Renoir. This revelation, this dazzling new illumination, is probably responsible for my later becoming an artist. I went back immediately to the bookstore and bought a big French book, the only one then in existence, on impressionism or the impressionists, and knew then by instinct, and very surely, that the future of art lay in that direction, and not with Dutch painting or the Old Masters. While I had been the first to draw, Eugene was the first to use color: I had never yet painted. The next summer, I did my first two oil landscapes: the sunlit garden seen from our porch, using impressionist techniques. I found in the house the volume of *Mir Iskoustva* ("the world of art") with color reproductions of the Shchukin-Morosoff collections. I begged my parents to allow me to take a quick trip to Moscow so that I might visit them, but my mother said: "First finish school; then you'll have the rest of your life to go there." And thus it is I never saw either the paintings or Moscow.

Actually, my parents were very hesitant about letting me become a painter because they thought that a banker or even a taxi driver (later in Paris) were more likely to earn a living. "Look at Wishnegradsky, the bank director," my mother would tell me. "He paints on weekends and does very well at it." Through the novels of Hugo, Zola, and Gide, I had discovered Paris: the Place de l'Opera, Montmartre, the Boulevards; now I saw it through paintings by Monet, Pissaro, or Sisley. Since I felt that impressionism was the only possible starting point for a young painter, it seemed obvious that Paris was the only city in the world where one could learn painting, and now my dream was to go there to live.

I took drawing lessons that winter. Once a week in my overheated bathroom, from five to seven, a nude model would pose and Naoumoff, an ex-academician, would correct my efforts to draw. All the professional models came from the Academy of Fine Arts: working-class men with severe moustaches, strong and squat, with knots of muscles, who would take conventional poses, and not very young women with sagging white flesh, but whose nakedness excited my adolescent lust. As for Naoumoff, he certainly knew his trade, I realize it now. All I learned and still know I owe to him. I drew on big white sheets of Waterman paper with charcoal because it erases easily. In this way I first discovered how to look at a model, to understand him, to draw him in my head before trusting him to my hand; how to start by setting the subject on the page—which is composition; to go from the overall to the detail by establishing key points, calculating angles and proportions. I learned to exaggerate when necessary to bring out character, to give life and intelligence to the line, to take into account the volume of reflecting light, and even to study anatomy. Naoumoff, tall, thin, with a little yellowish pointed beard and the unhealthy skin of someone who does not always eat enough, looked like Jesus Christ. After our session, he would usually come downstairs with me for dinner. He and Anatole disliked each other, Naoumoff feeling that my cousin was no more than a rich dilettante and my cousin that Naoumoff was a second-rate artist. Naturally, I admired my teacher. I visited his studio, brought first a canvas of an orchard in the impressionist manner, then one of a night dance at the side of a pond—probably inspired by Corot—and generally made propaganda that resulted in the sale of two oils to my friend Mischa Epstein.

Sometime in 1913, my stepfather bought my mother a country house in Tsarskoie-Selo (Pushkino), near Saint Petersburg, where the Tsar had one of his summer palaces. A merchant called Zolin sold it to him and included a horse and a cow in the deal. The horse, a trotter, was banned from the race course because it often broke into a canter. The cow, the trotter's companion, as well as our two stallions, stayed in the stable for lack of a meadow to graze in. I was the only one who visited the stables and our coachman Ilia's little apartment above to drink warm milk, which no one else liked.

Tsarskoie-Selo, which means the "Tsar's village," was a small town with sumptuous villas spaced along the avenue from the railroad station to the park, which was open to the public. The huge palace resembled the Winter Palace in size and style and was near the park's entrance. But while the Winter Palace was painted a dull wine-red, Tsarskoie-Selo was attractively done in more natural shades: its cream and light olive-green harmonized with the foliage, especially in the fall. And as I walked through the immense park covered with ponds, pavilions, and statues, nothing seemed to me pleasanter than the solitude of these paths. As for our country house, which was built of wood with two stories and painted white all over, it was not remarkable except for having been built by an Italian Court architect whose name began with an *M*; the only trace of his work was a very understated frieze dividing the huge living room that looked out on a small garden from one bow-window to the other.

The train ride from Tsarskoie-Selo to Pavlovsk, another of the Tsar's summer residences, only lasted ten minutes. Our coachman, Ilia, driving his two stallions, often raced ahead of the train on the road that ran parallel to the tracks. What Herculean strength a Russian coachman must have had to keep his troika flying! For the horses would go faster as he pulled harder on the reins, and more slowly when he loosened them. Only once, with Ilia at my side, did I try driving Solin's trotter in the park, and that was enough: I felt broken, as if I had been drawn and quartered, for several days.

As for the Opel and its chauffeur, Antoine, both of them would stay quietly in town for lack of room or use. My step-father had in fact ordered an Austin and a Wolsely in England, but we never received them, probably because the war threatened. In consequence, we had an open body built for the Opel so that we could use it in the warm season. In this car, transformed into a meteor with Antoine at the wheel, we reached the incredible speed of eighty kilometers per hour at a time when the world speed record was only one hundred and twenty kilometers per hour.

Our closed Opel was a double-coupé with windows that opened sideways. Since there could not have been more than ten cars in the whole city, and since ours looked like a Grand Duke's, all the policemen would salute as we passed.

I liked carriages more than automobiles, and sleighs more than either. With the disappearance of horses, a whole epoch ended, that of pre-war Saint Petersburg, the only one I ever knew. I cannot imagine the streets of my city as they must be today, without the neighing of horses, the hammering of hooves on the different pavements, the smell of horse dung and sweat, and the old hackney cabs. But not only such common smells remain from that time and place; there was also the smell of the private brougham, a mixture of waxed, varnished mahogany, copper, and tufted fabric—still sometimes found in a very old Rolls-Royce.

Occasionally on Sunday, if it were spring and she had no other companion, I would go with my mother to the Strelka, a fashionable promenade stretching along a promontory into the Neva and the gulf of Finland. There the file of barouches and landaus would proceed slowly in a great circle, with ladies seated deep in their carriages or strolling along a waterside path. Like all outings involving either of my parents, however, this seemed awfully dull at the time.

Uncle Otto and my cousins were all dressed by Knabe, the most famous tailor in town. Since there were no ready-made clothes, Eugene and I were introduced in turn to this temple of elegance. Once a year, my mother would take us and order two suits for each. Endless visits would center around first choosing an English material and then the fittings; my mother would criticize a shoulder that rose too high, or a fold; I would find the trousers insufficiently straight or complain that the lapel was cut on the bias and not straight as was the latest English fashion. One day, under the influence of the most elegant boy in my school, I took a piece of leftover material from my suit to the bootmaker so that he would cover the tops of my laced, not buttoned, shoes with it.

One of my friends, Mischa Epstein, son of a bank director, did not attend my school. Together with him, I went to an elegant shirtmaker on the Nevsky Prospekt who knew my stepfather to order modern shirts: soft, striped, with attached collar and double cuffs. How ridiculous seem the shirts everyone in my family wore, with long, starched, buttoned-on collar and cuffs, that would make a bump once they were tucked into long flannel underwear. A half-dressed man looked utterly silly. The first time I came down in one of my modern shirts, I was sent back to change by my outraged parents. "I will not have you come to lunch in your nightgown," my stepfather said.

The day I finished school was the finest of my life, At last, rid of the fear I would never be free of classes, I was a slave no more, but an independent person. To celebrate the great event, my stepfather offered to let me give a farewell dinner to my school friends; I invited some fifteen of them, along with the director, a kindly German who always wore a uniform and had been our algebra teacher. It turned out to be a very successful evening: We toasted one another, drank a great deal, and even soiled the carpet of the billiard room.

Actually, I knew only half of my mother's family. I had barely seen Aunt Eugenie and had never come across Uncle Max, who was an oil dealer in Baku: the handsome Max, allegedly beloved of women. Then there was short and fat Uncle Arthur, whom I had met only once, when I was a child— he who had carried his wife-to-be through the water in his arms.

It was Aunt Julie who would come to visit us in Saint Petersburg. She had been married for some twenty years to an English Jew named Jules Mayer, a lace manufacturer living in Nottingham. I was astonished when I discovered that my stepfather had to sign an affidavit every time she came to Saint Petersburg because she was Jewish. Aunt Julie had become more English than the English, for which we constantly teased her. It was really not very nice of us as she did not know how to defend herself and had to stand alone against the whole barbarian horde making fun of wicked Albion and boasting of its Russian superiority. No one could have been kinder, more devoted, and less selfish than this aunt of mine; she always thought of others, and her heart always won out over her mind. Her considerable bulk did not keep her from moving as lightly as a feather, from jumping on her toes, and tap-dancing in a complicated, castanetlike rhythm. Like all the English, she loved walking and drafts, and always gave off an air of freshness and health. I had what turned out to be the good fortune of not having seen her daughters since childhood, as a consequence of which my parents gave me permission to spend a summer holiday in England.

A certain Mr. Vann was to accompany me on the trip. Who recommended him? I really don't know, but one morning there appeared in our living room a strange character straight out of a Dickens novel. Without putting down his things, he strode in and, at my mother's invitation, sat down, depositing his bowler hat, stick, and gloves on the floor beside him. Then, hiking up his trousers, he crossed his legs, baring a hairy calf. While his manners did seem a little strange to me, I admired without reservation the way he was dressed: a wide-checked sports jacket, a club tie, grey flannel trousers, thick white wool socks, and enormous golf shoes. Mr. Vann had the common smartness of a Cockney, the stiffness of a retired sergeant, the suppleness of an athlete, and the look of a globe-trotter. I also thought he had something of Maupassant's Bel-Ami and was greatly entranced by his bovine forehead adorned with little fair curls, the reddish fuzz on his cheeks, his blue eyes and short nose ending in a little blond moustache that must have driven women mad.

On the day I was to leave, I found myself at the pier, on one of the city's deserted islands, with time to spare. Among the other travelers, I came across a fat boy called Frank who was also waiting for Mr. Vann. Time passed, and still there was no sign of our companion. Finally, when only a few minutes remained before sailing and I was feeling desperate, there appeared a cloud of dust on the horizon, growing ever larger as it came nearer, and finally out of a cab pulled by a foaming horse jumped Mr. Vann. "Quick, quick!" I began to shout excitedly, at which Mr. Vann calmly pulled out his watch, bade me notice that there was a whole minute still left, and added that his friend the captain would never leave without him. Mr. Vann was followed by Mrs. Vann pushing a perambulator.

Nothing much happened during the crossing except that the boy Frank, that mama's boy rotten with money, immediately offered me a ruble for each time he could have me. When I refused, he continued to chat without a trace of shame. At last we sailed up the Thames. I admired Tower Bridge and found everything in this strange land fascinating: the traffic on the left, the double-decker red buses, taxis able to turn in a tiny circle and allowed to drive up inside the railroad stations right up to the platforms. In Brighton-Howe, where we stopped for a while, all the houses were alike and the huge pier and its casino went far out into the sea. I remember that Sundays were deadly dull since it was forbidden to have fun or even to play cards. Mr. Vann introduced me to a few families where there were daughters; with one of these, a redhead full of freckles, I would play ping-pong and exchange kisses every time we changed sides. We would go swimming in a covered pool by the sea; among our little group, there was a very pretty girl, superbly built and the best swimmer. One day, somebody started a rumor that she was an illegitimate child, that her parents were actually not married. Immediately everyone shunned her like the plague including, I am ashamed to say, myself. The girl disappeared. It was here, too, that I bought a pipe, some tobacco, and a pouch, and started to smoke, but reluctantly: The pipe was too heavy in my mouth and the tobacco, John Cotton, it was called, nauseated me. I also bought some clothes and my longed-for trouser press, saw a few pantomimes, and went to the music hall, where ragtime so thrilled me that I bought the sheet music to take home. But since time was passing, I then went on to Nottingham—though I was not altogether enthusiastic about it. As soon as I arrived, my Uncle Jules honored me by taking me to the club where he bowled. I spent a good deal of time in Nottingham playing lawn tennis with my cousins Vera and Evelyn in their garden and fooling around with their fox terrier. My aunt was charming, and if it had not been for the outbreak of the war, this *dolce vita* could have gone on and on.

But as it was, I had to rush to London, where Mr. Vann was going from one shipping company to the next looking for a cargo ship, since regular passenger ships had already been stopped for fear of mines. He did find one such ship but would not book passage on it because of a bad feeling he had. And indeed, we stayed in London long enough to learn that the ship had been blown up by a mine. Finally we sailed from Leith, Edinburgh's harbor, bound for Bergen. The crossing was for me absolutely horrible, making me wish I were dead.

Return to Saint Petersburg · 1912–1914

Every time the ship rose and fell, every time it swayed from
side to side, my entrails, empty as they had soon become,
seemed to be torn apart. Everything, however, comes to an end;
we arrived in Bergen, crossed Norway and Sweden, and
reached Finland, arriving in Saint Petersburg two weeks after
we had left Scotland.

Chapter 4

War, Revolution, Finland

1914–1919

AND SO, I BECAME a University student, proudly sporting the compulsory uniform: bottle-green cap and trousers, black jacket. I don't know whether this uniform is still worn in the Soviet Union today, but you can see it on stage in Chekhov's plays. As for the University, it was on Vassily Island, between the Academy of Fine Arts and an old palace built in the Dutch style under Peter the Great. There, aside from mathematics and chemistry, I took a course in crystallography and one in three-dimensional geometry, for which I enjoyed doing figures in China ink on big white sheets of paper with a double pen, a ruler, and a protractor.

Enthusiastic, patriotic, and thirsty for adventure as I was, I wanted to participate in the war that had just begun. But, alas, I was too young. And there could be no question of my volunteering as an ordinary soldier in the Russian army: I would have had to share the fate of the peasants and workers who were covered with lice, fed on kasha and black bread, and lacked for everything—shoes and even guns, so that one front-line soldier out of three had to wait for his comrade's death in order to be armed.

I now had to give up all my romantic dreams and think of my future. There was the matter of choosing a career and a college, for without a degree, people at my social level were considered illiterate. I decided to enter the University, for which you needed Latin. Thus a man named Zavalevich was invited to spend the summer with us. During our many walks, my tutor, who had several degrees but still barely made a living giving lessons, talked to me at length about philosophy and religious sects throughout the history of Russia. For the entrance exam, I recited: "*Gallia est omnis divisa in partes tres, quarum unam incolunt Belgae. . . .*" and passed, along with Mischa Epstein and Hippolyte Kamenka, the son of another bank director.

At the beginning of the war life was in no way different from what it had been earlier. The Russians had only the faintest idea of what war was about because their last war, against the Japanese, had taken place so very far away. Even now, while one might easily find and point out Eastern Prussia on the map, there was far less certainty about finding, say, the Carpathians. A mood of optimism prevailed; the communiqués from the General Staff varied very little: Always so many kilometers gained, always so many prisoners taken. Ladies would visit the hospitals, send packages to the front, and organize collections. I accompanied the daughters of Baroness de Guinzbourg (her son, like Theodore, was a reserve officer) on their numerous visits to the palaces on the Millionaya where the aristocracy lived. Koussevitzky was then conducting in Dvorianskoye Sobranie (The Nobles' Assembly, the main concert hall), and Kohansky played the violin; Chaliapin sang and the divine Pavlova danced at the Maryinsky Theater; Francen and Dermos were at the French Theater; Rastelli juggled at the Winter Circus and, at the Wondering Dog, a fashionable nightclub, everyone applauded the satirist Vertinsky in his latest creation: "The Navy Lieutenant Schmidt wants to kill himself with his gun. . . ." What more could anyone ask? As for me, I attended the University, went to Rauha—a valley in Finland that was one of my favorite winter places in the world— for Christmas, and, at several costume balls, I danced to Drigot's Harlequinade, then very fashionable, among the Harlequins, Pierrots, and Columbines so dear to every Russian heart.

A speed-up course was started at the University—in 1915, I believe—so that students could be sent to the front as paramedics. In spite of the, to us, humiliating name of "Feminine Medical Institute"—all the more ridiculous in that the University never had a single female student—Mischa Epstein, Hippolyte Kamenka, and I enrolled in this course just in case the war should go on, though all the financial experts said this was out of the question because a long war would completely bankrupt all the belligerent nations.

When I found myself for the first time face to face with a corpse in the amphitheater, saw the livid flesh and smelled the disgusting odor, I nearly passed out. But by the second session we were not even bothering to put on rubber gloves. I told myself that this anatomy course would be very useful to me later on when I was drawing the human body. It was necessary, in order to pass the exam, to know perfectly a multitude of similar-looking little bones belonging to the fingers and toes, and so I bought myself a skeleton and put it in my room, hanging from its pole. I had forgotten to warn poor Agafia, so pious, so frightened of evil spirits. When she saw the skeleton, she almost fainted. Even later, every time she had to cross my room, she would spit toward it, mutter an exorcism, and cross herself abundantly.

In the meantime, little by little the war news got more and more disastrous; one could no longer ignore it or remain indifferent. On the front, defeat followed defeat; in the capital, the evil influence of the sinister monk Rasputin over the Imperial Family was growing. Nicholas joined his armies at the front, the Tsarina took over the government. In March, 1917, angry crowds in the streets made a revolution, the Tsar abdicated, the provisional government, later to be headed by Kerensky, was formed. I remember that day of the Revolution so well! From our windows, you could see people running in the street, taking shelter, shooting, falling. While the assistant director Guttman, a big, fat, shiny, bald man whom I hated, had taken refuge in our apartment and was exuding fear from every pore, my stepfather was crying for joy, declaring that the dawn of freedom had finally come to Russia and that he was living the finest day of his life. And in fact, the first weeks of the Revolution were a kind of golden age. There was calm, order, and joy, and all without any authorities, without any repression, all easy and natural. I wanted to contribute to this paradise on earth, so I enrolled in the militia and spent my nights protecting the rest of my fellow citizens. A Browning hanging on my belt, I spent my time in a smoky room where, actually, I was almost killed by a bullet from an imprudent novice.

Back at the Reformed School* where I finished my secondary studies, I had had a charming friend, the very young son of a very old general. General Roup was a hero of the Crimean War who had taken the seemingly impregnable Turkish fortress of Kars. Thanks to the recommendation of this venerable octogenarian, I was allowed to enter the Constantine Artillery School, the most exclusive Russian military academy. After a six-month course, I was to be sent to the front as an officer.

Now my dream was coming true. I would soon be going to war! And here I am in my new role as a cadet, proudly wearing yet another uniform, this time a big coat, braided trousers, saber, cavalry boots with spurs, crumpled cap dashingly worn like those of the smart Georgian horsemen, the famous daredevils of the Savage Division. It was impossible to pass a general on the street because, in order to salute him, you had to face him and wait for him to come three steps forward. When going into a restaurant, you immediately had to find the highest-ranking officer present and ask his permission to occupy a table. Every night when our classes were over, we would make our exit request, spoken all in one breath and at prodigious speed: "Your Excellency, the cadet of the Constantine Artillery School so-and-so asks for permission to leave until tomorrow." The early morning trumpet sounded at six and was followed by a parade of the six hundred cadets in the courtyard, then prayers, breakfast, and classes. Gun class: assembling, disas-

* The Reformed Protestant School.

sembling, lubrication, shooting. Artillery class: study of field pieces, of shooting, of aiming at an invisible target by triangulation. Riding class: riding without reins, saddles, or stirrups; obstacle jumping, figures, athletics on horseback. My dormitory friend was a Lett whom I nicknamed Little Eyebrows because, since his were exceedingly thick, he kept brushing them. Sometimes, the cadets would get back at dawn after a night of debauchery. One day, on the Nevsky Prospekt, I bumped into my friend Claudia and, courteous as a cadet must be, insisted on seeing her home. Not content with a regular cab, I hailed a luxury cab and, when we arrived, to my shame, I was unable to pay the fare. She teased me with this often afterward.

That same fall, an accident happened that could have had very serious consequences and could even have caused my expulsion from school. Cheery after a late dinner, three friends decided to take me on a visit to three kept women they knew. A friendly voice on the phone told us to hurry along. We jumped into cabs and, when we got to the house, we were greeted by someone we assumed was the doorman; he escorted us to the staircase, where we found ourselves surrounded by other men. Now a little uneasy, we arrived at a wide-open door giving on to a dining room in an indescribably messy state. The table with its cloth, glasses, silver, and bottle had been thrown over, the floor was covered with debris, food and red spots; my amazed eyes, looking over this chaos, finally stopped on a human figure, a motionless woman from whom was flowing a river of blood huddled against the wall by the passage. My legs buckled; I almost threw up. A murder had just been committed and, like idiots, we had walked into a trap. The men started to grill us and to examine our sabers; we were kept all night in this nightmarish apartment with its blood-spattered walls. The murder had probably been committed by drunken soldiers who, furious at not being able to take the victims' jewelery, started after them with their sabers. One of the girls managed to escape by jumping out of a third-floor window; severely injured, she was in the hospital, too sick to talk.

It was only at dawn that we were allowed to go, with the promise that our names would not be given to the newspapers. This being a Sunday, I went home along the empty street carrying my heavy secret, which, I felt sure, would shortly explode. My hands were shaking as I opened the paper. The murder was all over the front page; our names, however, were not mentioned. I never said a word to my parents about my adventure, but told Mischa Epstein every gory detail.

Two or three months after I entered the cadet school, the Bolshevik coup—the October Revolution—broke out. For a few weeks before, we had seen people meeting in the streets, demonstrating, and heard orators speaking to the crowds; unless I am mistaken, I once heard Trotsky himself. For some mysterious reason, throughout the entire two days of the Revolution all of us cadets were kept locked up inside the four walls of our school without any news of what was going on outside. Finally, on the evening of the second day, some ten cadets of the Constantine School who had been helping to defend the Michael School came back exhausted, in rags, saying that all was lost, that the Telephone Central, the Post Office, the main buildings were all controlled by the Bolsheviks. Everyone had tears in his eyes. Some cried openly, and we felt such rage, tension, and despair that, if I had been able at that moment to rush against the enemy, I would gladly have given up my life. Since all officers and cadets were being massacred or thrown into the canals, we were ordered to change into our civilian clothes and return to our homes for three days. Full of humiliation, hiding like a criminal, I went home hugging the walls. After the three days, with great caution, I ventured back to school; but when I saw that it was being guarded by a soldier instead of a cadet, I discreetly went away.

I don't know how many days or weeks I stayed at home waiting for something, anything, some kind of message for all of us ex-cadets. And suddenly, there was our message posted on the wall of a building on the Nevsky Prospekt. We were advised to take a holiday in the south of Russia where, I suppose, new anti-Bolshevik armies were being formed. And since I had not left Saint Petersburg for years and loved to travel, the idea of going off to the Caucasus, which I did not know and which Pushkin, Lermontov, and Tolstoy had so often described, pleased me so much that I asked my parents to let me go to Anapa and join a friend of Eugene's and mine, the infantry cadet Smetanich, a Czech. My stepfather gave me the money for the trip and promised to send me a monthly allowance. I left cheerfully, not knowing what troubles lay ahead.

With a large suitcase full of useless clothes, I took a crowded train to Ekaterinodar (today Krasnodar). In order to kill time on the thirty-six hour trip, I played cards and lost almost all my money. From the capital of the Kuban, a provincial hole, I had to continue by my own means: sometimes walking next to some peasant cart, sometimes riding in one, and sometimes alone. I felt happy, breathed in the pure air, my feet flattened the grass of the steppes, while on the horizon to the right could be seen the majestic, snow-capped peaks of the Caucasus mountains. Seldom did I come upon a farm in which I might stop, and then usually to be greeted by half-wild dogs. After a three-day walk, the sea appeared in the distance: Anapa could not be much farther. But, Lord, what disillusion was waiting for me there!

Except for a few villas up on the cliffs, the village was a morbid hole with two rows of widely spaced *isbas* facing each other; like in Western films, two rows of planks served as a sidewalk. The empty space in the middle, a sea of mud whenever it rained, was pompously called the main street. After a kilometer or two, it ended in a square plaza lined with some more *isbas*. Such was the charming village of Anapa where there was not a single tree, and, at night, not even one streetlight to illuminate the nothingness.

I was given a straw mattress on the floor in Smetanich's monk-cell, which was whitewashed, clean, and lit by a small window giving out on the sky and the steppe. There began a life of total boredom. There was absolutely nothing to do from morning till night. To kill time, we would sleep until noon, after which we would make our way slowly to the plaza and the Greek Dima's little tavern-restaurant; he was generous or stupid enough to feed a dozen officers wounded at the front and as penniless as Smetanich and myself. There was a sanatorium for convalescent soldiers in the neighborhood but, because the civil war was spreading wider and wider, the sanatorium was no longer receiving the subsidies of a non-existent government. In these circumstances, Dima's eternal mutton stew was more than welcome. A good part of the afternoon was spent playing cards. The first time I won a fortune in I.O.U.'s, I thought myself rich; then I understood that none of it mattered since money no longer existed.

Shortly after my arrival, I became friends with two Georgian princesses, Zuleika and Vagidé. The elder sister's forehead still showed the hollow made by a bullet that had been shot by her younger brother Murad when they were children. While playing waltzes on the piano, the princess would look at me with sad appeal, sighing for a life gayer than the one offered in that damned village. The gayer life, however, was actually being led by the handsome Prince Murad: He was providing for the Countess Tolstoy, and her one-year-old child; an abundant beauty in the typical Russian style, the Countess had been left quite resourceless by the Count, a general staff officer off to war against the Bolsheviks.

During the winter, the families with marriageable daughters who lived in the villas on the cliff gave a few balls. Then all the windows would be lit, the notes of a mazurka, a Spanish step, or a waltz would drift through the warm Caucasian night jeweled with huge stars, and one could hear the stomping of spurred boots shaking wooden floors. The officers led very fast lives, and competed with one another to do so. Of all of these officers, however, it was the little Tolichka-Bikoff who carried the day: He was a war hero, a knight of the Order of Saint George, and, moreover, an invalid who had lost all attributes of virility.

To celebrate Christmas and the New Year, officers' dinners were served in a barn on tables held up by wooden horses. Nothing was lacking: zakusky, meats, desserts, liqueurs, and wines. Where was all the money coming from? Smetanich and I, the only two cadets, owed an unquestioning obedience to the officers who made us take one drink after the other. Now and again, we had to help them out so they could piss or throw up. I did not yet know how dangerous it can be to mix liquors. With my neighbor to the right, I drank champagne, with the one to the left, wine, and with the one opposite, liqueurs. The result was terrifying. At one point, I slid under the table, my head began to spin, and I was sick. An unknown benefactor covered me with his napkin to hide my distress from the diners. But the hardest part of the evening, a herculean task, was that of getting home in the middle of the night. Arm in arm, Smetanich and I staggered on the planks in a darkness so total that we could see absolutely nothing, and when we tried to cross the street, we stumbled against a cow lying there, chewing its cud. It is pure miracle that I was able to fit the key into the wavering lock. Having made it to my mattress on all fours, I finally passed out.

This kind of life could not last forever; even the angel in-carnate Dima could not keep feeding us on credit and, since there was no communication with the rest of Russia, I could not hope to receive any money from my stepfather. Some-thing had to be done. The only solution I could think of was to try to make it to the nearest city and go to the local branch of the Bank of Commerce. This may have seemed reasonable, but of course I had no chance of success since I not only had no authorization from my stepfather to withdraw funds, I did not even have any proof that Mr. Schaikevich was in fact my stepfather, particularly as I bore a different name. But a miracle occurred, as other miracles were to save me later on. Was it my intuition or was it perhaps just my foolishness that allowed me to escape the deluge? There are great gaps in my memory of this period, and I no longer know how I managed to get through the long trip I then took, more than three hundred kilometers on foot, with no money, sleeping in barns, with or without companions; once I was badly bitten in the calf by a ferocious dog. But finally, filthy and exhausted, I arrived in the good city of Rostov-on-the-Don. Looking like a hobo in a world that was after all in those terrible times full of shady characters, I was taken into the bank director's office; and there the impossible came true. While I on my part did not recognize Bestchinsky, the director, that noble old man did not fail to know me for I had been present when he had dined at my step-father's. He opened his arms to me, put himself entirely at my disposal; I had but to command. This handsome white-haired gentleman to whom I owe an eternal debt of gratitude gave me a monthly allowance, put me up at his co-director's (a dry and formal man who gave me a miserable little room and never once asked me to a meal), and introduced me to his cashier, whose family adopted me, quite possibly because there was a very pretty marriageable daughter and I was considered a Schaikevich—that is to say, a millionaire.

Rostov was such a change after Anapa: life after asphyxia, relaxation after strife. For the entire first week, I rested without a worry.

Soon enough, however, I began to fret and wonder what to do next. On the one hand, I had promised to go back and save Smetanich (but, now that I think of it, why had he stayed? To watch over our belongings?). On the other, I was still a nondemobilized cadet. My duty was to join the army being organized by General Kornilov, though no one knew where this was happening as it was all kept secret. The soldiers whose advice I asked suggested that I get my friend first and then join up. But since there was fighting all around Rostov and all the roads were out, there was nothing to do but wait.

So I moved from the co-director's house, leaving my dark hole for a light room giving on to the main street. I bought the necessary clothes and took up new habits. At noon, after my usual visit to my friend Bestchinsky, I would walk up and down the main boulevard, give in to temptation when I saw halvah or nougat (Rostov was half Oriental), then would go back and lunch always in the same restaurant. Rostov was full of people, and the main street, with its shops and open-air cafés, was extremely lively. The main café, the meeting place of the male population every day at noon and five, was both club and stock market; middle-class women were excluded but prostitutes were numerous. Among these, the most elegant, the most respected, was the beautiful Bulgarian Donna whose price I never dared ask, sure as I was that it was too high for my purse. And at night, before midnight, I would go down into the cellar where Rostov's newspaper was printed; it was edited by the stepfather of a student of my cadet school whom I had met here. The cadet bore the famous name of Viasemsky but was not a prince. There, in the midst of metal printing frames and inking rollers, I would be plunged into an atmosphere of hysteria. Getting the paper out was a race against time; invariably this wasn't right, that had to be changed, something had been forgotten, but when midnight chimed the paper came out.

Like my cousins and all other young men of my period, I preferred the company of loose women to that of young girls of good family, dull virgins who only thought of getting a husband. So I rarely went out with the cashier's very pretty daughter, and all the more rarely since she showed a feeling for me that I believed was sincere. I saw it particularly clearly on the occasion of her best friend's wedding: We were maid of honor and best man, held the crowns above the bride and groom's heads, went three times around the Church, on to the City Hall and to a big family lunch. All the beribboned old ladies looked at us tenderly, which hardly seemed to annoy my companion, who never stopped holding my arm.

What I could not understand and envied was the irresistible

attraction exerted by her brother, who was not handsome and quite fat, on all the whores at the café. He immediately became the lover of Donna's younger sister, Valia, a serious and unexceptional girl. As for me, it was quite a while before I met Valia, barely of age, just in from the country, fresh, simple, and extremely attractive. Our first night was spent awake and in ecstasy. I introduced her to Count Tolstoy, the husband of the Countess stranded in Anapa, and he in turn introduced her to others. But Valia, unlike the cold Donna, too simple and generous, did not understand how to make a career. When I came back to Rostov after having been away for a few months, it would be just in time for her tragic end. I would find her in a hospital, terribly aged, ravaged by syphilis, and dying; I would bring her some flowers, promise to come back, but did not have the heart to do so.

One day, it seemed to us very suddenly, the word came that the Bolsheviks were winning and were going to enter Rostov the next day. People huddled together in one another's houses looking for protection; no one wanted to stay alone. All the windows that looked out on to the main street were empty. The street itself was deserted except for a few shady characters, vagabonds come from God knew where or simply spies and Bolshevik sympathizers. My host, who asked me to join him and a dozen or so friends and acquaintances, had just hidden two guns in the piano, which he thought an invulnerable hiding place. The waiting continued. The women were so panicky, so close to hysteria, that they spread a contagion of fear; I, too, even though I was sure we were in no danger, began to tremble like a leaf. Then suddenly, as if from a broken dam, came the victorious flood. Here was no army, but a horde; no well-ordered ranks, but a mob; no soldiers, but a sinister carnival; no human beings, but scarecrows. They were dirty, in rags, sometimes barefoot; they shrieked, brandished their weapons, and sang. There were men dressed half as sailors, half as soldiers, there were others dressed half as soldiers, half as civilians; men arm in arm with women who were half naked, shrieking and drunk. There were huge fur hats, caps, bare heads and chests. Some carried sabers, others handguns, others two or three rifles, others still had no weapons. But all had bands of cartridges slung across their chests. This nightmarish spectacle was completely hypnotic.

A few shots came from some windows, which were then immediately showered with bullets. Every apartment was searched for guns. When our host told some soldiers armed with bayonets that he had none, they went straight to the piano. I felt my heart sink as I thought my last hour had come.

It was getting ever and ever more dangerous for me to stay in Rostov. It was said that they were going to take a census of the male population, and a commissar had already taken over Bestchinsky's office. But I did not dare return to Anapa by myself; fighting was raging everywhere and I was afraid of disappearing without leaving a trace. So when by chance I met three Greek merchants who were going to Anapa, I promptly joined them.

Only before leaving, I made such a terrible mistake that it almost cost Viasemsky's life and mine. Since he was getting ready to return to Saint Petersburg (and why didn't I go with him?), I gave him a letter for my parents that he took without reading. I had written: "Dear Mama, the bearer of this letter, the Constantine School Cadet Viasemsky, will come to see you with my news. When the Bolsheviks came into Rostov, there was some gunfire, etc. . . ." Viasemsky was stopped purely by chance, my revealing letter was found on him, and he was only saved from being shot at the very last moment when the commissar turned out to be an old friend of his.

As for me, feeling perfectly innocent and quite unconscious of the near-tragedy I had caused, I was going back to my village, only this time by water. While, once again, I remember little of the trip, our arrival was unforgettable. It was in fact a new catastrophe.

In my absence, Anapa also had been occupied by the Bolsheviks. Smetanich and all the convalescing officers had disappeared—either mobilized or running away. There was not a soul left; I had walked right into a trap. I rushed to the house of Zuléika and Vagidé, who told me that their youngest brother, Ostap, was fleeing that very night by boat. At midnight we set off, flattening ourselves first against the walls of the *isbas*, then against the cliff, and went down to the cove where Ostap had hidden his little boat. We spent the whole night sailing toward Kertch. Once we arrived at that Crimean port, we separated, and I found a big freighter laden with refugees due to leave in a few days for Rostov. From then on all was misery, roasting by day on the overheated metal deck, shivering with cold at night.

I can still see myself ringing futilely at the door of my lodging. Silence. The house seemed dead. I kept on ringing, and a window on the second floor opened just a little; a furious voice muttered in a whisper: "Get away!" Startled and uncomprehending, I stayed rooted in place when the voice, now apparently desperate, hissed: "Get away, you imbecile, you've caused enough trouble already with the soldiers who came at night to shoot you and gave me lots of trouble. Just get the hell away, you horror!"

This time, in a panic, I ran to the cashier's, and his family told me what had been happening. I was being hunted, an outlaw, and could find no refuge with friends or in a hotel; I could not even leave Rostov without a permit. Was I to sleep in the street? Once again, I was saved by Bestchinsky, to whom I owe so much and whom I never saw again. He gave me money and a letter to his agent, took me to the little boat that shuttled between Rostov and Azov and for which no permit was yet required. I hid myself in the country with the agent for at least a month.

In the meantime, important things had been happening. The Germans had occupied all of the Ukraine including Kiev, where Count Mirbach, their Gauleiter, had been murdered. And unhappily for me, the front had stabilized between Rostov, already freed by the Germans, and Azov, still in the hands of the Bolsheviks. I waited from day to day and, seeing that nothing seemed to change, set out once more for Rostov, accompanied by the agent's son, who came with me to try to pass through the lines. We arrived in town that same evening without having met a soul.

I was free. I had escaped from the Bolshevik hell into a city I knew well and where I had many friends. This was the time when I found Valia disfigured and dying. But by now I missed Saint Petersburg and my parents so much that finally I could not take it any longer. Everyone advised me to stay in Rostov and wait, that to try to get to Saint Petersburg might mean my death, but I would not listen. So, armed with a letter of recommendation from Bestchinsky to his colleague at the Kiev branch of the bank, I boarded the train for Kiev.

There, two problems awaited me. When I went to the bank, I was refused all financial help and was humiliated when the director offered me the charity of a few rubles. Then I found out that there were no more trains between the German Ukraine and the Bolshevik area in northern Russia. Purely by chance, I overhead a conversation about a hospital train soon to be put together for Saint Petersburg. I ran to the station and was able to buy one of the last tickets for the two passenger carriages to be attached to the convoy. How pleased I was! But my good mood darkened when, the next evening, near the border at Orcha, I found out that all the passengers except for me had a pass. I began to imagine myself rotting in the fields, penniless, in the middle of this desolate country, with no houses or villages, unable to go either forward or back since there would be no more trains. The train stopped at a small station. Soldiers armed with bayonets told us all to get out, then stood in front of the carriages. While all the travelers lined up in front of one window, I walked up to another window to ask if I could purchase a ticket to Saint Petersburg. "But you don't need one," said the clerk, "since yours is good until the next stop. Just get off and buy your ticket there. Now go back to your carriage. You need nothing more." The guards let me through, thinking I must have shown my pass, and I went back to my compartment, trying to look as small as possible. A mistake made by the clerk in Kiev, who should have given me a ticket to Orcha only, had actually saved me so far. Suddenly, the door opened and a two-man patrol came in. One of the soldiers stopped in front of me. "Your pass," he demanded. "Leave him be," his friend interrupted. "Can't you see he's just a kid?"

Back, at last, in Saint Petersburg, I found our apartment—empty. Only Madi was there. My parents had gone to Finland with Eugene; Aunt Mania, Uncle Paul, Claudia, Anatole, and Theodore were on holiday in the Tsarskoie-Selo house, to which I went the very next day. When I walked in to the living room, I saw my uncle and my two cousins playing bridge. "So there you are," they exclaimed without interrupting their game. "We're awfully pleased. We thought you were lost." The greetings I received upstairs from Aunt Mania and Claudia were a lot warmer.

A year had passed since I had left for the Caucasus, and everything had changed. I found out that Trotsky had offered the Ministry of Finance—or something like that—to my step-father, who had preferred to go into exile, like a number of his acquaintances. They were all sure they would be back soon. The Bolsheviks put no obstacle in the path of those who wanted to leave Russia, with the exception of young men of military age, for whom the border was closed and guarded by soldiers who did not hesitate to shoot. And so a whole new industry was born around this mysterious border: illegal traffic in messages, packages, documents, and especially young men—for whose escape the peasants in the vicinity took great risks and demanded high ransom from their rich parents. Over-night, some of these peasants had amassed large fortunes from their new industry. They were mostly Finns; the best-known and most reliable was a man called Toika, and my parents had used him to release Genia. Another of them, who was supposed to bring Anatole his rolled-up Dutch paintings, which were worth a great deal of money, vanished forever.

Life in Tsarskoie-Selo as well as Saint Petersburg was becoming intolerably restricted and there was a shortage of everything. Nothing was normal any more. Food was a problem; the lines in front of the bare shops kept getting longer, and while one was clandestinely offered fine red apples in the streets, they hardly satisfied one's hunger. Then one day my brother arrived from Finland. My parents had been weak enough to let him come back because he missed Claudia and Anatole. This return, as you will see, almost cost him his life. Besides, it was for nothing because almost immediately after, Claudia and Anatole themselves left to join my parents in Finland. For me, then, and now for my brother too, life became an endless wait for Toika, who seemed to have disappeared.

In the meantime, autumn had come and, one morning, instead of Toika, a big, fair man, typically Russian, was sent to us by our parents. He told us to meet him that same evening at the Yacht Club pier on the Neva. Among innumerable boats, a fine twelve-meter yacht, similar to the one I had sailed on Lake Ladoga, was waiting for us. Had our man bought it, stolen it, or was he supposed to bring it to Finland with Prince M., our future companion? In any case, as soon as we hoisted sails, the sad truth came out: Our guide knew no more than we did about sailing, and there was not a single maritime map on board.

In addition, the weather was dreadful—we could see nothing. When we passed from the mouth of the Neva into the gulf of Finland, it was pouring rain and we had to cross an area controlled by the guns of the famous Kronshtadt fortress before we would be safe in Finnish territorial waters. Preferring the sea air to the smoky cabin, I was at the wheel, holding it in the direction I had been told. After several hours, the weather cleared a little and we saw the dark coastline on the starboard side and the silhouette of the fortress forward on the port side. None of us knew that the channel on one side was too shallow for our tall keel, while the one on the other side was too narrow for us to get through unnoticed. Soon the yacht began to behave strangely. It jumped, then lay down on its flank: We had just run aground on a sandbank. Our situation was critical. Even if the yacht were to hold together through the night and not drop us into the sea, we were too close to the border not to be suspected by the Coast Guard, who would find us in the morning. So the first thing we did was to destroy all papers and documents. Huge, black, tattered clouds fled across the sky with incredible speed, and the moon, coming out between them, dramatized our somewhat unenviable position. Suddenly shadows appeared: fishermen rowing in their tarred boats. I tried to grab one of these boats by lying down on the front of our yacht and, holding on to the ropes with my left hand, reaching the boat with my right. But because of the tide, each time I rose, the fishing boat would sink, and as soon as it rose, I would sink. The only time I was able to get hold of it, I thought my arm would be torn off. After a few unsuccessful tries, the unenterprising fishermen disappeared, and we went back into the cabin to wait for the day and the end of the storm. We were wet to the bone, had lost our food, and could attempt no escape since neither my brother nor our traveling companion, Prince M., knew how to swim.

The sky finally began to grow lighter, the rain stopped, the sea quieted a little, and, a few hundred meters away, we saw the deserted beach of Oraniyenbaum, on which there was neither house nor person. All was not lost yet if we could move quickly. Simultaneously we all turned on our incompetent guide: It was up to him, we said, to do something to save us. Wordlessly, he stripped to the waist, plunged into the waves and disappeared. We waited for a long time, not knowing whether he had reached the shore, whether he was coming back or had abandoned us. And suddenly, I saw a little black spot between the crests of the waves; then it grew and I realized it was a head and a rowboat. Having stolen the little boat, our savior had had great difficulty rowing back because the current was so strong. Finally he had jumped out and pulled it with his hands. In a few minutes we were aboard and heading for the beach, which we crossed at a run, bending under our heavy suitcases. Somehow we reached a little railroad station and took the first train for Saint Petersburg, where we arrived safely twenty hours after we had left with such high hopes!

A few days later, Eugene was thrown into jail, and because of me, though it was not my fault. As we were both dying of fear and boredom, I said to him one morning, "Why don't you go see our friend the painter M.G.? I went to his studio yesterday and admired his new paintings." My brother followed my advice and disappeared. Everybody who walked into the courtyard of the artist's building that day was arrested and thrown into jail. It took a week of inquiries before Madi was able to find out which prison he was in. No communication with the prisoners was allowed, no package could be sent to them. Eugene's life was in very great danger: It was the period of shootings and numerous drownings from rafts ordered by the sadistic Djerjinsky, head of the secret police. My parents were advised of what had happened, and Anatole tried to get in touch with his acquaintances among the Bolsheviks. We might have been able to free Eugene by paying a large sum of money, but we might just as easily have lost him to a charge of corruption. My parents were wise enough to choose the more prudent alternative and let events take their course.

After three months, Eugene was released for reasons no less mysterious than those for which he had been arrested. We had been gravely worried because of his delicate health but, to everyone's amazement, he came back in the pink of condition and the best of moods. He had seen unbelievable misery and endured privations, but he had behaved with the same courage as during our unfortunate escape attempt on the yacht. A short time after he was freed, Toika took him through the border— but I anticipate.

When Eugene was taken to jail, I had at first refused to run away to Finland without him. But in the end I gave in to my parents' insistence that I come away from Saint Petersburg so as not to complicate things, especially since I could in no way help my poor brother. Toika, having returned to life, came to get me at dawn one morning with a horse and cart full of hay so I could hide in case of danger. I left immediately just as I was, walking with Toika toward that mysterious border about thirty kilometers away that no one really knew, except of course for the peasant smugglers who lived right near it and the Red border guards. This line, invisible to the eye, here would go through the middle of a meadow, there cut a path or a line of trees. It would have been as difficult to cross, if you were not familiar with it, as for a blind man to find his way in an unknown country.

We crossed the city and its suburbs, then the countryside, and the closer we got to Finland, the more people we met and the more suspicious we seemed. Toika was not chatty and gave me no information. At a particular moment, we found ourselves on a long, straight road, and he let me know that the moment of decision was near. On our left, not a house, not a soul in the middle of the fields; on our right, a thickly planted pine forest. Each ditch, each tree trunk might be concealing hidden Red guards ready to shoot. Toika stopped suddenly, looked around, tied his horse to a pine tree, put his finger on his lips, and then leaped toward the forest while I brought up the rear. We ran, then fell, motionless, into the grass. The birds were singing, and I could see before me a little brook, then a clearing. We jumped over the water, ran a little farther, and stopped. We were in Finland, on Toika's property, and promptly went to his *isba*. His family was waiting for us; never did soup taste better to me! Only we were still eating when all faces suddenly froze; a suspicious noise had alarmed the whole family. I was taken by the hand, pulled outside, and hidden in a haystack. Bewildered, understanding nothing of this new danger, I finally came out to be told that the intruders were Finnish soldiers; and that, had they found me, they would have taken me in for a three-week quarantine. Toika set me on the paved road I had to follow, and I went off with a song in my heart, which changed to a song loudly sung as the sun rose and I came closer to Tursevo, where my parents awaited me.

The year we spent in Finland was a time of waiting. We waited to return to Saint Petersburg. We waited for the end of the great battle between the Red Army and General Yudenich's troops; for several weeks, from our side of the gulf, we could see its effects across the water: a blood-colored sky, violent explosions, and the muted growling of guns. Finally, we waited for the exit visas on our Nansen passports so that we might go abroad. Thanks to the intervention of Sir Basil Zaharoff, supposedly the richest man in the world and a friend of my stepfather's, my parents left Finland long before the other refugees. Claudia and Anatole, properly married, followed them six months later, and Eugene and I left at the end of that same year, 1919.

All this waiting was painful to the grownups but not the young people. For us it was like a holiday: We were living in an area we were familiar with, in comfortable villas surrounded by Finnish servants, and in a society of other refugees we knew well, the Blocks, the Senutoviches, the Maximoffs, the Walters. The parents would visit one another and play bridge while the children would gather in groups and have a "jolly good time." Not far from our dacha was the dacha of writer Leonid Andreyev, who lived there with his family. With what avidity I listened to his conversations with Anatole on literature and art, or to their evocations of fabulous Italy! He seemed such a strange character, this big, intellectual *mujik* with monkish long black hair. He dressed like a peasant: Russian shirt belted onto the loose trousers and boots. He spoke old Russian in a very deep voice, with a sing-song like in Church, pronouncing *a* like *o*, and *o* like *ô*. And it was not only his appearance and language that belonged to the last century, but also his frame of mind, for he thought his genius had been reincarnated in his youngest son, Sava, who was brought up and worshipped like a Buddha by his wife and himself to the neglect of their other children. All kinds of people we knew came to Tursevo on their way to Helsinki or to Viborg. Sorin, a friend of Anatole's and a famous portrait painter, told me about the impressionists whose canvases I had not yet actually seen, and I asked him silly questions like, who's the greater painter, Cézanne or Renoir, Monet or Van Gogh? Roerich, the famous painter of theater sets and polar landscapes, encouraged my Cézanne-like attempts at doing apples on a cloth out in the open and my brother's dark Dutch still-lifes painted in a cellar by the light of a single candle. He gave me a letter of introduction to his friend and colleague, Maurice Denis, in Paris, and pleaded our cause to our parents, saying that we should be allowed to become artists.

It was Anatole who, at the beginning of our stay and to give our little group an occupation, thought of the studio. He rented an old barn and got hold of an ancient piano. Every morning, to the sound of his arrangements of Chopin and Schumann waltzes, guided by the genius of Kroll, the young director, we learned the noble art of pantomime: how to walk in time, how to move with grace, how to express different feelings, joy, fear, anger. A few months later, having reached a state of great perfection, we gave a show at the Viborg Theater for the Russian refugees who had been dying of boredom. It was much talked about. I can still see myself on the stage, with the auditorium in darkness, perfectly at ease, making wide gestures. I am Pierrot, I dance with Columbine-Claudia a languid tango on a big barrel. But Harlequin comes in, provokes me to a duel, we have a swordfight, and, fatally wounded, I collapse as the curtain comes down to general applause.

There was some flirting and two or three affairs. The famous aging dancer Egorova appeared one morning on the doorstep of our villa and said she felt ill; having lain down on a bed, she asked me to lock the door and sit next to her. There was an embarrassed silence for a half hour, after which she got up and left. My mother found her behavior suspicious and rude. Egorova finally managed to seduce young Levitan, a protégé of my cousins, the Efrons, and got him to marry her. As for me, I had no adventures except for an innocent flirtation with Claudia, whose nape I would kiss when I found her alone at breakfast.

This winter spent in Tursevo shone with an incomparable splendor because of our youth, our *joie de vivre*, our toboggan rides, the logs burning in the fireplaces and the country buried under the snow and reflecting the sunshine. How sorry I feel for those who have never known the wonders of a northern winter! There are months of silence, of isolation so that one feels as if on another planet and reality becomes unreal. I can never forget our visit to a brother of Aunt Mania's who lived in an isolated village. As Claudia, Anatole, and I were getting ready to board the train, my cousin realized he had forgotten an important document, so I offered to go back home and take the next train. Only, when I arrived at the village's station a little later, the promised sleigh was missing. There wasn't a soul around, not one *isba* anywhere near. Night was falling and my only choice was one of freezing in the unheated station or walking a few kilometers to the house. And so I started off along the edge of a forest, walking with difficulty, sinking above my knees at every step and getting snow in my *valinki* ("boots"). I don't know how long this torture lasted but finally I pushed open the gate of my uncle's house in a state of dumb exhaustion. The spectacle of a group gathered before a bonfire confused me still further. Not knowing what I was doing, I advanced like a sleepwalker toward my uncle and, to every one's amazement, kissed his gloved hand; then, seeing a big dog chained to its kennel, I went straight to him, sat down, and started to caress him. Accidentally turning, I saw my uncle and his guests frozen in wonder and heard someone shout:

"Get away, Caesar will eat you alive!" And, in fact, the animal, who had never been caressed by anyone but its master, realized its error and was about to get me when I moved away.

While that whole winter of waiting was a continuous party for the young people, it reached its peak at Christmas and the New Year. All our group, including Claudia, Anatole, and Kroll, was invited to spend ten days on the estate of Gourevich, the millionaire, in the north of Finland. The splendor with which we were received, the generosity with which we were treated, were worthy of old Russia. This visit was like a farewell to our past, to our life that was soon to change so drastically.

Half a dozen peasant sleighs picked us up at the station and, comfortably reclining under sheepskin covers, we flew for several hours on a magic carpet through the white spaces. The dazzling whiteness of the snow made our eyes sleepy and the ringing of the little bells lulled us; were we actually asleep? After having shown us our rooms, our host took us to a huge whitewashed empty sitting room and told us: "My dear friends, this room is yours. Cover those walls with frescoes, paint anything that goes through your head. I want to have a cabaret and a big party for New Year's eve. Go ahead, you'll be given everything you need, brushes, paints, ladders; I count on you."

While the show we put on may not have been in perfect taste, the enthusiasm it provoked was beyond anything. After the Viborg pantomimes, I did a wild dance, leaping into the air like a madman and Serge Walter, our favorite pianist, soothed us with waltzes: He played so well he seemed to have four hands. We took some sleigh rides, played all kinds of games, and time passed so fast we never noticed it.

But by the time we had returned to Tursevo, everything had changed. Our little society scattered. Some left for Helsinki or Viborg, others just stayed in, waiting, as we were, for exit visas. My parents were gone, Anatole and Claudia followed them, and now our dacha seemed empty, cold, and hostile. My

mother told us to sell anything that could be useful to the
incoming refugees, so we got rid of absolutely everything:
sheets, blankets, my mother's old dresses, cooking utensils. To
our amazement, we each made £70, which we were to spend
on clothes in London. Two princesses insisted on my turning
the villa over to them and told me to come to lunch if I would.
Deserters, shady characters, started to come around. They
would wander into unbarred gardens and shout insults. Two
of them, armed with bayonets, even threatened me. I don't
know how it happened, but one of them gave me a gun, I
aimed at a crow all the way on top of a distant tree and fired.
I am normally a bad shot because my hand shakes, but, a
miracle: The bird fell, pierced through the neck by my bullet,
and, after I returned the weapon to the appalled soldiers, they
promptly and respectfully left.

Finally our visas came. We said good-bye, leaving poor
Agafia in tears, though she was to join us later in Paris (and,
by the way, everybody had completely forgotten about Madi,
who was still watching over our apartment in Saint Petersburg).
In Helsinki, waiting for a cargo ship, I found myself once
again in a lively and cheerful city, full of open-air cafés. There
I saw my first French officers: I envied their sky-blue caps, their
khaki uniforms, their Parisian accents! I met an officer's wife
who had a weakness for me and left me an unpleasant souvenir.
During the crossing, I noticed sadly that I had caught the clap.
Once in London, I had such cramps that the doctor at the
Strand Hotel had to give me morphine injections, and I had
to confess to Aunt Julie. We bought a whole wardrobe and I
ordered some suits from Davis, the famous tailor, on whom I
had the temerity to force my own taste. Two weeks later, we
arrived at the Gare du Nord in Paris, were met by an employee
of the bank, and were told that all our suitcases were lost.

PART II

FRANCE

Chapter 5

Paris
The Académie Rançon
The Triangle
The Riviera

1919–1929

My WISH HAD COME TRUE. I was in Paris, the only city in the world where one could learn to paint. The past no longer mattered; I thought only of the future.

It was a month after Genia and I arrived from London that the suitcases we had lost during the trip were finally recovered thanks to the efforts of a private detective sent by Sir Basil Zaharoff and of a young employee of my stepfather's bank. Since the bank in Saint Petersburg and all its Russian branches had been nationalized, a new business headed by my stepfather was created from the Paris, Brussels, and Geneva branches.

And it was only a few days after our arrival, with Roerich's letter of recommendation in my pocket, that Genia and I took the train to Le Vésinet where the famous painter Maurice Denis lived. The maid who opened the door told us that the absent master gave no private lessons but that he taught in a free academy, or art school, in Montparnasse, whose name and address she gave us: Académie Rançon, on the rue Joseph Barra. And having made sure of the arrangements for our painting lessons, we were delighted to have a few weeks of freedom so that we could become more familiar with Paris. During the day, I visited churches and museums with Genia, but in the evenings, alone, I liked mixing with the crowds on the boulevards and sitting at sidewalk cafés, for I was impatient to have a more intimate contact with this city I had loved from a distance for so many years, and also to sleep with a Frenchwoman so as to lose my foreigner's virginity. Was this need for physical contact not also a spiritual need? The shows of the Médrano Circus evoked Toulouse-Lautrec and Seurat; the place de l'Opéra, the Saint-Lazare station, and the boulevards, Monet and Pissaro; and Paris women, Renoir. As for the day-to-day life, the theaters, markets, department stores, they all reminded me of Zola, Maupassant, and the Goncourt brothers.

And so began that long, very long romance between me and France, a passionate romance that lasted until the end of World War II. I was actually the only one in the family to love our new country and want to be part of it. My parents and my cousins, who joined us there, liked France well enough —as did most foreigners—but knew it little and understood it less. Too old to put down new roots and shake off their preoccupation with the past, they stayed mostly among Russians. Before the war, of course, my parents had visited France regularly. But what had they known? The elegant sections of Paris, the place de la Concorde, the place de l'Opéra, the Bois de Boulogne and, outside the capital, only Nice, Cap d'Antibes, and Monte Carlo. Even my brother, born in a city built partly by Italian architects, came to prefer Italy, a country that is somehow closer to our Russian ways. For there is a wide gulf between the Russians and the French, between generosity, impulsiveness, sentimentality, and lack of balance on the one side, and wisdom, measure, discipline, even thrift on the other. A ruined Russian nobleman, a refugee in Paris with still a million left, would prefer to spend it magnificently and then become a night watchman rather than live as a petty bourgeois. At the beginning of our stay, there were many small features of daily life that surprised me, as they did my mother. How could parents take their children to the Casino de Paris to see naked women? In a park, a nanny would call to her charge, "Come here, *ma cocotte*," a word that, to us Russians, meant streetwalker.

I preferred to live exclusively among the French—the Parisians in Paris, the fishermen, peasants, and petty bourgeois in the provinces. I even became jingoistic. I assimiliated the ways of thought, the manners, the language, and wanted at any cost to be mistaken for a Frenchman. But, in spite of my perfect knowledge of French, a small speech defect—the *r* rolled a little too strongly—always betrayed me, for there is an age beyond which you really can no longer change your accent.

At the beginning of my stay, struck by the grandiose spectacle of Parisian life, I had thought I would never be able to assimilate; there was an invisible barrier. Then, one morning, the miracle took place and the angel Gabriel visited me. I was sitting in the Cour Carrée of the Louvre. The sun was shining, pigeons flew about, the noises of the city barely reached me. I was alone, admiring the architecture when, suddenly, I felt as if a light had come to me. When I left the Cour Carrée that morning, I was "French." From then on, I felt perfectly at ease.

Later, I was to be the only member of the family who wanted to become a French citizen. When he had arrived in Paris, my stepfather had obtained from Millerand*, as a rare exception, naturalization papers for himself and all his family to be made final in two years. But nobody bothered with them; the papers were lost. And when, later, I applied for my citizenship papers, I had all the difficulty in the world and only succeeded thanks to the help of a minister, an uncle of Christian Dior's: In a France bled white by the war and needing men, only illiterate foreign workers could become citizens.

One may love countries and cities as one does people, and as one travels or strolls along, collect the impressions given by towns, by nature, or by historic places as one would collect stamps or objects. Having become familiar with the principal monuments in Paris, I began to visit less well-known areas and to walk into endless numbers of old courtyards in quest of old facades. This is how I discovered the splendors of the Marais. These princely dwellings were then so little known that there

---

* Alexandre Millerand, president of France, 1920–24.

wasn't a single book about them. Not a single photograph had been taken in the area (which should actually not be surprising since Huvet, the curator of the Chartres cathedral—who, like Quasimodo, lived in the cathedral towers, where I visited him —was at that time the first to publish photos of the sublime details of this unique building). Still, here and there on newsstands I managed to pick up the remains of an out-of-print series of postcards showing Paris's old facades. Thus I was able to put together a unique collection, which I used as a guidebook. But, finally, what I really admired most was not so much the buildings, but Paris itself: its tree-lined streets, its incomparable unity, its fantastic views.

I disliked my parents' temporary apartment as much as the modern buildings of the rue Bayard, that insipid, middle-class, dead stump of a street between the avenue Montaigne and the rue François-Ier. Several Russian refugee families lived in our building, among others the Abelsons, whom my stepfather knew and whose son, a young buck of my own age, had arrived in Paris before me. He offered himself as a guide to the city's lovelife and took me to the Grand Café, on the boulevards, in the space now occupied by American Express. There, seduced, she said, by my pretty face, a handsome brunette called Yvonne took me under her protection. She nicknamed me Pépé, which I thought at first was "Bébé." There was another woman, a redhead, whom I thought more attractive, but rumor had it that she had a disease so I never dared make a real approach to her. After one or two drinks, Yvonne and I would make for one of those discreet and respectable little hotels on the rue Godot de Mauroy where one could rent a room by the hour and which made me think I was living in the pages of a Maupassant novel. Not all our rendezvous were so pleasant, though; I remember being in a nasty little hotel of the Cité Bergère when, in the middle of the night, Yvonne had such terrible cramps in the lower stomach that I had to run out and get a doctor. It was only later that I realized I had witnessed a miscarriage. It also happened several times that Yvonne left me, though we had a rendezvous, and picked up a client at the café. My pride was finally hurt and I dropped her. I think I could have replaced her with my dancing teacher at the school where I was learning the new steps. We would go out to dancehalls for practice and the fragrance of the sweaty young body glued to mine was very exciting, but my shyness and my fear of a refusal kept me mute.

The Paris I knew and loved, the Paris of the twenties and thirties, was, it seems to me, a more intimate place than it is today. In any case, in those years the City of Light dominated the world. People spoke of the *douceur de vivre*, and a German writer created a sensation by calling his book "Is God French?" When I arrived there, the red taxis that had helped win the battle of the Marne were still plying their trade against the grey of the city's medieval patina. Lined with clubs and private houses, the Champs Élysées was barely lit at night. At the corner of the rue de la Boétie, the princely Massa house still stood surrounded by its gardens. And one morning in front of the Petit Palais, Citroën launched his Citroën-Trèfles. The mirage of Byzantium created by the Sacré-Coeur corresponded to the oriental impression of the old Trocadéro. In front of the Louvre, as in the old prints, barges unloaded bricks and sand on the quays. The pony-driven cart of the Petit Gervais cheeses rushed through the streets and the troika of great white horses of the Planteurs de Café Caiffa shook the pavement. Later on, from my studio on the avenue Malakoff, I was to see a shepherd passing with his flock of goats, selling milk to the tune of a litle reed pipe. At night, by the Madeleine, under the light of the stars and the Chinese lanterns slung between the trees, in a honky-tonk atmosphere, violins would play dance tunes. Everywhere there seemed to be poetry in the air and, feeling happy, I would join the crowd of strollers and good-natured streetwalkers wrapped in furs given them by American soldiers.

The Paris I was to make my own was that of Raquel Meller

singing "La Violétéra" at the Olympia Theater; of Mistinguett singing "Mon Homme" at the Casino de Paris and stealing the show from Maurice Chevalier; of the Médrano Circus clowns, the Fratellini, and its trapeze artists, the Rixfords and the Cordonas who flew through the air, of the female impersonator Barbette, of the Boeuf sur le Toit; of Cocteau's Six. And there was the Russian Ballet, with Karsavina, Massine, and Lifar—a completely new venture of collaboration between painters, composers, and dancers—Diaghilev calling on the genius of those future giants, Stravinsky and Picasso.

There were so many surprises, so much that was new. From the United States came films with Chaplin, Garbo, cowboys, gangsters: We laughed, then we cried. There was jazz, the Blues, the Hoffman girls, and, finally, the Blackbirds led by an ebony goddess who soon conquered Paris, Josephine Baker. She danced to the electric rhythm of the Charleston and her naked breasts did not shake! From a mysterious and barely explored Africa came a new primitive art. Montparnasse replaced Montmartre. Among the artists, Gris was starving, Vuillard was still hidden, Chirico and Rousseau were just making their appearance. People were beginning to buy contemporary painting; it was the time of cubism, surrealism, neo-romanticism, and a number of other "isms." The major art galleries were gathered on the rue de la Boétie, the lesser ones on the rue de la Seine. Art was torn between traditional and modern, and museums of modern art were being born.

Wanda Landowska was reviving the harpsichord, Bach, Scarlatti and baroque music. The designer Paul Poiret made color fashionable, Coco Chanel introduced sport clothes. In tennis, Suzanne Lenglen played like a man and the Musketeers proved that the word *impossible* was not French. The Parisians discovered the Riviera and Saint Tropez in the summer. French flyers made it from Dakar to South America and competed for long-distance flight records over Asia; and Lindbergh crossed the Atlantic.

The Académie Rançon, where we were to study and live the

life of Montparnasse for two years, was at the back of a small, abandoned garden on the rue Joseph Barra. Sleepy, charming, the street could have belonged to any little provincial town. On the side opposite the Académie was the long wall of a convent garden, with the treetops showing above it, and beyond this, small gardens in front of little houses. At certain times, we would hear the convent bell tolling, but footsteps were rare and cars never came through. Against the white wall, we would now and then see the nuns in their black habits slipping past. The street's only animation came with the arrival and departure of the students at the Académie Rançon. At one end of the street was a run-down building full of the studios of well-known painters: Kisling, Pascin, Hermine David. Zborowski, the private dealer, also lived in this building, and Modigliani had just died there. At the other end, the street opened into the rue d'Assas, opposite the Académie André Lhote. A few meters away was the rue de la Grande Chaumière, well-known for the Académie of that name; though as short and narrow as the rue Joseph Barra, this street was very animated and full of studios, of art-supply stores, and small shops. It ended at the crossing of the boulevards Montparnasse and Raspail, heart and center of this tiny closed universe that, having replaced Montmartre, had now become world famous. There, facing one another, were the restaurant Bati, where everyone ate in the basement, the Dôme, where everyone met to talk, and the tiny Rotonde, abandoned since the days of Lenin. Painters, known, unknown, or misunderstood, students and models, all gathered in one big Montparnasse family. There were no tourists, no taxi stands, no expensive hotels, no movie theaters, no nightclubs except for the Jockey, whose star was the notorious Kiki; and so little traffic that, even at noon, a child could safely have walked across the intersection. And yet, this little universe was responsible for a major artistic revolution through a dozen so-called "free" academies that had made the Academy of Fine Arts obsolete. Among these was the Académie Rançon, less popular than the Grande Chaumière but more renowned because of the great number of famous painters who taught there—men like Maurice Denis, Bonnard, Vuillard, and Sérusier, the disciple of Gauguin and Valloton. They had come together by chance: They had all been Nabis and, when one of them, an obscure painter named Rançon, died, leaving a penniless widow, all his friends decided to support her by founding an academy where she would keep the fees while they taught without charge.

After opening the rusty garden gate and walking under a large tree, one entered a passage on the right of which was the office where the respectable widow ruled. She was dressed always in black, her white hair pulled back in a bun, cold, distant, masculine, hairy, with no thumb on one hand. After greeting her, one passed into a very large studio, surprisingly light since its window gave onto the dark garden, but actually lighted through a skylight—the whole sky seemed to come right in. In the middle of this studio was an enormous cast-iron stove called a turtle with a long, bent exhaust pipe, which warmed us in winter. In a corner, on the garden side, was a small room belonging to the good Concetta, an Italian model married to a factory worker and now the Académie's housekeeper. Plump, her eyes popping out of her flat face, she was a mother hen to all her students. She was also an excellent cook and sometimes invited one of us into her cage to share her delicious dinner.

There were about twenty-five students: a few Rumanians, including Catargi, the son of the ambassador to Belgium, two Russians, Genia and I, one Australian, Edouard Goerg, and, for a short time, Douglas Fairbanks, Jr. Latapie was "*massier*," a rank corresponding to corporal in the army and given to the oldest or most advanced student. While we rarely saw this tall, thin young man, the same was not true of little Pierre Charbonnier, his assistant, who was very diligent. Like all the rest of the students, I unreservedly admired his nudes, which seemed to me "perfect." And so, when on Saturday at noon, it was Vuillard's turn to criticize our nudes of the week, he would usually stop in front of Charbonnier's canvas and teach us by pointing out his successes and failures. Two girls, one fair, the other dark, Thérèse Debains and Isabelle Ischval, did wonderful drawings. Two seventeen-year-old Parisians also came, one to talk, the other to fetch him at noon: Christian Bérard, nicknamed Bébé, and one Christian Dior. Then there was Gaston Roux, who was later to be successful. And a pleasant nobleman, Jean de Gagneron, who, alas, had no talent at all.

The morning's model would keep the same pose throughout the week. In the afternoons, whoever wanted to would paint a little still-life arranged on a stool next to the wall. This arrangement hardly varied: Cézanne's eternal apples and his white napkin—only rarely Picasso's fruit bowl. Even the technique of small parallel strokes was influenced by Cézanne, whose work then dominated Paris and was imitated in all the free academies. Our day's learning would end with rapid sketching from five to seven at the Académie de la Grande Chaumière, where the housekeeper, like Concetta an ex-Italian model but tall and thin and called "that big stick of a Rose," earned extra money by reselling to the students at a bargain abandoned painted canvases that could be covered with a layer of grey and painted again.

According to the very rigid rules of Nabi or impressionist teaching (I cannot, today, separate the two), our palettes were divided in two: on one side, warm colors, the cadmiums; on the other, cool colors, the chromes—it would have been considered a crime to mix the two. All subjects, nudes, still-lifes, or portraits, were treated in the same way. We started with a rough drawing done with a stiff brush in a dark color; this was to remain and serve to indicate the subject's main colors. Then came two more colors, the light and the shadow, which created the volume. Both light and shadow had to be all warm or all cool and the opposite of each other. Black, so beautiful in Manet's paintings, was banned because it does not exist in nature. Since white is a cool color, it could be replaced, if you wanted a warm one, by Naples yellow. And so on. Since it was impossible to reproduce exactly the colors of our subjects, there was a transposition of reality that took us away from realism and thus gave a certain abstract charm to those works of Bonnard and Vuillard we so admire today. Once you were used to it, this theory was extremely simple, even when you had to take complementary colors into account: red and green, yellow and blue, orange and purple. To give a simple example: a warm red apple had a green, i.e., cool, shadow; a cool yellow apple, a blue and warm shadow.

None of the famous painters teaching at Rançon lived in the neighborhood; they only appeared on Saturdays, which is to say, rarely, and so, for me, they all remained gods who occasionally came down from Olympus—unlike certain other artists, just as well known, whom we would often see at the Dôme and several of whom became our friends. At the Académie, we were taught mostly by Sérusier, then by Maurice Denis; Vuillard and Valloton both came regularly, Bonnard, never. Outside, we saw mostly Hayden who, at one point, wanted to marry Thérèse Debains. After lunch at Bati, he would invite us upstairs to his studio (it was in the same building), show us his cubist paintings, and explain the movement's mysteries and rules. Influenced by him, Christian Bérard once brought to Rançon a cubist Pierrot he had painted at home.

The Russian Lipschitz, heavy, serious, and a collector of art objects, would come to the Dôme with his young son and his wife, the big Bertha, whom everybody hated and mocked. Louis Marcoussis painted cubist subjects on glass and his wife Halika had created what was called "quilted romances," artistic arrangements of plush objects, wires, in boxes. We would have a drink with Marc Chagall, the poet and critic André Salmon, the critics Fels, Charensol, Waldemar George. Moïse Kisling, full of fun and jokes, would join us. I used to go to his lunches and met there the most beautiful and best-known women in Paris and admired large-eyed portraits of flowers, barely begun but already sold.

One man whose work and appearance I disliked so that I refused to meet him (a decision I now find idiotic), and who had the solid appearance and vulgar expression of a butcher, was Fernand Léger. Man Ray, that remarkable photographer, as far as I was concerned, should never have picked up a brush, and I hated Marcel Duchamp, that handsome esthete, amateur, and parasite who was taking it easy at the house of Mary Reynolds. Pierre Roy, this Landru, this Bluebeard, clad in black—this correct gentleman who liked very young girls— would carefully paint charming little still-lifes in a mixture of naturalism and surrealism. When Chirico, then unknown, arrived in Paris for his first exhibition at Paul Guillaume's, where nothing sold in spite of the very low prices, he was brought to Avenue Malakoff by his second wife, Raissa Kroll, whom we had known so well in Finland. His big, badly knit body ended in a horselike head, and a defective jaw made him produce sounds that were like a bugle call rather than Italian-accented French. As for his work, Chirico could be compared to Dr. Jekyll and Mr. Hyde: He had a double personality, for aside from his now-classic metaphysical paintings, he painted portraits and nudes of Raissa that were so realistic, in such bad taste, and so devoid of all talent that even later, when he was universally admired, no one would buy them.

Our little group from Rançon—Bébé, Thérèse, Genia, and I —when we went to the galleries went mostly to Paul Rosenberg's gallery on rue de la Boétie to see Picasso's latest cubist canvases, his ballet drawings, and his portraits, as admirable and realistic as those of Ingres; Rosenberg himself would show them to us in his office. At Paul Guillaume's, we looked at our first di Chiricos and Douanier Rousseaus. At Hessel's, our friend Jean Aaron would show us paintings by Madame Hessel's old and faithful lover, Vuillard. At Bernheim Jeune's, I saw my first Chagall. But it was the tiny little Pierre Gallery (Pierre Loeb) on the rue Bonaparte that first exhibited Miró.

Paris between the wars had a unique climate, for the famous, the beginners, as well as the students, which helped bring on the golden age of modern painting. The students had a chance to become known to the public by showing in the salons, of which there were three: the Autumn Salon, the Tuileries, and the Independents. Having once attracted notice there, you might be offered a contract by one of the numerous small Left Bank galleries. In exchange for a monthly payment that allowed you to live modestly and improve your skill, the gallery owner would receive a number of your works. It would therefore be wrong to suppose that painters were exploited by the dealer. All the expenses—for advertising, for exhibiting, for promoting an artist—were borne by the dealer, who bet on the future of his stable just as it is done at racetracks. All the risk was his. The painter, once successful, had most of the profit. I myself one summer received 600 francs a month as per my contract and lived in Port-en-Bessin, where I was able to pay the full rate at the best hotel on the cliff, twelve francs a day, and still have enough money for my paints, canvases, and small daily expenses.

My stepfather had by now rented (but, alas, not bought) a private house at 46, Avenue Malakoff (now Raymond-Poincaré), at the corner of the rues Saint Didier and Lauriston. I was given a huge studio on the third floor of this house, but never felt really comfortable there, never really at home, and so, much to my mother's displeasure, it was never properly furnished. As for the family's way of life, while it could in no way be compared to that of Saint Petersburg, it was still very prosperous. My stepfather provided abundantly for the needs of his large family right up to his death, after which the family collapsed. We had two footmen (one won a fortune at the races, and the other jumped to his death from the Eiffel Tower); two maids, Agafia, who had joined us from Finland, and a kitchen maid; and a Belgian couple in the kitchen who stole so openly that they were soon replaced by a cook. My mother was still dressed by the great couture houses; twice a year, my parents would still go off to Monte Carlo where they always had the same suite at the Hôtel de Paris. Anatole and Theodore, who had arrived in Paris soon after my parents, got very large sums of money out of their father; and even Genia and I, who lacked for nothing, were given allowances. Penniless refugees would be fed in the kitchen and often given a few francs by Genia and me as well as warm clothes. Our house was well-known to them. Sometimes we would be unpleasantly surprised: Thus a young man, after weeks of being kept, failed to show up for the job I had found him at Les Halles, but came back to ask for more money; another one, to whom I offered five francs, answered, "I don't want this; I want ten francs or nothing."

Agafia, in spite of her advanced age, faithfully continued to serve my mother, who would ring for her constantly, making her run up and down the stairs. This killed her, Agafia complained, for her legs were painful and she wanted to "throw them out of the window." On Sundays and holidays, her only entertainment was attending the Russian Church on the rue Daru where she would go not only to pray, but sometimes to clean and even wash the floor of the vestry. There, as at home, she felt she belonged, was loved and respected by all the priests, including the metropolitan. The grace, the amplitude of her movements, almost in slow motion, during the service, her serious and almost transfigured face, her kneeling and bowing were of a rare and moving beauty. On the whole, she can hardly have felt she was in exile since she had her family and her Church, that little piece of Russian earth. (This Church would accept refugees of all religions; thus a service was to be celebrated there at the death of my parents and my cousins.) Even in the kitchen, surrounded by French servants, Agafia could relax: She had created a dialect, half French/half Russian, that they alone understood. She had remained a virgin and was therefore still frightened of unknown men, especially the French, so famous for their lusty ways. One day as she was crossing the place de l'Étoile, her purse opened. Unaware of the heavy traffic, she fell to her knees to pick up her money. A passerby rushed to save her. "Disgusting man, disgusting man!" she shrieked. Toward the end of her life, she would see devils everywhere, especially in her dreams: They would enter her room and carry her to the Pit in a coach. I was away from Paris when she died; she was staying with a Russian family from whom I rented a room for her after my mother died. With her disappeared a large portrait I had painted of her, which I miss, for I never had any photographs of her.

My parents had for their private physician old Dr. Mendelson, whose wife was killed, along with about a hundred other people when during the war a shell shot by Big Bertha fell, one Sunday morning, on the Church of Saint Gervais. He would come for lunch once a month, bringing his eighteen-year-old daughter whom Genia and I liked as little as we liked her father. This sad and unpleasant man (I only liked cheerful, athletic doctors like a Dr. Aitoff who took care of me) somehow managed to convince my parents that we should spend our first summer in France taking the waters at La Bourboule. In fact, he received a commission from the hotel.

Up to this point, Genia and I had been inseparable, at home, at the Académie, traveling; we would paint the same subjects and then criticize each other—a practice that would stifle the free development of our separate personalities—and while we may have begun to realize this, we were not yet mature enough to work independently. And although we were inseparable in this way, we did have separate private lives; years earlier, my brother had asked me always to respect his privacy. Whether it was for love of Claudia or for other reasons, he never had intimate relations with women. As for me, when the need called, I went to the brothel on the rue Croix des Petits Champs, behind the Palais Royal, where the madam greeted me as a friend and the girls preferred the young rooster to the more demanding old goats. Not that I didn't sometimes have little adventures. I never slept with the kitchen maid, whom my mother allowed us to paint in the nude (she slept with the cook and I always avoided our servants), but on the other hand, I did have an affair with a professional model with alabaster breasts who seduced me, then began to pose badly, to come later and later, and who finally disappeared. This taught me never to mix work and pleasure. I did, however, have another adventure with a black model. I had never known a black model before and, since there were very few in Paris, they were extremely popular. What made our rendezvous in a hotel on the rue Godot de Mauroy particularly memorable was the shock I felt when, after having watched a familiar person walk into the bathroom, I saw, amazed, a complete stranger come out toward me. It was all like magic: I hadn't recognized my black friend, who had changed her coiffure and, instead of slicked-back hair, was wearing a huge Afro.

After two years at the Académie Rançon, Genia and I felt we had learned enough to fly with our own wings. And since I had a huge, almost empty studio, I suggested to Thérèse and Bébé that they come and paint there and share the cost of a model; they were delighted to accept. At the beginning, Jean de Gagneron joined us but Genia made such a scene when, one day, our friendly aristocrat was so bold as to proposition the model that he was really offended and never came back.

After two years of work, my brother was beginning to be free of his dark colors and the chiaroscuro of the Dutch masters, whom he had followed under Anatole's influence. Bébé had practically never touched a brush at the Académie but, naturally gifted, had learned just by watching us work. Thérèse, so good at drawing, had more problems with painting; and, as for me, tired of impressionist rules, I abandoned the divided palette and started to paint freely.

I had been lucky to meet, in Thérèse and Bébé—right at the beginning of my stay in Paris—two cultivated people who were typically French, both physically and mentally. How I envied those who were lucky enough to have been born French, or, even better, Parisians! Thérèse, who came in every day on the train from Versailles, where she lived with a widowed mother and two younger sisters, reminded me of the statue of justice in the Chartres cathedral. She was fair and wore her braided hair rolled up over her ears; she had blue eyes, thick arched eyebrows, and a very low voice. I liked listening to her discussions of painting with Bébé and to their commentary on the first volumes of Proust, which were then being published and which most people did not take seriously. Charmed though I was by Thérèse's mind, I felt no physical attraction. She was simply not my type; I only loved brunettes.

Bébé was seven years younger than I. Very fair, with striking blue eyes, white teeth revealed by an overly short lip, a small beaked nose, this Parisian to his fingertips was slim, well-dressed, and neat—the very reverse of what he was to become later—which is fat, dirty, and bearded. He was one of the very few people, along with the composers Sauguet and Poulenc, and esthete Jean de Gagneron, to speak perfect French, French as brilliant and fascinating as his mind. He was loved by some, hated by others, but he never went unnoticed. His father, the president of the Paris Society of Architects, was a pompous, conventional, and very masculine fascist, who had mistresses and loathed his son because the latter was cultured, refined, and even, unconsciously, effeminate. Bébé was also, to his father's displeasure, beloved of his mother, a very elegant little woman—unhappy and unhealthy—who had been born the daughter of Count de Borniol, a family famous in Paris for its chain of funeral parlors.

Bébé, whose parents lived at the rue Spontini, spent increasingly less time at home, where he felt lost and lonely, and now spent virtually his entire life at the avenue Malakoff. In the morning, he would come and work; in the afternoon, we would go together to see art shows in the rue de la Boétie or in museums; and in the evening after Thérèse had gone back to Versailles, we would go to the Foire du Trône, to the Médrano Circus to see the Fratellini brothers, or simply to a movie. My parents finally accepted Bébé, whom they hadn't quite trusted at first but who won them over by his youth and charm. When both Anatole and Bébé came to dinner, there would be duels of

ABOVE The family Manassevitch. Seated, first row center, in black gown, the maternal grandmother, and holding hat, the grandfather. LEFT Aunt Eugenie. BELOW Leonid's mother, at left, and at right, a photograph of his famous 1908 impersonation.

TOP LEFT Family group: Leonid at left, his mother holding the baby Eugene, known to the family and friends as Genia. BELOW LEFT Leonid. BELOW RIGHT Young gentlemen: Genia, left, and Leonid. FACING PAGE, ABOVE Mother, in Monte Carlo. BELOW Uncle Otto, Monte Carlo.

730.

ABOVE Left to right: Leonid, Anatole, Claudia Pavlova, and Genia. BELOW Toupsik. FACING PAGE, ABOVE Ischia, 1926. Left to right: Leonid, De Angelis, and Eugene Berman. BOTTOM Toulon, 1926. Back row, left to right: René Crevel, Viot, Poupet. Front row, left to right: Christian Berard, two sailors, Leonid.

FACING PAGE, ABOVE Leonid, left, and Pierre Charbonnier in St. Tropez. FACING PAGE, BELOW Left to right: Pavel Tchelitchew, Edith Sitwell, and Allen Tanner. Guermantes, 1929. THIS PAGE, ABOVE Left to right: Leonid, Petroff, Kristians Tony. St. Tropez, 1926. BELOW Kristians Tony, left, and Leonid on the quay at St. Tropez.

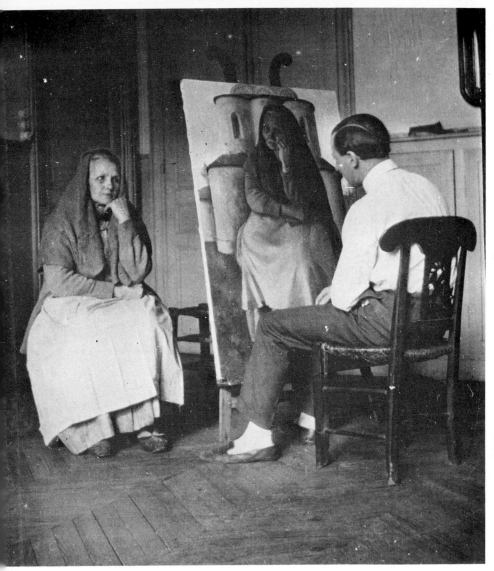

FACING PAGE, ABOVE Christian Berard. FAC-
ING PAGE, BELOW Years later, with Prince
Leone Massimo, at left. ABOVE The young
painter paints his old nanny, Agafia.

With wife, harpsichordist Sylvia Marlowe,
in Connecticut.

wit between the two, one so Russian, the other so French, for Bébé was familiar with Russian literature and music as well as with the Diaghilev ballets. For him, all that was Russian was charming, a feeling to which he remained loyal all his life, even in his love affairs. In love with the musical sound of the language, he would make me repeat sentences like "I love you," "I'll kill you," or pronounce city names like Tsarskoie-Selo.

During the winter, Thérèse became my mistress. One evening, we were both invited to a cocktail party given by a young decorator-architect who had suddenly become fashionable and whose secretary happened to be one of Thérèse's schoolfriends. For the inauguration of his Auteuil penthouse, there was a flowing bar and some twenty guests, mostly gay, for whom I was asked to demonstrate the high jump; then we fox-trotted. While I was dancing with Thérèse I became aware that she was losing her control: Her thigh rubbed against mine so provocatively that I looked around to see if anyone had noticed it, after which I led her to a chair. We said nothing about it at the time. It was only the next day that I phoned her and went to see her in Versailles. I made no allusion to the incident during our walk in the park. When, tired out, we reached the edge of the fields, I finally asked her a single question: Had she known what she was doing? When she said she had, I embraced her, kissed her, and made love to her, quite clumsily. To my great surprise, she cried afterward. It broke my heart and, from that moment, I loved her.

After that I took a bachelor's flat on the rue de Lisbonne and, every day, when the model was finished posing, Thérèse and I would leave Bébé with Genia and go off by ourselves. Thérèse, like most Frenchwomen, was passive, voluptuous, and quite non-sensual. During Thérèse's and my idyll, Bébé, who had been my friend, grew closer to Genia. Then he began to isolate himself in a tiny room in a house belonging to his mother on the rue des Saints-Pères, on the facade of which a black panel bore in gold letters: "Borniol Funeral Parlor." It is there that he painted his very first—yet already mature—

paintings: two of these showed a sitting acrobat, a third, two little boys, his cousins. One wonders how, in that dark closet giving out onto a courtyard and where a couch took up half the available space, he was able to see anything. I suspect that unhappiness caused him to make this amazing leap forward. He also worked with our model, Lucienne Baptiste, small, thin, a real Parisian *titi*, whose daughter would later claim Bébé as her father. It is quite possible that he made love to the very liberated and agreeable Lucienne. What is certain is that, in his solitude, he realized that he loved Thérèse, but told no one.

I smothered Thérèse with presents. On our walks we would go into little antique stores near Saint Germain-des-Prés and look for opaline bottles of which she already had a collection. I insisted she take an otter hat brought back from Russia and my old Wiesbaden watch. I became her "little Lou" and wore a Louis XIV medal she had given me hanging around my neck. I was in my period of fascination with the Sun King; we walked in the Versailles park so often I knew it perfectly. I collected old books on Louise de la Vallière, read French history and, under Thérèse's influence, was mad about Marcelline Desbordes-Valmore's poetry.

The summer was to separate us. As she had done every other year, my friend was to spend her holidays with her mother and sister at Le Pouldu, a little Breton fishing port. She did not want me to follow her because her mother still did not know about our affair. As for my mother, she probably didn't know either because she had only met Thérèse on the staircase once or twice by chance when she was coming to work. Anatole, who now lived in a modern studio in Auteuil with an attic and a garden, suddenly developed a strange idea: He decided to go to Berchtesgaden and, naturally, my brother wanted to accompany him; this influenced my parents, who asked me to go along. I could not have cared less where I went if it meant that I had to be away from Thérèse.

I found those weeks a bore. The sun hardly penetrated the dark pine forests covering the mountains. The company was typically Russian, always the same discussions about art, always the same irritatingly monotonous walks, no amusements. I found it all especially annoying when confronted with my family's perfect harmony. Anatole and Claudia were settled in the only large hotel, Genia and I, in a neighboring chalet. The place could not have been more unsuitable for painting; Genia did not work and I only made a copy from an antique Aphrodite that reminded me of Thérèse. At the peak of my distress, not having received any of the promised letters from Le Pouldu, I finally ran away to Britanny. I stopped for just one afternoon at La Baule, where my friend Mischa Epstein was staying with his family. I can still see myself after my visit with Mischa, standing in the train with my forehead pressed against the window of the corridor, full of dread for some great trouble ahead. The evening was growing dark when I got off at the little Quimperlé station and walked toward the only house in the valley, an inn. I borrowed a bicycle from the innkeeper and immediately started pedaling toward Le Pouldu. There a fisherman pointed out to me a villa isolated in the middle of fields. A light was still burning. I knocked at the door: it was opened, oh miracle! by Thérèse herself. We walked away and sat leaning against a haystack. Yes, she hadn't written, hoping I would understand why and become free of her more easily, because her position was so difficult. I understood nothing and was just happy to see her. I don't know what she had thought to begin with, but, staring ardently into each other's eyes, we finally embraced and nothing else mattered.

There followed four weeks of perfect happiness which brought us much closer than our Paris meetings. Every night, I would pedal fifteen kilometers to join Thérèse at our hay-stack and get back late in the night. I spent my days painting two very dark landscapes, visiting the neighboring village of Quimperlé on its hill; I walked through the forests to see the Druids' sacred places, admired the small church of Saint-Fiacre, and went one day to Belon in my innkeeper's little truck, where I bought such a huge lobster that I was barely able to digest it cooked that night.

Then came the day when Thérèse told me that friends of her family would be coming and that, for the last week of her stay, we would no longer be able to meet. But, on the other hand, she promised she would arrange to spend the last night in Quimperlé with me.

What a memorable night! Thérèse was crying, afraid to return home. And, to make this end of our holiday even more lugubrious, a storm burst upon us so violently we thought the end of the world had come. Amid the ceaseless thunderbursts and lightning, a thunderbolt seemed to strike the inn, shattering the centuries-old oak before my window. We were too frightened to sleep all night. Had it been a warning of the gods? We left separately the next day and, except for one occasion, I saw Thérèse no more.

The summer now over, something mysterious was happening in Versailles, where Bébé now went every day. Thérèse no longer came to Paris. Finally one evening, when Genia was away and my parents in Monte Carlo, Bébé, in my stepfather's little study, announced that he had a great sacrifice to ask of me: I must give up Thérèse. They had both discovered that, without having ever told each other, they had been in love since the beginning at the Académie Rançon. This was the first bad blow: Thérèse had never loved me. Besides, he added, I probably already knew that, for years, Thérèse had not been free because she had lived, without her mother's knowledge, with a traveling salesman who had said he would marry her; but now, he, Bébé, thought he might become her husband. It was this second blow that completely did me in, for what was left after such double treachery? For a long time I could not say the fatal word, after which I collapsed, lying on the couch all night without moving, tears running from my eyes and unable to breathe, left with a hiccup that stayed with me for almost two years. Bébé, who had not at all expected this reaction, was terrified; sitting on the carpet, he begged me to be calm, stroked my hair, kissed me. Was it chance or an effort to appease me that led his hand, at one point, to caress me? Anyway, we spent the night together.

Until some time later, summering in the little village of Sainte Maxime, I was to remain indifferent to women. When she saw me looking so withdrawn, my mother told me I shouldn't take it all so tragically, and Anatole, always a romantic, exclaimed one day: "Ah, Youth! How wonderful to suffer for love!" while I thought, "The idiot, he doesn't realize that I am dying." It still surprises me today that I stayed faithful to Thérèse in my heart and continued wearing her medal around my neck.

Except for Genia, none of us was actually painting any more. I couldn't concentrate, and Bébé and Thérèse were too preoccupied with their own lives. Outside of his afternoons in Versailles, Bébé spent all his time with me. God knows what would have become of me without this faithful friend and nurse. As for our intimacy, it was not in me to receive without giving something back and, as we did not go beyond manual relief, I accepted it with a sort of *schadenfreude* because, like Thérèse with me, I did not want to hurt Bébé. All our friends now thought of us as a couple, which seemed to make them respect me more.

Torn between Thérèse and me, confusing love and friend-ship, Bébé, still a naive adolescent, was only now beginning to discover his own tastes. Soon there was no longer any question of marriage. Had they even slept together? The visits to Versailles became rarer, our walks through Paris took more time. This is when we explored courtyard after courtyard in the old neighborhoods and discovered so many architectural treasures. Sometimes we would spend our Sundays outside the city, in Verneuil, in Chartres, in a little restaurant on the banks of the Oise or the Eure or even in some suburb which still felt exotic.

Then fate made me in my turn Bébé's nurse and caused him to need my help. First, he grieved deeply for his mother's death. Now truly an orphan, since his father had rejected him, he became all the closer to my family. He had some kind of heart disease—whether real or imaginary, I don't know. He would suddenly start choking in the streets; breathing hard, his forehead running with sweat, he would stagger, lean on my arm; then I would take him to a bench or jump into a taxi with him and go to his doctor's. During one of these attacks, one evening in the Trocadéro gardens, we were pushed away from a bench by two policemen who followed us, shouting insults. This reminded me of Masaccio's fresco in Florence, the expulsion from the Garden of Eden. I must have had a very red face and Bébé, hiding his face with his hands, whispered: "What a shame, the brutes, they don't understand anything!" When Bébé had to serve in the army, in Coblenz, I sent him one of the postcards of old Paris from my collection every day with a few words of encouragement, but this separation marked the end of his "friendship" for Thérèse. This was when I saw her again for the only and last time. She called me and I took her to Houdan, where we ate one of those famous chickens. She cried again and took refuge in my arms, but, though I ardently desired her, I remained cold.

Actually, the needle had pointed the wrong way for all three of us: I loved Thérèse, Thérèse loved Bébé, and Bébé loved me. Thérèse abandoned me as Bébé did her and as I did Bébé as soon as I was myself again—which is to say, in love once more.

A few months after my break with Thérèse, I was finally able to start painting again. To start, I obliged myself to a strict hourly discipline so that I could recover my taste for work. Later, I painted a very large canvas for one of the salons, and when I saw it hanging between the works of two celebrities, Warroquier and Favori, I thought my career made. Léon Kochnitzky, a Belgian cousin of Aunt Mania's, came to see my painting and brought with him the Brussels critic Paul Fierenz. Inspired by Renoir, my canvas showed two bathers by the side of a river with the Maintenon aqueduct in the background. I had asked our model Lucienne Baptiste to pose for one of the bathers, and I painted the other from a photo of the Aphrodite and the drawing that I had done of it in Berchtesgaden. I'm sorry I have lost the photograph of my painting but I still have a small, bad silkscreen, quite different from the big canvas but with a sitting figure that looks like Thérèse; I never had a photo of her. The atmosphere of both compositions is very romantic. In the little one, there is even a winged cupid crawling near Thérèse, which I had added for balance.

Bébé and I were supposed to spend a summer in Italy, and my parents approved of the trip. Of course, we knew most of Italy's treasures from books and reproductions and I actually wondered if the reality could match my imagination. Genia left for Venice before Bébé and me, and I accompanied my friend to a place near Dreux where his grandmother owned a small chateau. I settled down in a neighboring farm, a charming place called the Gué des Grues. Its shallow, swift river, where trout could be caught, was bordered with willows. Bébé would come and visit me every day. I was now working better than in Paris as I liked living in the country and had a natural bent for landscape.

It was time to go to Italy; Genia was already waiting for us in Venice. But I was badly upset by a letter from my parents: They felt I had not deserved this treat, they said, because I had not been serious enough or done enough work. Quickly putting together a few paintings, I rushed to see Moïse Kisling in Paris and, after I received his approving comments, took him to my parents, who were only too happy to change their minds.

Having passed this crisis, I spent three unforgettable months in Venice, Florence, Rome and its neighboring towns. These constant distractions were excellent for my morale, though my spirits sank again every time we stopped at a post office and picked up the inevitable letter to Bébé from Thérèse where my name was never mentioned. We would run around from morning till night, wanting to see and know everything, and come back to our hotel dead tired, only to start again early the next day. Since we were also spending too much money buying postcards, along with Anderson and Alinari photographs, we sometimes skipped dinner. Still, we had much more money than we were to have later on, because our parents, unaware of prices, had provided abundantly. Aside from our allowances, we each had 75 francs a day, and this in a country where life cost just half of what it did in France.

Italy, which had few tourists then, reminded me of Stendhal and Corot. In Venice, Bébé and I stayed at the Albergo Vittoria behind the Piazza San Marco, in front of the gondola basin; it was an old palace made into a hotel. One could still visit the Palazzo Giovanelli with Giorgione's "Tempesta." I liked Rome better than Florence. We were most impressed by the works of Carpaccio, Masaccio, Mantegna, and especially Piero della Francesca. We went back to Paris exhausted, thinner, and very happy.

This first trip to Italy was followed by others, but without Bébé, who was serving with his regiment at Coblenz. The following summer we visited Orvieto first, then the Roman *campagna*. We felt really at home in Orvieto thanks to Aldo Prosperini, a young man of my age. and the son of the owner of the Albergo della Posta. Every morning all the housewives would sing the song of the Gigolette loudly as they cleaned. In basements, under the shade of the arcades, peasants would drink the local wine. Picturesque oxen slumbered near the medieval gates. And the women's multicolored costumes flashed in the vineyards. A young farm girl called Peppa posed for her portrait.

After Orvieto, Genia went to work in Tivoli and I was off to the Villa Adriana. We would meet only on Sundays or on the Saint's Day of one of the villages to hear the Mass and admire the old costumes, taken out of their trunks by the young women for the occasion: They were so starched and stiff that they looked like medieval suits of armor. I saw Palombaro and stopped thinking that Mantegna's landscapes were fantasy.

I was delighted to end this Italian stay with a three-day visit to Naples—against my brother's advice, for he thought it a ridiculously short time to see so important and beautiful a city. I came out of the train at the Porta Capuana well after midnight but just could not stop walking, making my way amid an army of sleeping children—whose beds had been taken out of their rooms because of the heat—under lines of laundry, until, finally exhausted, I started to knock on closed hotel doors, which would not open. Finally, I was taken by a night watch-man into a sort of storage room under a staircase. I slept there among stacks of folded metal beds. When I woke up in the morning and saw through the opening of my cage only the feet of people walking up and down the stairs, I thought it so amusing that I stayed in my little room for the remaining two nights of my visit.

The summer following, we were lucky enough to be able to go to Spain. This was quite a feat for refugees like Genia and me who only had Nansen passports. This is how it happened. When Claudia and Anatole left Finland, they went first to Berlin, where they met refugees from Saint Petersburg ballet circles: the dancers Smirnova, Romanoff, and Oburoff, with whom they set up a company, the Romantic Ballet. Two Russian painters, Leon Zack and Pavel Tchelitchew, designed the sets. Everyone eventually moved to Paris, and in due course Anatole introduced Tchelitchew, whom we called Pavlik, to our family. Here, too, he met Bébé. The two geniuses got along badly, jealous or admiring in accordance with the mood of the day. When the Romantic Ballet was invited to Spain for a tour, Anatole got 50,000 francs from his father for various expenses, such as new sets for the ballet and new Groult dresses (she was a cousin of Chanel's) for Claudia. Since we wanted to go to Spain and paint there, Genia and I were given walk-on parts.

I can still see myself on stage in Madrid in front of a packed audience, with King Alfonso XIII in his box. That was when I became aware of the difference between the hard work put in by the dancers and their airy appearance, between the sweat, panting breath, effort, holes in the floor to be avoided and what the audience saw, which was grace, lightness, smiles. . . . At the end of the show, an aide-de-camp asked four dancers to come and meet the King. Claudia, however, was not among those invited. Anatole took it so badly that he left for Paris with Claudia that very evening, in an amateur's thoughtless gesture that ought to have cost him a lot of money for breach of contract. After that, Genia and I went off to paint in Toledo. In this sun-scorched country, the few trees seemed miracles. In the evenings, on the miradors, the young girls accompanied by their duennas would stroll past the cadets of the Alcazar. We met several of these young cadets but must have offended them by something we said about religion or Spain, for they dropped us. A painter called Marañon introduced us to the mysteries of bull fighting and took me to a brothel where guitarists were playing in the courtyard. We saw several *corridas*, including a supposedly comic one, with clowns, which nevertheless ended in the death of an innocent little calf. We also witnessed the sinister ceremony of the Corpus Christi.

Our work was going well, but the July nights were just as hot as the days, and we found them intolerable. We wanted to leave Spain but our parents' money order, delayed by a mis-understanding, seemed as if it would never come. We took a big chance and, with the little money we still had left, took the train for Orvieto, spending a sleepless night on a bench of the Rambla in Barcelona, almost without food, and finally arrived in Italy at the Albergo della Posta with about five lire between us.

That was the last summer that Genia and I were to spend completely together. Twice more I would join him for a month before our final parting, but he preferred Italy, and I, France. Even at Avenue Malakoff, we were spending much less time together. While I would spend my winters on the Riviera, he would stay in Paris. From being a recluse, he had grown into a great socializer, seeing the architect Emilio Terry, Marc Chadourne, a writer, Gertrude Stein and the Polignacs, and painting a big portrait of Marie-Laure, Vicomtesse de Noailles. He sold the big Italianate paintings done in Paris to Zborowski and, with my mother's help, moved to an apartment of his own in the Grenelle quarter where the rooms were painted one red, another yellow, a third blue, in memory of Anatole's flat in Saint Petersburg. It was there, I think, that he did his very best work: stable yards with figures and farm horses, snow falling on stacked logs, beggars lying under the bridges, and "The Sleeper," a portrait of our cousin Andrey. For several years, until our stepfather's death, all went well with him. Then he took an apartment with Claudia and Anatole in a sumptuous house on the rue des Lions. Soon he had to pay all the bills and in addition was pining away and beginning to paint poorly, until my mother saved him by sending him to the United States. There, in Hollywood, he met his second passion, Ona Munson, who made him completely forget his old love.

As for my own work, it, too, was changing—as was my attitude toward it. Little by little, work was becoming my main preoccupation and I began to order my life around it. I thought continually of painting, training my memory to retain colors. And I would often draw subjects in my head—a pleasing face, for instance. More and more, I was giving up portraits, nudes, and still-lifes for landscapes. One winter, for the first time I exiled myself to the Riviera, but not to any of the famous resorts. I went to an unknown little port, Saint Tropez, then terra incognita, a paradise known only to a few simple souls, a few Parisian painters like Segonzac, Durey, Kisling, Mouillot. I had gone there first to join Pierre Charbonnier, who had rented a little Provençal house. Pierre was in those days a truly happy man. Fortune had smiled on him: He had married Annette Natanson, with whom he now had a two-year-old son, Pilou, and while the rest of us were still mere apprentices, he had already launched a great painting career. His father-in-law ran one of the main galleries in Paris, Druet, on the rue Royale, in front of the Café Weber, and was the brother of the famous Thadée Hatanson. He was constantly showing Pierre's work and sold his little Riviera landscapes—each painted in quick session, fresh and really quite charming—like hotcakes. Though his life at this time was proceeding so very brilliantly, Pierre was later to spoil everything. He was never to progress as an artist. Instead, he was to become infatuated with Annette's sister, leave his wife, his child, and finally to stop painting altogether and disappear.

But to return to the happy beginning. If you have never taken the train for the south on a nasty winter evening, you can't imagine how I felt on waking up after Orange and seeing the sun, a countryside fragrant with eucalyptus and flowering mimosa trees, a blue sky without a single cloud. The south of France, land of youth and gaiety! How privileged I felt to be one of the few to enter this paradise!

The little fishing port of Saint Tropez, jewel of the Mediterranean, presented a unique spectacle of multi-colored sails and hulls surrounded by Provençal facades painted in pastel shades. I took a room in the Sandstroëm farm in the midst of the vineyards of the Côte des Carles, not very far from Colette's villa. Sandstroëm, the future mayor of Saint Tropez, a handsome Swede with a meticulously trimmed beard, was so clean that, every night in the kitchen, with the door open, in front of people, he would wash his buttocks in a tub, splashing about like a duck. His wife had the blotched, faded face of peasant women. Later she was to develop an almost maternal feeling for me. There was only one hotel, Sube. Sénequier sold nougat in his little shop. The beautiful Emilienne exerted her powerful attraction on everyone. The composer Durey, one of the "Six," though he never wrote much, forced a local young girl to marry him. We would have drinks at the home of Marie, Segonzac's ex-model. We played bowls, we danced waltzes with small steps, I ate bouillabaisse on Auguste's fishing boat, and often visited the Charbonniers. It was paradise!

My painting then imitated Charbonnier's. I walked around looking for a landscape like a hunter for his prey. In fact, I wonder which the impressionists loved more, painting or nature. After several hours spent out in the open, in the sun in front of my canvas, it seemed to me finished, I never knew how to continue or change it once I was back in my room. When Saint Tropez, inevitably, was to become fashionable, I would switch to Marseille.

In Paris, I had lived in my parents' house. In Marseille, I had what became my own home: the room in which I always stayed in the Hôtel Nautique, Quai des Belges. To me Marseille was a call from Cythera, from the fabulous isles of the Pacific, it was the remembrance of novels by Conrad, Stevenson, Defoe, Manfred. My window was wide open and looked out onto the handsome sailboats, the forts, the tugs, and the sleepy quays. Occasionally, an archaic tram pulled by two sorry old horses would pass by. A lost taxi would zigzag dangerously, as if drunk, between the fishmongers' stalls and the drinkers coming out of the bars. My host, M. Pignari (whose daughter was a famous pianist in Paris), sometimes asked me to pay for the room with a painting. Some mornings, I would forgo coffee and croissants and breakfast in the local fashion: sea urchins washed down with white wine. I would lunch in the little Gorlier restaurant with my cheerful friend Kisling, that perpetually black-suited gentleman in his eternal bowler, Pascin (who was soon to commit suicide), and the agreeable Eichaker, who would lend me his empty studio giving out onto the harbor. The evening meal was naturally eaten at Toussaint's, the friend of the painters who held open table in his basement on rue des Martingales. In the summer, I swam at the Catalans; in the winter, when the weather was bad, I might go to the movies as often as three times a day, using free passes. The newest American films would come through on their way from Paris to Nice. Movies were my element; I loved their atmosphere, even in small theaters that showed bad films. In Paris, I once watched a movie seated on a barrel, and in Naples,

I watched a show at ten in the morning and waited while the film was stopped long enough to calm the children who were shrieking warnings to the cowboy-hero.

Most of the time in Marseille, I was alone, and I enjoyed my solitude, if you can really call it that, since I could see people I knew whenever I wanted and the busy life of the harbor went on all around me. When he got out of the army, Bébé came and kept me company, but then he moved on to Toulon. At times, my half-empty little hotel would suddenly be crawling with new arrivals. I thus met a charming adolescent Englishman, Edward Ashcroft, a poet and the brother of the famous actress, Peggy Ashcroft; the rich young American Philip Lasell, who danced bare-chested to the music of the blues, invited us for drinks at Cintra's, and wanted to sleep with everyone; the painter Dora Bianka, who cried on the shoulder of Toussaint's sister—Claire Smadja—because I did not want her. (Years later, it would be she who didn't want me.) One morning a Lancia driven by Fernandez, Darius Milhaud's nephew whom I had met at the composer's house near Aix, stopped in front of the hotel. He had brought from Paris for a short visit Bébé and Georges Geoffroy, who were always fighting, Georgette Camille, Henri Sauguet, and Leone Massimo, a Roman prince whose passport finally revealed to us all his numerous titles. I liked showing Marseille to people with Bébé. First we would take the new arrivals to Basso's where we would eat the then fashionable hearts of palm, or to Pascal's fish restaurant where the waiters were old and bearded; then on to Aline's where we would see two curious things: porno films and the famous voyeur's mirror— reflective from the front, transparent from the back.

I had many visits during the course of those Marseille winters. I remember Cocteau and Jean Desbordes having lunch at Basso's with Bébé and me—their elbows on the table, their shirt and jacket sleeves rolled up, showing and admiring their hands. I was never able to find Cocteau either handsome or likeable, but thought he showed taste in his choice of lovers.

His bulging forehead, frizzed hair, wrinkled eyes. chiseled features, and nervous hands with El Grecolike fingers, all this displeased me—not to mention his narcissism, amateurism, snobbism, eclecticism, and dandyism. Whether it was the young novelist Raymond Radiguet, the female impersonator and trapeze artist Barbette, the jazz pianists Wiener and Doucet, the nightclub Le Boeuf sur le Toit, the French composers Les Six, or Diaghilev's ballet troupe, there was always too much Cocteau in any of them for me.

As for the arrival of the Rolls-Royce driven by a uniformed chauffeur and bringing Antonio de Gandarillas—Madame Erazuriz's nephew and, along with Emilio Terry, the most elegant bachelor in Paris—that memorable event took place after one summer when I had met the young novelist René Crevel in Sainte Maxime. Crevel, now suffering from a tubercular lung, was being taken to Morocco by Gandarillas and the English painter Christopher Wood, who limped like Lord Byron. I introduced Kit to an extraordinarily beautiful, and insatiable, Spanish woman, who could spend whole nights in a semiconscious sensual delirium. It seems that she gave him a certain disease. On the night of their departure, I went to the Hôtel de Noailles and, for the first and last time, smoked opium. I had seven pipes, woke up after the others had left, and was sick as soon as I tried to drink a cup of coffee. After that, I slept for twenty-four hours. I had in any case been in no danger since I much preferred life to illusion.

My painting improved greatly during my stay in Marseille. I began to choose my subjects better and gave up country landscapes for the forts, the quays, and especially the sailboats, the first sign of my growing love for the sea. And while I was still working mostly outside, the mental level of my work was already much higher, for I was composing, eliminating, changing, and arranging my colors in a more abstract manner and according to an overall harmony. I even painted a triptych with a sailboat in the middle and, on either side, the harbor reflected in the windows of Eichacker's studio. But I did not yet feel any need to give up working outdoors. On the quays I met a one-legged young man and, unusual for me, painted two portraits of him in my room under the influence of Bébé's "The Sleeper." I did it half in oils, half modeled in wax, like the portrait of Walter Shaw, which is now in Virgil Thomson's collection.

The Germans partially destroyed the Marseille harbor, one of the most beautiful in the Mediterranean, but it was "progress" that finished it off. Nothing is left now of its old charm. The traffic on its quays is worse than that of Paris or New York. There is no trace of the sailboats or even of the freighters; the water has now virtually disappeared under the crowding of small power boats. Balzac or Eugène Sue might have described the city's old quarter, spots like the red-light district of the rue de Bouterie—that rue de Lappe of Marseille, only more dangerous—where even the police would hesitate to venture. From the rue de Bouterie a number of tiny, narrow streets descended to the harbor. Laundry hung on ropes stretched between the roofs and hid the sky. In the middle of the pavement was a gutter with a steady trickle of sewage. It was in one of these little streets, the rue des Martingales, that Toussaint lived and, opposite, had his basement where several of us used to meet every night. Once inside the clean and brightly lit cellar, we would forget the horrid squalor we had passed through and relax at a long table, on benches, among barrels of wine. Nowhere in Marseille did one eat better: an aioli that would make you feel drunk; gobis, mudfish with a crayfish flavor that one could not buy anywhere else; sea-urchin omelette and the freshest shellfish brought in by Claire, herself a fishwife. As for Toussaint, he was a legend, and one was proud to be numbered among his friends.

When I had first arrived in Marseille, not yet acquainted with Toussaint, and unaware of the real danger, I was driven by curiosity to the rue de Bouterie. Every door opened either to a prostitute's bedroom or a shady bar. The street was crowded with gangs of Algerians and sailors out on the town, both of whom exchanged insults with groups of transvestites, painted, bejewelled, and calling one another by women's names. Suddenly, I felt a sharp push in my back, fell on my knees, and when, bewildered, I got up again, I noticed that my lost beret was now in the hands of a woman who was waving it from a third-floor window, shouting: "Come on up here and get it, darling!" Later, when I knew Toussaint, the tables were turned; I only had to say one magical word, Smadja, the name of Toussaint's brother-in-law, and any would-be attackers would become friends, tell me they were sorry, and ask me to have a drink with them. Smadja, who regularly visited all these prostitutes, had them thoroughly in hand because he gave them credit on underwear, perfumes, and cosmetics. Without this, the girls could never have survived the costs of their trade. While Smadja appeared to be the master, it was Toussaint who was the hidden power. Smadja was an Algerian Jew, tall, thin, and very neat, a real Middle-Eastern type; he made a sharp contrast with his wife and brother-in-law, who were Corsicans, squat and short and whom I thought the ugliest people in the world.

Toussaint always conducted himself very properly and soberly. He didn't smoke, ate little, and hardly drank at all. You would never have guessed he was friendly with the most important men in Marseille; yet at election time, the Minister Cachin would summon him to Paris. He was a white slaver and probably involved in drug traffic. In the time I knew him, his wife, the beautiful Esperanza—a formidable woman, the prop of her husband as well as his love, and a great cook—twice went to Shanghai with a group of girls. The Toussaints had two daughters in their late adolescence, whom their mother would lock in when she left her cozy apartment decorated with mirrors, ottomans, carpets, and little occasional tables; I only met them twice by chance; they never had dinner in our basement.

Toussaint, as I said, was ugly. He looked just like a bulldog. His flesh was unhealthy, swollen, and flabby. He had little molelike eyes, from the corners of which ran a yellow liquid, a few rotting teeth, a broken boxer's nose, and two paralyzed fingers on his right hand. He could neither read nor write, signed his name with a mark, and never had a passport when he went abroad. We never knew exactly what he did, but were given an inkling of it by the following story, told me by the writer Joseph Kessel. Toussaint and a friend, on their way to Buenos Aires with two whores, lost all their money gambling on the ocean liner. "Don't worry," Toussaint told his friend. When they got off the ship, he had his taxi driver pay the porter, went to the most elegant hotel in town, booked a suite, and had the doorman pay the taxi. Then he chartered another taxi, went slowly around all the bars until he found some men of his own kind who helped him out.

I was lucky enough to be in Marseille for the wedding of Claire Smadja's eighteen-year-old son, Dédé, to a young working girl; it was a spectacle worthy of Maupassant's *Maison Tellier*. Some twenty open carriages, each pulled by two horses, were waiting for us when we came out of the Catholic Church (only Smadja himself was Jewish). All the women from the brothels in their Sunday best made a ravishing bourgeois picture, along with beribboned children and men in morning coats. The whole procession went off to a small country restaurant where a gigantic meal lasted well into the night.

But even my friend Toussaint, with all his power, probably couldn't have straightened out my difficulties with the postal employees who kept refusing to cash my parents' money orders. The first time they made trouble, my name had been given an extra "n" by mistake; the second time, I had forgotten to provide myself with the small change that the postman was demanding as the delivery charge.

Whenever, during my visits to Marseille, my parents were in Monte Carlo, it was my duty to pay them a short visit. This particular duty I always regarded as a bore. I would arrive in their suite at the Hôtel de Paris dressed like a "hippy," so that they would immediately buy me a whole new set of clothes.

The first time my stepfather gave me 100 francs to play roulette—he gambled very moderately, only for fun—I lost the money. After that, I held onto it for other pleasures. It was here, too, that my parents introduced me to their fantastic friend Sir Basil Zaharoff, who ate at a round table separated from the rest of the dining room by a screen. They told me how this ex-oarsman of the Bosphorus who had been knighted by the King of England, aside from his incredible financial career, had lived through an adventure worthy of a fairy tale. Once while traveling on a Spanish train, he saved the wife of a royal prince from the violence of her drunken husband, after which the Duchess Villafranca de los Caballeros, a member of the House of Bourbon, went to live with Zaharoff and took her two daughters with her. When she became a widow, she married him. Since the Duchess was lucky at roulette and my mother wasn't, my mother gave her a certain sum of money to play for her, which grew to 50,000 francs. My mother then bought some phony porcelain from a ruined Russian princess, thinking she was making an excellent investment for her children's future.

Between visiting my parents at Monte Carlo and returning to Marseille, I would sometimes spend a few days in the Hôtel Welcome in Villefranche, a very beautiful but snobbish place where I felt squeezed in between the mountains and the sea as if on a raft. Glenway Wescott and Monroe Wheeler lived there in a villa, as well as Jean Guerin of the Guerin Shoe Company. When the U.S. fleet came into harbor, Kiki, of Le Jockey, a nightclub, would come from Paris to join her lover Jeff, and great drinking parties would follow. In the course of one of these, she was thrown into the jail at Nice for having insulted a policeman. Neither the painter Man Ray, her Paris friend whom I warned by cable, nor my cousin Theodore's lawyer, who happened to be staying in Nice, was able to shorten her one month sentence. I would also see Cocteau there; he liked Villefranche. I would see him in his room, with all the lights on, the curtains drawn, in a litter of papers, photos of

American actresses, and records. I would also meet him on the little beach where he went with his admirer, Maryse Robinet d'Uris, a rich young girl from Dijon whom everyone ridiculed by distorting her name.

The summer of 1925 was memorable for me, a summer that brought many changes to my life. For one thing, I freed myself of Thérèse's spell by tearing her medal from my neck and flinging it into the sea. I began to break the ties that held me to Bébé, and, after two years, needed to love and be loved. Then, purely by chance, I "discovered the window," and this window completely changed my style of painting. It had been my little group, along with a few already famous people, who had opened a whole new era of sea, beaches, sunbathing, and sports on the Riviera. Now the word was getting around Paris: If you were a young painter and wanted to be successful, all you had to do was spend the summer in Saint Tropez or Sainte Maxime.

This particular summer, in 1925, was a season of *sturm und drang*, of passionate youth, of pleasures and dramas, of laziness, and of progress in my work. Most of us that year happened to be living in Sainte Maxime at the Hôtel des Palmiers, whose palm trees cast their shadows on the little square in front of the gulf. It was a tiny square. On the left was a little dike, on the right, one of the best bars of the region with two luxurious bedrooms, and, farther on, the deserted beach. The village consisted of a dozen houses; half a dozen little villas spread out among the green hills were the rest of this earthly paradise. In front of the beautiful gulf, on the almost virgin shores, one felt at the end of the world. At a half-hour's distance in a little motorboat whose purring would put you to sleep, the jewel of the Mediterranean, the little fishing harbor Saint Tropez lay scintillating: a bouquet of multicolored sails on a background of pastel Provençal facades.

In our little group were Pierre Charbonnier, his wife Annette and her sister, Denise; René Crevel, who was the darling of Paris society, and his American friend, Eugene

McCown, a midwestern dandy who would charm us at the piano with his rendition of blues and of Gershwin songs that we were hearing for the first time; the famous Misia Sert's nephew, Jean Godebsky, with his mother and half-paralyzed father known as "wild-hand Chipa"; the painter Louis Marcoussis and his wife Halika; Laglenne, the flower painter; that "giddy young thing with the straw hat," the future English critic Raymond Mortimer; an ex-student of Rançon, Bresson, with his Rumanian "fiancee"; Maryse Robinet d'Uris, Cocteau's special admirer; Tilia Perlmutter, a Jewish refugee from Poland whose sister had been Radiquet's mistress and who posed for us; Bébé, and I, not to forget that ravishing "African," Rosine (sunburned so very dark) who made everyone fall in love with her. Her mother was Ex-Yaune, the vaudeville star, and had entrusted her to us in an attempt to save her from the big, bad wolf incarnate in an unscrupulous Dutchman who was trying to seduce her. "The handsome Leonid," as I was called, and the irresistible Rosine fell in love but, though I was burning to be with her, I never touched this thirteen-year old girl. When, at the end of the summer, I left for Ischia to join my brother, she apparently wanted to commit suicide. Her mother at first hoped I would marry her and, later, in Paris, accused me of having made her pregnant. (Rosine became the actress Rosine Doréan and married Claude Dauphin.)

From day to day different people would join our excursions: the two nieces of the couturier Poiret, Mesdames Vins and Woirin; the movie-maker Chaumette, René Clair's brother, accompanied by his girl, Nadia Bentz, covered with hickeys; Georges Poupet, who worked for the publisher Grasset; and Jacques Viot, surrealist poet and a salesman at the Galerie Pierre.

As for our audience, the people for whom our little group provided distraction, it was made up of the biggest names in theater and vaudeville: Sacha Guitry and Yvonne Printemps, Jules Berry and Suzy Prim, Dranem and his wife, Odette

O'Niel who swam topless, and Ex-Yaune, with her lover, a doctor. I should add Bidou the newspaperman, Gaston Ravel, the movie-maker who bought my first picture through his secretary Tony Lecain, and two young women, rich and free, who lived at the Hermitage: the little English girl, Mils, and Odette Thornhill, whose lover was young Felix, owner of a fishing boat; and, finally, a few couples from the villas.

The summer was a mixture of chastity and vice, of affairs and breakups. Charbonnier was openly courting his sister-in-law Denise. McCown, abandoning René Crevel, left for Italy in Dick Windham's Rolls-Royce. Marcoussis went to Collioure and watched his mistress drown. Laglenne and McCown would proposition me; Jean Godebsky, who was on the very warmest terms with one of the Poiret nieces, kept pushing me into the arms of the other. I was in love with the infant Rosine. Annette was unhappy, Crevel and Bébé were always crying. Bébé in fact pursued me so with his jealous scenes that finally, in despair, I beat him up in front of Godebsky's parents on the beach. Some occasionally went to a senator's villa in Saint Tropez where, it was said, there were orgies and opium was smoked, as in Beauvallon.

I remember a boat ride—there must have been some twenty of us—during which Viot kept his hand in the trouser pocket of his sailor of the day, fondling the boy's sex organs, and neither the young women in the group nor Godebsky's parents seemed to notice it. Everyone apparently had a weakness for Viot, especially the women, who wanted to convert him. What surprised Bébé and me was the way he kept repeating, "If only we could hide it all in case things get tough." The next winter, he was to sell some impressionist paintings belonging to Pierre Loeb for fifty thousand francs and, with a phony passport lent to him by Poupet, vanish from Paris for three years. We later found out that he had traveled in Asia, lived in China, and then, ironically, become a Justice of the Peace in Tahiti. When he came back, his friends would manage to hush up the theft. The thing that I was really to find revolting was the sight of him one day at the terrace of the Deux Magots looking with pleasure, in the company of some other Dadaists, at photographs of crucified and tortured Chinese.

As for Tilia, I had met her in Montparnasse through Cocteau. She and her sister Bronja, both of whom lived in poverty, were very unlike; while Bronja, the younger, was amusing, liberated, and practical (which she was later to prove beyond doubt by her marriage to the film director René Clair), her older sister was bland, brainless, a good girl, a good friend, probably a virgin, and the eternal victim. Sometimes she would pose for painters, but fully dressed. In order that she should have a little fun and enough to eat, Bébé and I brought this not very pretty albino blonde to Sainte Maxime. As soon as we went out anywhere, she would hang on my arm, which bothered me, but I was afraid of hurting her. Whenever we sat at a café terrace, she would ask, "Am I allowed a cup of coffee, a drink, a cigarette?"

I don't wish to boast, but of the three people who were painting that summer, I worked the hardest. Bébé did two magnificent portraits of Crevel. Bresson spent a month on the same still-life, changing it every day; I liked each new variation equally but always regretted the previous ones. As for me, the hotel had given me a tiny maid's room overlooking the dike in which I would isolate myself every day from six to eight, nine to eleven, and two to four. At eight, I would go down and have breakfast on the little square in the shade of the palm trees with those who were already up. Between eleven and twelve, I'd swim and have lunch. Then while everybody else had a siesta, I worked again. After four we would gather together for some engagement. We'd go for a boat ride across the gulf or walk in the cork tree forests behind Saint Tropez, following roads toward the lost villages of Cogolin and Grimaux or toward Ramatuelle, where the Kislings and the Salmons lived. Sometimes we'd meet friends near the harbor and then all cheerfully dine together, singing old sailors' songs: "Valparaiso," "The Girls of Camaret," "La Paimpolaise," "There Was a Little Ship."

One morning, on my way to my little painting room, I saw through the open window a painting composed so perfectly that, instead of going out, I started to paint it, using the window as a frame. The subject was a fishing boat loaded with wine barrels that was tied up to the little dike. While I had now and then painted "from" a window before, this time I was doing it "*through*" a window, and I can hardly explain how satisfying I found this new way of working. The quiet of the room, the feeling of being sheltered from the wind, from prying glances, from changes of light, the ability to concentrate, think, study, and organize my composition, eliminating useless details and harmonizing the colors—all of it seduced me. It was a lucky, lucky day; not only had I happened on a perfect subject, but without knowing it I had also made a great stride forward. That canvas was the best of the summer. My friend Marcoussis to whom I showed it the next day encouraged me, and gave me some precious advice derived from cubism. In the future, nature itself was no longer to be my goal but my pretext. I would always look for another window, a hangar, a roof; once I even climbed to the top of a water tower. I would choose subjects carefully so as to make them "my" subjects. From then on, as I said, I would train myself to remember colors and draw mentally. Finally and truly, I would stop being an amateur and become a professional. All this happened that summer. Viot, who admired my new paintings, talked to Pierre Loeb about them and during the following winter, I had my first one-man show in Paris at his Galerie Pierre.

I think it was Pierre Charbonnier who, with his father-in-law's consent, presented the show later called "neo-romantic." To him, it was just another chance to show his recent paintings at the Galerie Druet. He invited some old comrades from the Académie Rançon (a good advertisement for it) and some other friends to participate; and thus he managed to create a whole that was both homogeneous and varied, and therefore interesting. As for the show's timing, the winter after Sainte Maxime, it could not have been better. This show caused a great sensation because of its originality, its freshness, its humanity and the future promise of its young talent. It was Waldemar George, the most eminent critic of the period, who dubbed the show "neo-humanist" or "neo-romantic"; that last title remained. The participants were: Pierre Charbonnier. Thérèse Debains, Christian Bérard, Kristians Tony (recommended by Pasquin, whose favorite pupil he was), Tchelitchew, De Angelis, a hairdresser from Ischia who had been discovered and sponsored by Genia, Genia, and me. For those who might think this a surprisingly diverse lot of artists to be yoked together, I can only say that the impressionists were no less different from one another; and while only four of this group of eight painters have survived, only a dozen of the forty impressionists are remembered today.

To Charbonnier's little Riviera landscapes, fresh, quick, and seductive, people would compare Thérèse's nostalgic evocations of Brittany. Then came the primitive work of the Italian. Then the fantastic drawings of the Dutch Kristians Tony (his real name was Tony Kristians), done in a process peculiar to him; they would show feats of medieval warriors, or of robots, or of monsters. The portraits by Bérard and Tchelitchew made an enormous contrast: Bérard was a colorist and looked for an inner resemblance, while Tchelitchew concentrated on an outer resemblance based on asymmetry and particular features. Genia showed big compositions with Paris beggars sleeping under the bridges and scenes of the Umbrian countryside, and I, already attracted by the sea, offered views of the Marseille harbor and of the sailing and fishing boats of Saint Tropez.

The exhibition had considerable success, and the neo-romantic movement influenced a lot of painters as far away as the United States. But there were no sales. The dealer Pierre Colle became interested in Bérard, and Pierre Loeb showed me in his gallery on the rue des Beaux-Arts. Loeb drew a profile of the artist for the catalogue cover of every show, and René Crevel wrote a verse preface for me entitled "To the music of a pianola," in memory of the waltzes we danced in Saint Tropez imitating the sailors. The man who had showed in the gallery before me, Helmut Kole, a friend of Uhde's, had painted a canvas called "The Oyster-Eater," which I found so pleasing that I started to do still-lifes with oysters, mussels, and shellfish. Several critics—Fels, Charensol, and Claude Roger-Marx— mentioned them in the papers, and Janet Flanner talked about me in her "Letter from Paris" for *The New Yorker*. I sold only one painting, my best canvas, that of the window in Sainte Maxime. But for that one at least I had three offers. My mother bought it at the opening to bring me luck; Aunt Julie, whom I hadn't told, wanted it the next day; and, finally, I sold it to Fernandez, who didn't want any other; and everybody paid me for it.

While this show wasn't a financial success, the next show in Brussels really was. Though I had never been in Brussels, I felt at home because I had both relatives and numerous friends who lived there. Half-brothers of Aunt Mania's, my cousin Léon Kochnitzky, my cousin Nadine Effron, who was a social leader, the painter Olivier Picard, the Rumanian ambassador, whose son was the Catargi of the Académie Rançon, old Baron de Haulleville, the father of Eric (who married a Nys and became Aldous Huxley's brother-in-law), all entertained me and several bought my canvases. The exhibition opened in midwinter, the water froze in my room at a little Ixelles hotel, and from Léon's apartment, the roofs of the city buried in snow looked like Breughel's paintings. The Galerie Manteau was at 46, Boulevard Waterloo in a sumptuous building; in the hall was a most beautiful round Louis XIV table, supported by three dolphins. When I arrived at the gallery, I heard Madame Manteau calling her clients: "Well now, my good Mr. Van Geluff, won't you come by and buy a painting by that excellent painter, Leonid," and immediately Brussels' poshest tailor, as fat and placid as Madame Manteau, arrived and bought two. It was that simple!

After my show with Pierre Loeb, the Galerie d'Art Moderne offered me a contract. Its location on Boulevard Raspail was out of the way and the sale of books and records in the basement detracted from its seriousness. For one reason or another, my painting began to deteriorate—perhaps I was too sure of receiving my monthly check. Probably also my choice of subjects was bad, and then, it may be that progress only takes place by fits and starts. Since I loved books, a part of my fee went back to the gallery every month. I fell in love with the Canal Saint-Martin and, wanting to imbibe its atmosphere, I rented a room in a shabby little bar on its quay. The room was full of lice, fleas, and bedbugs, and I would go there early in the morning to paint. But barges and locks were no good for me.

During this period, too, I invited Aunt Mania to lunch several times to distract her from her sorrow at Uncle Paul's recent death from cancer. I also wanted to show her this little-known part of Paris, which felt like Holland.

From the discovery of my "window" until 1929, when I gave up the Riviera for northern beaches, my work was to continue indifferent or bad.

That same winter after Sainte Maxime, I finally broke with Bébé, who was so unhappy he refused to see me again. Our farewell scene took place at the home of our friend Louis de Lasteyrie during a weekend in his historic chateau La Grange. Under the influence of Cocteau, Auric, and perhaps some others, Bébé began to smoke opium, also to design theater sets. He became the undisputed master of that craft, but to the detriment of his easel painting. He became a snob, hated or loved by Paris society, moved in with a Russian I never liked much, Boris Kochno, grew fat, dirty, and bearded, often sleeping fully dressed and even wearing shoes under the sheets. In a word, he became the very first hippie.

I don't remember the year or the month on which I visited

Saint Tropez for the last time; it was out of season and there was no one I knew except Tony, Henri Méry, and Nora Wiener, whom I met then. The mistral was blowing when I arrived at the Hôtel Sube and I was careless enough to open the door to my balcony; three men closed it with difficulty. Tony Kristians stuck to me like a leech, which amused me at first because he had a unique and brilliant kind of wit. But he was a drunk, and arrogant, always fighting and really not likeable. He had a narrow head, long nose, flaxen hair, blue eyes that seemed blindly to look inward, and he had very ugly hands—in sum, a typical Dutchman. Nora, Tony, and I began to swim in the nude at a little creek; soon Tony was no longer wanted, but being jealous and without pride, he refused to leave us alone. When I spent the night with Nora in her pavilion far out in the woods, he came at dawn to surprise us, after which we stopped speaking to him. And then Nora stopped inviting me to spend the night. Whether because she thought I was intimate with Tony, or because she was in love and offended by my lack of enthusiasm, or because she regretted having confided in me, I cannot say. All night out in the woods she told me about a lover who had just left her and I consoled her, telling her she ought to paint, for she was gifted and was doing portraits of friends in Bébé's style. After our one night, we twice took our pleasure on a deserted beach where we swam in the warm water and caressed each other in the sun, on the sand. Soon I returned to Paris and hardly ever saw Nora again. Afterward she painted a great deal, married a well-known composer, and became a leading hostess of Paris.

In the course of all these years since 1919, the time of our arrival in Paris, little by little my cousins showed up. Except for Anatole and Claudia, who were staying in Berlin, we had had no news of them. Theodore was the first to turn up, arriving from Constantinople, followed by Anna Tupsik, a young and beautiful gypsy. Then came Gregory, from the Caucasus, duly married to Vera Wtorowa, the daughter of a ruined but once-rich Muscovite merchant, for whom he had fought a duel. Happy in his marriage, Gregory converted to his wife's Orthodox faith and was the only one who lived within his means, like a petty bourgeois, first on his salary, then on his pension from the Banque de l'Union Parisienne.

As for Theodore's Tupsik, who was the best girl in the world, with a golden heart—also primitive, illiterate, fiery—she shocked my mother at first, who then grew used to her, respected her, finally loved her. As soon as Tupsik arrived in Paris, she fell half in love with me; and since Theodore was so much older than she, we felt no compunction about deceiving him. We would make love at avenue Malakoff, between two doors, in boxes at the movies, and in little hotels far away from the center of town. She was my slave, my comrade, and my friend because I never really loved her. Not only was she not jealous, she even pushed me into the arms of her friends. I went off with one of them for a weekend in La Rochelle, driven by Fernandez, but dropped her when we got back, as I did an overripe Georgian princess.

In the winter of 1928 after a short illness my stepfather died. Even on his deathbed, my stepfather was too shy to ask his sons to come closer and kiss him.

As long as Uncle Efim had been alive, we had all had luxurious lives. After his death came the deluge. My mother's stocks went steadily down; Anatole and Theodore immediately used up their small legacies. Slowly, the family began to disintegrate.

Chapter 6

The North and Mollie

1929–1933

A NEW PAGE of my life opened now, marked by two main events: I gave up the Riviera for northern beaches and met my bad angel, Mollie.

Here I was in Boulogne-sur-Mer, and life was smiling. The Channel and its vast spaces, its low tides, its subtle colors, its huge empty vistas with sometimes the silhouette of a fisherman on the horizon—all was a new, prodigious, and attractive world for me. It immensely furthered my paintings. What I began to paint then, I am still painting today. I had found my theme: sea, space, and solitude. My Boulogne canvases were the first "Leonids" (I had signed Leonide Berman, Leonide B., just Leonide, then, after a critic thought I was a girl, Leonid, and, finally, I used just the initial and the date). My work of that summer—1929—was very well received and in consequence it sold: Emilio Terry, the architect, Paul Chadourne, the writer, and several Americans bought paintings, and Alfred Hitchcock bought many drawings. Some of my landscapes were plunging views of the cliffs with shrimp fisherwomen on the shore. There was a painting of women tarring nets; their faces were covered with handkerchiefs that looked like masks, very like Chirico. In another work, a small figure of a fisherman appeared on the horizon behind a trawler stranded in the front plane; this figure gradually came closer until it reached the front and became part of the landscape, filling it and giving it meaning by tying it to human activities.

Mollie was Irish—her name had been Cushla (an impossible

name in French). She had come to Paris on the recommendation of her London doctor for a rest from her conjugal life and especially to have a little fun. In fact, the illness was her husband's. He was a career diplomat named Sly, an ex-consul in Yünnanfu, China, where he had lived with Mollie for seven years after marrying her, then a seventeen-year-old orphan. Afflicted with incurable cancer, he had suffered the amputation of his rectum and part of his intestines and become an invalid. Aunt Julie had met Mollie in England, two ladies of our acquaintance who lived in Calais knew her well, and our friend, Dr. Rosen, who was a ladies' man, knew her even better.

After a very pleasant interlude during the winter, Mollie and I decided to meet in the summer on one of the Channel beaches, halfway between London and Paris. I was impatient to start work and left for Boulogne during the first nice days of spring. There, I rented a room on the quays. Mollie, who had leased a fisherman's house in Andreselles, arrived with her five-year-old son as soon as school let out for the holidays. She was accompanied by her faithful maid and friend, who was delighted to see her mistress having a gayer and more normal life than in London. Handsome little John, with his black, curly hair, was an intelligent and neat child. He won me over immediately and soon was telling his mother that he loved me more than his father. Such words go straight to the heart of a mother who has a lover and believes in providence. At first, to keep up appearances, I would walk home to Boulogne along the beach, but soon we were putting on a little act merely for John's benefit. I would pretend to leave a few minutes before he went to bed and then would return.

I was ecstatic. For the first time in my life, I was working a great deal, had a mistress, and was leading a family life. Like little David Copperfield in Dickens, I felt I was living in a boat by the shore. At night, I would hear the roar of the sea, the moaning of the wind, the bleating of a foghorn. During the day, I saw the gulls on the deserted beach, fishing boats on the horizon, and the mailboat coming in and out of Boulogne harbor. The house was low, almost without openings, and all white; it stood on a tarred base, had a thatched roof with narcissus growing on its crest; along with another half-dozen cottages lost in the dunes, it made up the hamlet of Andreselles. Every morning and evening, a small flock of cows would come through the village, and one of the animals always stopped by our wall with a long moo that would startle us as we were making love. So we soon called it "making moo" just as Swann had said "making cattleya" with Odette.

Then the holiday came to an end. John went back to England with the maid; Mollie and I went off on a little trip before separating—first to Amsterdam, then on to a houseboat on Leyden Lake where we saw Tony, and then, finally, to Brussels where Mollie became very sick with an abscess.

One night, several weeks after my return to Paris, I was awakened by a violent ringing of the bell, and, when I rushed to my studio window, I saw Mollie standing next to a taxi and waving to me. Unable to believe my eyes, in a panic, I quickly grabbed some clothes and rushed down the stairs, past my mother's room, pursued by her questions. You can imagine our emotion as the taxi took us through a sleeping Paris. Mollie was hysterical; she had fled from her home, sent me a cable I never received, and then not found me at the railroad station. I was stunned and annoyed, never having thought of this possibility and, frankly, never having wished it. My career and my independence were too dear to me. And then, I was not in love with Mollie. Had I received her cable, I probably would have left Paris. I consoled her, comforted her, and told her I was very happy, which was cowardly and untrue. The only thing I was thinking about was finding a hotel room, but everything was completely full because of a convention or the Exhibition. The only way we were able to end this senseless driving about was to take a room in a prostitute's hotel on place Clichy where, ironically, we were given the same room in which I had slept with my ex-model, Lucienne Baptiste years before.

The next day, I found a little bachelor's flat. Though a sad, dark, and bourgeois place, it was still a refuge and was located just around the corner from me in the rue Lauriston. Once Mollie was installed, I rushed home to see my mother. She took small comfort in the thought that my friend was not a loose woman, but a married "lady," so she agreed to go and se her. Both women cried. After that, my mother became very kind and generous; she rented us a modern little house with garden in back of a courtyard at the bottom of picturesque rue Lepic.

It was there, after a few weeks, that Mollie's illness appeared: an unreasonable and incurable jealousy. In the street, in restaurants, at the theater, anywhere, she would make a scene because I had looked at a woman whom, in fact, I had not even noticed. According to her, it was improper to look into a woman's eyes when you were speaking to her. So, little by little, I began to be on my guard, to cheat, to lie, which is difficult because one tends to forget just what it is one has said. I would look away as soon as someone pleased me. Our scenes would sometimes end in blows when we got home after which, exhausted, overexcited, and crying, we would be reconciled by making love with a five-fold passion. I still feel ashamed when I think of a dinner given by Mollie in our little house to her two friends from Calais: They were neither young nor pretty but, since I was their host, I was smiling and pleasant. Unable to contain herself, Mollie literally threw them out before the end of the meal. I myself was becoming somber, irritable, sly, nervous, nasty, hysterical, and a liar: I no longer recognized myself.

I must admit, however, that Mollie's situation was extremely difficult, torn as she was between her son, whom she missed, and me. She even returned to her husband, only to leave once again because she could not live without me. Her husband came to Paris and begged us to separate. He even sent us a priest, who preached to us about our duty and threatened us with damnation, but nothing helped; on the contrary, all these attempts just made us more obstinate.

Mollie had some money of her own. The next summer, she rented a little villa at Mesnil-Val, on the cliff above Le Treport. I painted its owner, a shrimp fisherwoman, with her net and her basket; she lived in the basement and did our cleaning. Little John was naturally not allowed to join us but Mollie bought a little Sealyham from the captain of the Dieppe–Newhaven packet, who raised the breed. All the village children went crazy about this dog when they saw him because he had a "black eye," which is to say, a black ring around one eye. He was "my" dog, as no other had ever been. His name was Friday, and he would sleep with his snout on my foot. Since we didn't know anyone, all remained peaceful, and this charming summer allowed me to do a great deal of work. I painted small canvases representing fisherwomen working on the beach and pebble pickers with their white draft horses against the chalky background of the cliffs. When they were shown the next winter in the new Galerie Jacques Bonjean, at the end of the Impasse La Boétie, these works were snapped up.

In spite of this success, the winter was sad. The jealous scenes got so bad that twice I went to spend the night at a hotel. We had moved to one of the new buildings near the Porte de Châtillon. Not far away, in front of the Belt Railroad, the Austrian painter Floch had his studio, and opposite were the magnificent stables of the Planteurs de Café Caiffa. The building was shaped like a rectangle with a fountain in the middle. The names of the sixteen superb, huge, white or dappled horses that I often drew were written in gold letters on red plaques: Zanzibar, Madagascar, Mombasa. They made me dream of faraway places.

But what actually brought a little diversity into the monotony of our life together—because of Mollie's jealousy, we hardly ever saw anyone—were our frequent visits to England, where Mollie had relatives and friends. I had an exhibition in a fashionable gallery in Knightsbridge. We stayed in one flat near Victoria station, in another near Harrods, in a villa in St. John's Wood, and in a village that later became a movie production center. I met an aunt of Mollie's who drank too much and hid her gin bottles in the water tank of the toilet, and an uncle who was too tall for his tiny cottage so that he had to keep diving forward as he walked around in order to avoid the beams; he never once hit his head. This dandy had the most beautiful shoes I ever saw and immediately thrust into my hands, as a mark of great favor, a brush and some shoe polish. I admired the Christmas pantomimes in London, the Christmas trees near Trafalgar Square, and I even remember Midnight Mass in Saint Malo cathedral.

For some time, Mollie had been urging me to live in the country. Now she learned by chance that two of her old friends from China, the Bochers, were living outside of Nantes. She wrote them and they promptly invited her to visit. They were settled in a handsome and comfortable estate in Trentemouet on the banks of the Loire. A high wall covered with trained fruit trees shielded a big old house and its vegetable garden from the neighbors' eyes. The sanded, raked paths, the perfect flowerbeds, made gardening just as pleasant as the hours of relaxation spent chatting in front of a big log fire in the huge fireplace of the living room. The Far Eastern furniture and tapestries gave the whole interior an atmosphere of travel and adventure, so much so that young Panouillot de Vesly, who sold us a second-hand Citroën Trèfle, had the idea that the Bochers smoked opium. I became great friends with the master of the house and worked next to him in the vegetable garden while Friday avidly ate the big white worms called "Turks;" I admired this aristocrat who was not afraid to dirty himself by cleaning out his hen-house.

The aging Bocher was tall, stylish, and liked the good life. He had been sent to China after a wild youth and had stayed

for twenty-five years in Yünnanfu, where he had been a neighbor of Sly's. He had finally married his housekeeper, an efficient
woman and a great cook who looked after everything,
especially spoiling her big child. Everything was elegant at
Guy Bocher's, even his farts, performed in the living room in
front of everyone without any embarrassment; on the contrary, with an amusing ease, he would comment, "Well, there!"
and look, smiling, straight into your eyes. I have never eaten
better boiled beef or shad in a beurre blanc sauce; the fish was
a Nantes specialty that was caught right in front of the house.
I did several paintings of net fishing that was done with two
boats. The nets, having been brought in, were hung to dry
from tall pikes on the little beach, and were draped in festoons.
My friend Prince Leone Massimo happened to be visiting one
of the neighboring castles, and I introduced him to Mollie and
the Bochers.

I was very fond of the maritime city of Nantes and its numerous canals, which later filled with silt. The slave traders' old
houses leaned dangerously on the Ile Teyder, between the two
branches of the Loire, and the tramways, after going past the
handsome Louis XIV facades on the quai de la Fosse, went
on through the old city. The purchase of postcards took me
to a publishing house whose owner asked me to do a series
of views of Nantes in China ink. He gave me much information about the neighboring areas, which led me to spend a
summer on the island of Noirmoutier.

The island is linked to the mainland by a road passable only
at low tide. I arrived at the entrance to this road after it had
already been chained off, but, unaware of the danger, I removed
the chain and started across. I was soon sorry. In the middle of
the two- or three-kilometer crossing, the water, which comes
up, they say, with the speed of a galloping horse, was already
reaching my ankles, and stalled my Citroën's motor. I had to
push at a run with Mollie holding the wheel.

We rented another picturesque, thatched-roof cottage in

an isolated area of the island called Barbâtre, surrounded by salt marshes that had stagnated and been abandoned; as a result, they were full of the most fantastic colors and wonderful to paint. A little wall set off the courtyard whose old fig tree broke as soon as I climbed it to pick some of its fruit. In the center of this flat and treeless little island were a few old windmills made into houses, and at the other end was the village from which the island took its name. There the salt marshes were being fully worked; the village, adorned with little salt mounds, also boasted the Bois de la Chaise, a hotel, a little beach, and a small group of tourists. But we never went to this little outpost of civilization. We made friends instead with an old spinster, Clemenceau's former maid—who lived in a pretty cottage full of local furniture—with a few old captains who, in their impeccably clean houses, showed us the models of sailboats they had built, and with the fisherman Armand Palvadeau, who provided us with fish and sea-spiders and in front of whom, exhibitionist that I was, I nearly drowned one day in a rough sea.

In the fall, we went back to see the Bochers. They were thoroughly fed up with the climate—for Nantes is the rainiest of French cities—and talked about moving to the Dordogne, where the weather is better, land cheap, and where, above all, one could raise poultry and make a lot of money. They were absolutely sure of this and kept showing us figures to prove it. And since Mollie had long wanted to leave Paris, their suggestion that we precede them did not fall on deaf ears. In spite of the snow and the cold, or perhaps because we yearned for a warmer climate, we left in midwinter. Hardly had we passed the gate when the Citroën's motor exploded: Some water left undrained, had frozen. The car had to be repaired before we could set off again. Being inexperienced, I had traced a straight line from Nantes to Bergerac on the Michelin map and thought to save time by traveling on all the roads, whether large or small, that were closest to my line. This, of course, turned out to be pure folly. I got lost in forests, found myself on impossible little unpaved roads, on sections of road under construction; I was several times unable to turn back and found myself out of gas in a lost village on Sunday. And, as if all these difficulties were not enough, the Citroën itself was still behaving strangely: It was equally capable of going perfectly or of jerking slowly forward and stalling altogether. Once, when the car had broken down on a main highway, I signaled a big truck and it stopped. Two giants asked me what was wrong and, having listened to my explanations, advised me to try starting again; whereupon, to my amazement, I went off like a bird. I floored the accelerator for fear that the two men might think I'd been making fun of them and beat me up. We finally arrived in Bergerac, an exploit that seemed all the more extraordinary to me in my state of complete exhaustion from having driven all the way. Mollie had never learned to drive.

I cannot say how long we stayed in Bergerac, or even the length of time it took us before we came back for good, ready to settle and raise poultry. First we had to return to the Bochers', then on to Paris and give up the apartment. We exchanged the Citroën-Trèfle (its mystery was solved by a mechanic in a little village who found an extra level control in the carburetor) for an old Ford that we so overloaded on the way back that its defective tires were constantly punctured.

We went to the Hôtel de Londres and since it was out of season and empty, the owner, the handsome Chateigner, gave us all his time and became our friend. He asked me to decorate his bar as payment of our bill. I hung two of my paintings and created a frieze made of photos of the innumerable castles of the region. Since all the hotelkeepers were chefs who worked for ambassadors, princes, and millionaires throughout Europe during the off-season, the food was exquisite. For years, Chateigner had been in the service of the Duke of Connaught. While we saw a lot of him, we spoke to his wife only twice, in her room. She was either ill, unhappy, or imprisoned.

The medieval Dordogne, land of the Sleeping Beauty, wild and picturesque, captivated us as it had everyone else. Fortresses transformed into castles hidden in dark forests, perched like eagles' nests above smiling valleys or reflected in the handsomest rivers in France, animated the landscape. Every day, an agent would show us ravishing sites, but nothing suited us: The houses were too large or not romantic enough. Mollie had written her bank to send her a sum of money for the purchase of an estate but her trustees refused to do so because they feared it might be a bad investment. Thus we were forced to rent, which turned out to be much more difficult. One day, we saw a place we adored! It was a ruin perched on a cliff dominating the countryside; it had no well, no access road, no comforts, and was far away from other dwellings. The agent had not wanted to take us there and Chateigner, whom we showed it to the next day, forbade us to think of it further. But on the way he had an idea, to put us up close to the hotel in a peasant house belonging to one of his ex-waiters. The house was on good land, it could be had for almost nothing, and its owner, a man named Rapnouil, could surely help me start raising poultry. As for Chateigner, he promised to buy my whole production in advance. What more could we ask?

After a short visit, we settled the business. Rapnouil, a sharp Gascon with his long musketeer's moustaches, had nothing to lose: We were renting an empty house, which, furthermore, we were going to improve. A bricklayer opened a doorway and plastered the walls, but we had to abandon a hut that had been made into a bathroom because we could not get water to it. Rapnouil, who lived in Mussidan with a young and pretty mistress, agreed to go halves with me in the raising of rabbits. I provided the capital, he would do the work, and his fat wife, the legal one, our neighbor, would clean the house. All seemed perfect. Elie, the most helpful of our three neighboring farmers, plowed a field so that I could grow potatoes and, all around my "estate," I stuck poplar branches into the ground to serve as an enclosure.

Our enterprise, called a "warren"—which literally means a small wood—consisted of raising mostly wild rabbits. The animals wandered about as they chose, which gave them a very desirable gamey taste. Rapnouil therefore enclosed part of his wood with a tall wire mesh held by deeply sunk posts so that the wild beasts would not be able to get in. We populated our warren with rabbits, chicks, and ducklings. Left to themselves, the rabbits served the females too often, the females gave birth abundantly, with the result that there were no new rabbits: The babies were too weak and were eaten by birds or even their cannibalistic parents. The chicks disappeared completely, I don't know why. Only the ducklings prospered and became fine ducks, which were plucked and brought to Chateigner. But by the time I had given Rapnouil his half of the proceeds, and deducted the installation and feeding expenses, the result was so discouraging that I dropped the whole business. We had gone into this on the Bochers' advice; they themselves only came to the Dordogne several years later.

My business failure, which I saw coming from the beginning, depressed me terribly. It took away my only occupation in this backwater, and my only hope of making money, for this time away from Paris and its stimulating atmosphere, I was unable to paint. All I did was cut wood and go to the spring for water. They say that troubles never come singly: I learned that my gallery, the Galerie Bonjean, had just closed as a result of the famous Oustric Bank failure—a collapse that also ruined the father of my friend Christian Dior, who had invested his whole fortune, some sixty million francs, in it. I was in a humiliating situation vis-à-vis Mollie, since she now had to keep me. I could not ask my mother for money. She was ill, her bank stocks were constantly dropping in value, and she had just gone to enormous effort and expense to send Genia to the United States.

My only distraction in this period of idleness was the contemplation from my little hills of the farmers' labors taking place all around me. Inspired by the "Very Rich Hours of the Duke of Berry," I started to write little prose poems entitled "The Twelve Months of Bergerac." The manuscript is now lost except for the month of October. Here are a few extracts that depict my mood and that picturesque corner of the Dordogne.

On All Saints Day, I helped Elie pick up the acorns in the bushes. The cart, loaded to the top, crashed through the underbrush. . . . Nothing stopped the oxen: supernatural creatures. . . .

The Dead, Pergolesi's solemn work, evokes tempests and shipwrecks, tormented souls and funerary chapels. . . . Nature itself seems to pause.

The watch of Le Maine [a hamlet]: The geese signal the coming of strollers by their guttural cries. The Dordogne is unaware that time is passing, that the world is changing. As in a convent, I live with the living silence of the earth. . . .

On a clear day, slightly veiled by cirrus clouds, the inhabitants of Le Maine and Le Roc started to gather in the grapes.

The still has just arrived.

I go off with Elie to pick up the chestnuts. We move with great difficulty, each bent on his furrow, sifting through the thick layer of dead leaves with little sling-shaped sticks. And since no one is speaking, *"le boun Diou era como nou aou."** From afar, one feels the pulsing of the countryside, all its sounds seem near and alive: the creaking of a cartwheel, the wind blowing through the woods, the tapping of wooden clogs on the road, and the hard blows with which the metal binding of barrels are reinforced before the new wine is put in. . . .

Went with Mayor Chadourne, son-in-law of the beautiful Vincent woman, and with the surveyor of Villemblard to the Town Hall of Saint Julien du Crempse to help them move the heavy detailed tax maps.

Since yesterday at Le Roc, two old madwomen have been fighting.

* Local dialect in the original.

The North and Mollie · 1929–1933

Crouching like a wild man in front of his house, my tanned body wearing just a loincloth, I take the cornstalks out of their straw.

I was in a shipwreck lost on some South Sea island, rejected by a society with which I have broken. I feel so terribly alone. . . .

Dordogne is a very old rough country that has known how to keep its old carts.

The countryside is constantly changing. A plowed field, an orchard, a vineyard have multiple faces.

This is the time when cows give birth and I hear their mooing in the stables.

The hours that the little steeple of Comsegret throws to the neighboring countryside . . . lost in the forest, I wandered for a long time.

Every morning, the fogs imbue the country, veiling the farms and their trees; hours without measure, the flames crackle in the chimney. . . .

It is fall and yet, according to Elie, the winds are following the sun and looking for rain.

Just as the movement of the tides changes the curve of the shores, that of the seasons transforms the appearance of the countryside.

Now that the harvest and grape gathering are over, one can see the hens following the farmer who, bent over his plow, opens the earth. . . .

The country now wakes up in white, the moist valleys are dyed in the down of the rushes; the water willows follow the edge of the vineyards. The farmers stay at home and begin their winter's work.

It was while everything was collapsing for me that we received the news of Mollie's husband's death, brought about by a chill caught at his mother's funeral. Mollie would finally be able to have both her son and me. We went to Paris to establish a residence there and were married a few months later in the Mairie of the Eighth Arrondissement. John's holiday with us in the Dordogne was delightful; I loved that child. Several times, we went along on the curious badger hunts in the wild forests of Mussidan. They were led by the area's best hunter, young Count Jean de Corbiac (*corbiac* means "white crow" in the local dialect). You introduce a terrier into the badger's lair (I had Friday), then, hundreds of meters from the opening, you find out, by keeping your ear to the ground, where the weak sound of the dog barking 'way underground comes from. The dog does not attack the badger, whose claws make it too dangerous. You then dig a trench, take the dog out by its tail, following which you pull out the badger with a pair of giant pincers and kill it with a revolver bullet in the temple. The farmers would tell the hunters about the lairs because the badgers did so much damage to their crops. Standard hunting dogs are indifferent to the animal, unlike terriers who have this enemy in their blood from birth, as the puppies we had from Friday and his companion, Dawn, showed us clearly.

But after we had returned John home to England, our quarrels started again. We found each other more and more irritating. Mollie made a scene because I looked at the peasant girl who brought us milk. She quarreled with the bricklayer and his family whom we were driving to Paris in our Ford and made them get out at Orléans. Finally she had a fight with our neighbor and cleaning woman, the fat Madame Rapnouil, who in revenge, since her outhouse was not far from our door, would show Mollie her big, bare buttocks every time she saw her. There was no sense in living in the country any more. I was becoming hysterical, surly, and nasty; I hardly knew myself and had lost all control. I would even take vengeance on our dog, whom I would beat and then cover with kisses and tears. When we moved to a little villa in Bergerac, I found even the perspective of life in a small provincial town, let alone the country, unbearable.

Then the young Corbiac started to see Mollie, coming for tea while I was driving around in my old Ford trying to sell land for an agency to which he had recommended me. During several fights with Mollie, I had shouted that I was leaving. One day, she answered coldly, "Well, then, why don't you?" I threw some clothes into a suitcase, slammed the door, and never saw her again.

The North and Mollie · 1929–1933

When I left, I was more or less thinking of a temporary separation, but many months went by before I received a letter from Mollie: She wanted a divorce. She married Count Jean de Corbiac and lived, I presume, right near where we had been together, in the family castle at Comsegret. So ended a troubled and, to my mind, shameful period of my life.

Chapter 7

Léon Kochnitzky
and
Granville

1934

WHEN I ARRIVED back in Paris I was in a pitiful state and knew neither where I should go nor what I should do. I was penniless, but I still didn't want to end up at my mother's. I had always felt at home in Paris but now I had come back as a crushed stranger. I had not held a brush in my hand for two years, didn't even know whether I would still know how to use one. I was ready to do anything, sweep the streets, even. . . . And when, leaving the Montparnasse station, I almost ran into Pavlik Tchelitchew and Alan Tanner coming out of a newsreel theater, I quickly hid, ashamed as I was of my miserable state. "These are privileged people," I said to myself, "people without a care who can afford to spend their money on pleasures!"

From the station, I ended up at Leone Massimo's; he now lived on the place Vintimille. His faithful cleaning woman, Madame D., had served him for years and knew me well; she let me in and told me the prince was in Rome at his dying father's bedside. The good woman felt sorry for me and not only took on herself the responsibility of putting me up for two or three days, she even served me meals.

I must now stop and offer a small digression on my friend Prince Leone Massimo. One of Napoleon's relatives once expressed his surprise to one of Leone's ancestors at the fact that, unlike the Orsini and the Colonna, the name of Massimo appeared not to be found in history books. To which the ancestor replied modestly, "Sir, we have been hearing this reproach for a thousand years!" Leone had been leading a bachelor's life in Paris, studying composition with Cliquè-Pleyel. With his father's death he confined himself to Rome and his Italian castles, to become the head of the family, to marry a royal highness, and have children. He was the same age and height as I, a little heavier, with a magnificent, typically Italian head, and finely chiseled features reminiscent of the warriors in Mantegna's frescoes. We had often strolled down the Champs Élysées and stopped at d'Ayetz, the famous tie shop in the arcade, where Leone's friend, Jacques Dupont, was working. Under the influence of Christian Bérard, Jacques had started to paint. After Leone's final departure from Paris, Jacques Dupont became the faithful and constant friend of the composer Henri Sauguet, and in his own right a well-known painter and set designer.

From Leone's, I went to the Rond-Point des Champs Élysées, where Raoul Leven had a bachelor flat, in the hope that Raoul would let me sleep on his couch. He owed me a big favor for having introduced him to Walter at the Quatre-Chemins bookstore. Walter had been wounded during the Russian Revolution and had married a Gabrilovich from Rauha. He became known for his elegant publications of Diaghilev's ballets and impressionist drawings; he made his bookstore into the best gallery in Paris for drawings.

Instead of putting me up himself Raoul, who frequently dined with his elderly sister in her tiny apartment near Clichy, took me to her place. There, for two or three weeks, I dined and slept on a mattress on the floor, in the passage, near the entrance door. I am ashamed to say that I later forgot to reward this admirably helpful and charming spinster.

One morning I said to myself, Why not go and see your Belgian cousin Léon Kochnitzky and see what he's doing? He was then living in Paris at 116, rue de Vaugirard in an apartment bought from Marie Laurencin. It must have been around ten in the morning when a very fair, stunted servant in a striped yellow waistcoat showed me into the living room. There two men with ruffled hair, barely out of bed, draped in their robes, were lying on the couch, conversing: my cousin and the poet Eric de Haulleville. They greeted me with great signs of joy and Léon asked me if I would share the breakfast they were expecting. This relaxed atmosphere, this lazy, idle life, this insouciance on the part of people without any financial means was a shock at first. Then I calmed down: They were surviving, so why shouldn't I? It is true that Eric had his family and that Léon, though ruined, was always being saved by his cousin or his friend Count d'Urssel, the director of the bank where he had his overdrawn account. Léon asked me how I was doing and, having listened to me, he started to scold me: "You must not do just anything! You're a painter—start painting. We'll put together a group, your mother, a few friends, myself, we'll each give you a hundred francs a month on which you can live in the country and work. In exchange, later, you can give us paintings." "But, dear Léon," I answered, "how can you give me a hundred francs a month when you're five hundred francs short yourself?" "Well, that's just it, my friend" was his sublimely kind answer. "It doesn't make any difference whether I'm five or six hundred francs short!" And indeed, it was Léon who saved me. My mother, Leone Massimo, and he agreed to help me for six months, and Christian Dior offered me his house in Granville, which had been seized by the tax collector. I owe him my undying gratitude!

Meanwhile, as I was waiting to leave for Granville, I began to lead a very pleasant life. Léon liked my company and, as for me, I have always adapted easily to other people's ways of life, especially now that I was no longer feeling desperate. We chatted, we strolled through Paris. The penthouse-like apartment had a magnificent double view of Paris. The place was divided in two by a corridor; on either side was a big room and a bedroom, separated from one another by a bathroom. The rooms were painted in Marie Laurencin's colors, pale blue and green, and were furnished with Karelian birch furniture, including a magnificent lyre-shaped console; books, manuscripts, and modern paintings lined the walls: a Braque and a Picasso, both large cubist works, two Mirós, one of the best metaphysical Chirico's, and a painting by the Breton painter Tal-Coat. Léon had bought the apartment a few years earlier at a time when, strangely enough, he had wanted to get married. Now that he was ruined, the apartment was all he possessed, along with his few paintings, the future of which he believed in more than I did. Often when he woke in the morning he was so short of money that he didn't have enough for the paper and cigarettes. Robert, his servant, hadn't been paid for several months. But Léon always managed. The first time I saw him operate I was dazzled. We went and had lunch in the neighborhood's best restaurant; he had been a frequent customer there when he was rich and so was still respectfully received. We had some pâte d'oie from Strasbourg, wild hare, dessert, a bottle of burgundy, liqueurs, and then he was given change for a bad 100-franc check and so was able to live for a few more days.

I called Léon cousin because we had an aunt in common: Aunt Mania. He was a typical Effron, tall, heavy, with frizzy hair. Like Bébé, he had been handsome, so handsome as a child that a chocolate manufacturer had stolen his portrait and been sued by his parents. Even now—and he was seven years older than I—his chubby face often took on the expression of a pampered child; for he had been completely spoiled, especially about food; he loved sweets although he was forbidden to eat them and would consent only to eat veal, sole, and asparagus. It was therefore quite an accomplishment when I made him try oysters. He had been converted to Catholicism and was very devout. Either loved or hated by the people who knew him, this brilliant man was a linguist, an orator, and a wit. He was also extraordinarily erudite, but always remained an amateur in everything—poetry, music, collecting. During the attempt on Fiume, he had been d'Annunzio's right hand. He had been Nijinsky's lover, a frequent visitor at Landowska's Saint-Leu-La-Forêt, a passenger on the zeppelin during one of the first trans-Atlantic crossings, one of the first to climb

Léon Kochnitzky and Granville · 1934

Machu Picchu and to photograph Brazil's baroque churches. In Paris, he wrote for Prunier's famous music review and, in Brussels, he would publish, every two or three years, an elegant thin volume of his latest poems. When his parents died, he and his younger brother invested a large fortune in an Italian spaghetti company, which failed. At his house, I'd meet Eric, Olivier Picard, Jacques de Pressac (who became a Pétainist), Léon's cousin Nadine, a man-eater who almost seduced me, her daughter Ninette, with whom I flirted, the charming, gifted Marquise Yvonne de Casa-Fuerte. Time passed quickly, and in February I left for Granville.

When I arrived on the shore of the Channel, the customary bad winter weather was in full force. It was raining, windy, and very cold. I felt miserable but it was too late to change my mind. My whole future hung in the balance. So I went to a tiny street address I had been given, and rang the doorbell. A shrunken little old woman, dressed in black with a white cap, an old servant of the Diors, had been warned of my coming; she took a bunch of keys and led me toward the cliff; once at the summit, she opened a squeaky gate on which the name "La Lude" was written in large gilt letters. On my left, shaded by some pine trees, was a dainty little villa perched on the rock. Its small rooms, walled in mahogany or teak, resembled the cabins of a yacht. For my hibernation, I chose one that, away from the winds, looked out onto the garden. It was also larger and simpler than the others and had a stove so that I could have some heat. After warning me that the water, gas, and electricity had been shut off and that I should block my window carefully so that no light would reveal the presence of a clandestine visitor, the laconic old crone withdrew and I felt horribly lonely, lost in a universe full of hostile forces. I started to improvise my life as if I had been shipwrecked. I put some pails under the drainage pipes so as to gather rain-water; I found a great quantity of superb candles in a chest— they had been bought for Christmas. I picked up some dead wood around the house and filled my stove. With the coming of night, my isolation seemed all the more dread: The shuddering and moaning of the house, the noise of the sea and the wind, made me think the storm was rapidly worsening, and, unused as I was to this kind of confrontation with nature, I began to shake in fear of being thrown with the house into the abyss. I hid my head under the blankets and finally went to sleep. How great was my surprise when I woke up in the morning only to look out on a calm and sunny sea! I soon settled into my new life. I lived and worked in that one well-heated room. I took only one meal in town, lunch, in a little restaurant with the only two people I knew in Granville, two young Parisians who had also come there to work for a season: Marcel, a bricklayer, and Petit, a pharmaceutical apprentice. My domain was soon explored. On a steep path snaking down the wall of the pine-shadowed cliff, I could go down to a little beach from which I never swam—there or anywhere else. La Lude's garden was linked to a big winter estate, "Les Rumbs," by a tunnel under the little street that went along the lonely hill to the cemetery.

I grew so absorbed in my work that I forgot my isolation and even came to like it, especially when the weather warmed up. I received no letters. I painted with great enthusiasm, like a sick man returning to health, several canvases at the same time, comparing them, constantly making improvements. I was too poor to buy another tube of paint if I ran short—later I was even to be unable to afford the luxury of sitting at a café terrace. I convinced a traveling salesman to take me with him in his little truck when he was doing his rounds. I would wait for him on the square in front of a grocer: Once I even had to spend a night in his room and share his bed. But when we went to the seaside I was able to draw and thus brought back new subjects from Carteret, Port Bail, and Bréhal. In this last place, men in water to their knees were mowing down the seaweed —it was nature's own surrealism—then they loaded it into huge baskets.

Just beyond my tunnel under the road, in front of a

now-empty colonnaded basin, was a fine terrace with an endless view of the beach, the ocean, and on the horizon, the Chansey Islands. There, away from prying eyes, where no one could come and bother me, I painted my largest and best canvases, representing the endless equinoctial sands with carts pulled by three horses in a row picking up the gathered seaweed. I was unaware of the great progress I was making, not realizing that these canvases would end up in American museums and the best private collections and that, starting at the end of the year, I would be earning a living, then and forever.

Summer holidays were coming, but I had no news from Genêt, where my friends, the Waldemar Georges, should already have arrived. Léon's money order for that month had not come. I was in critical financial straits, but I risked the last of my money and took the bus, aware that, if I did not find them, I might have to walk back thirty kilometers.

My friends had in fact just arrived, and I spent a charming weekend with them and came home with some money—life was rosy again. Not only was old Madame Lavallée, the famous art critic's mother-in-law, a veritable dream of an old-fashioned woman, but the white, thatched-roof cottage seemed to come out of a fairy tale. The cozy, comfortable interior was furnished with antique rustic furniture, a willow-lined path led from the entrance gate to the little house sitting right on the shore of Mont-Saint Michel Bay; it had the most amazing view. The low tide would uncover the salt meadows on which flocks of sheep grazed. One could not have imagined a more extraordinary place!

Throughout all the colder months, I had lived in La Lude, a summer villa; now, I was told to move down to Les Rumbs, the big winter house. It was a change for the better. The big house was built in the middle of a completely neglected park; one could no longer walk down the paths that once three gardeners had kept clear. The inside looked like a graveyard; the furniture, swathed in dustcovers, reminded me of tombstones, and big potted palms were dying in the summer garden.

I chose a big servant's room under the roof. It was light and cheerful, I saw the sun in the morning and heard the birds singing.

The Dior family had come from Granville. Christian's grandfather had started their fortune by hauling fertilizer with his brothers. Later, they had trucks, then cargo ships importing or exporting Brazilian fertilizers. After Christian's father lost his fortune, his mother died of grief and he himself got tuberculosis. Like me, he was saved by several friends who sent him for a two-year cure to a sanatorium in Font-Romeu. He came out completely cured, started designing dresses for Lucien Lelong, met Boussac, the textile producer, and with his new friend's millions, became the worlds greatest couturier.

One day, near the stables in the underbrush, I found the rusting frame of an old bicycle, which I sold for twenty francs. Fortune was now smiling on me. With the Waldemar Georges in the neighborhood, I no longer had to worry. Then I heard from my American friend Virgil Thomson that he had arranged a contract for me with a New York gallery owned by Julien Levy. I would be shown during the winter and, in the meantime, would receive a hundred francs a month. It was at this time, too, that I received the letter from Mollie asking for a divorce. It was as a winner that I went back to Léon in Paris. I gave him one of my best canvases and was proud and happy to be able to invite him, in my turn, to the best restaurant!

Chapter 8

After Granville

1935–1939

I HAD STARTED living with Léon again, but I now had a separate maid's room, larger than the others, with a balcony, which I rented from the building's manager, a Dr. Pfuhl. I slept there and kept all my belongings there but as soon as I woke up, would go down to Léon's for my bath, breakfast, and even for meals. The tables had been turned: Now I was helping Léon. For a long time, we had lunch almost every day in a little restaurant called Chez Georges, on the rue Mazarine, where we drank a delicious Traminer. Later, there was a period when we would dine in a little Spanish restaurant near Saint Sulpice, sitting at a table next to that of Picasso and his companion, Dora Maar. I admired this genius, but I was afraid that if I ever met him he might disappoint me. Today I realize how idiotic that was. Twice a week, in the morning, Pivègne, a wonderful masseur discovered and made popular by my brother—Virgil Thomson and his friends swore by another Russian, Dobrinin—would come to us. Separately, we would do exercises, then have a massage. I have never felt younger or lighter while, under my very eyes, the fat and flabby Léon grew muscular. One thing I especially admired in my cousin was his ability to go to sleep immediately, any time, anywhere, anyhow. For his taste in lovers I had less admiration than I had for Cocteau's. He liked common, squat, and ugly little guys, workers, firemen, but he was so discreet I never met any of them. Once again we were spending our days chatting and strolling through Paris. One day, in a junk shop on the rue de Rennes, we found an old canvas, possibly by Arcimboldo, and we bought it for a hundred francs. Later, in a moment of crisis, Léon was to resell it to Emilio Terry for a thousand.

My career now seemed solidly established. After my first show at Julien Levy's, others followed regularly. My work pleased people so much that it sold out and Julien, a rich and brilliant avant-garde young man who was educating American millionaires, knew how to place my canvases while creating the first modern art collectors. He showed all the great names of the School of Paris: Duchamp, Brancusi, Chirico, Dali, Ernst, Tanguy, Tchelitchew, the surrealists, my brother, etc. He had all the advantages of a modern art dealer: money from his father, flair, a wide range of acquaintances, and a wife who was a superb saleswoman. For a painting about 18-by-8 inches, I would receive a hundred dollars, which, once exchanged for francs, and especially considering I lived inexpensively in the country, made me feel rich. Later I had a contract, and Julien bought my entire production. On Emilio Terry's recommendation, I opened an account at the Westminster Bank on place Vendôme, where I was impressed because you could walk right in with a check and have it cashed immediately.

My room was really only for short stays since I spent little time in Paris. I was always working on the coast and would come back only to rest and have some fun after my periods of isolation. I think I must have known all the ports, visited every beach, every village between the Belgian border and the Landes, including Arcachon. The abundance of maritime themes created for me a world I appropriated; I painted oyster beds, mussel beds, and salt marshes, which no one had ever tried before. After two, three months of complete solitude —sometimes leaving for the coast so early that I suffered from the cold and, as at the Île d'Oléron, my fingers would freeze in an unheated hotel room—after that primitive life, I would come back for a few short weeks to Paris, to pleasures, to civilization. I would relax, see friends, lead an idle and cozy life with Léon, then go off again. I still loved the movies and continued to see Tupsik. At one time, there was a little Spanish seamstress who would visit me. My parents had had a tailor from Odessa who had done a lot of work for them: Now he had his own little business with seamstresses who worked for him, and she was one of them. Even though this tailor was very ugly, none of these girls could resist his male charm. Nothing held me in Paris for long. I always left with pleasure to go to a new place along the coast where sometimes, as in Esnandes and Le Gros du Roi, Léon would come and visit me for a few days.

My frequent absences from Paris combined with the fact that my paintings were selling in New York, not Paris, caused a divorce between my life and my career. I was living in France but was becoming better known overseas. I did have a gallery in Paris, Renou et Colle, where I had shows but sold very little. Everybody knew and liked my work but the newspapers rarely mentioned it, and my paintings were not going into museums and private collections. But buyers kept coming from the United States; I got to know them and came to depend more and more on the New World. Julien Levy, this handsome, rich, and brilliant young man, came to Paris. I met him at the house of his mother-in-law, Minna Lloyd. I often saw Minna along with her daughter, Fabienne, who, for some mysterious reason, nicknamed me Dudule; it was there that I met Dali who, like Balthus, also showed at the Renou et Colle gallery. Julien had come without his wife and since, like all foreigners, he was convinced that all was sexually possible in this city of perdition, I arranged an evening at the house of a courtesan whom I knew. But it was her friend who, after an intimate dinner, came out of the next room, frightened and horrified by Julien's demands. The following year, he came back, accompanied by his new mistress, the lovely Muriel, who later became his second wife. Then came James T. Soby and A. Everett Austin. The first was a millionaire collector of modern paintings, including the neo-romantics; and the other, the director of the very first Museum of Modern Art in America, the Wadsworth Atheneum in Hartford. Jim Soby took photos of Genia and me on my balcony (Genia had come back to Paris for a few months), and asked me to join him in Italy. I met him at Cesenatico with his future wife, Nelly, and Chick Austin. We drove to Venice in his Lincoln-Zephyr. I stayed at the Albergo Bucentoro, Chick (who gave me a red madras shirt I still own) stayed at Harry's Bar, and Nelly and Jim, at the Lido Excelsior where I joined them for a swim every day of their two-week stay.

The years after Granville and before the war were all spent mostly in working. To describe them is to talk at some length about places and paintings.

1935. Oléron, Étretat, Genêt, and Port-en-Bessin. In Saint Trojan, on the Île d'Oléron, I painted oyster growers with the fort of Le Chapus in the background. It was so cold in March that I had to make a heroic effort not to run back to Paris. In Étretat, the cliff enchanted me as well as the *"calloges"* where the fishing gear was stowed away. I was drawn to Genêt, of course, by the Waldemar Georges and by the unique land-scape and to Port-en-Bessin (where in the best hotel I paid twelve francs a day for full pension) by the beautiful dikes, the trawlers, and the picturesque fish markets near the harbor, where the prices were still announced in eighteenth-century currency: Louis, pistoles, and crowns. Arranged in big round baskets, there would be sole, plaice, and ray, with their white bellies up; I made many photos of these arrangements, which looked like giant white flowers.

1936. Le Grau du Roi, Fitou, and Bazière. Le Grau is near Aigues-Mortes. There is fishing in the *graux*, or canals, with a net called a globe, brought up from the depth with a windlass and seen nowhere else in France. I visited the Camargue, flirted with a young and pretty little maid in my hotel; she offered herself in marriage in the park at Nîmes. I painted the vivid landscape with its flocks of sheep and fishing in the neighbor-ing ponds. Near Toulouse, I painted white oxen at their labors, often saw Henri Sauguet, a native of the city then visiting his parents with Jacques Dupont, and I went to the library to do research for an article on the Lauraguais Churches called "Steeple Walls."

1937. The year of Esnandes and Venice, and my American friends. The little village near La Rochelle was an inexhaustible mine for the raising of mussels and quite unknown outside the region. There I met the Fougeroux family, of whom I'll speak later because I spent several years with them during the German occupation. As for Venice, I went there in the fall, as I have said, to meet Jim Soby and to paint the laguna. I introduced Saint Christopher into one work and the fall of Phaeton into another. I visited Florence in order to draw and later paint the sand gatherers of the Arno.

1938. I went to Ambleteuse, near Boulogne, and to Pourville, near Dieppe, and took up old themes again: plunging views of the cliff. I spent more and more time in Seclin, near Lille, where I was invited by the Effrons and painted some of my best canvases (one of them is in Oliver Smith's collection in New York) while neglecting Léon and Paris.

1939. I worked part of the year in Seclin with excursions to Saint Omer where the ponds and canals came to possess me, with their small boats used to transport horses from the farms to the fields. It was then that rumors of war sent me fleeing from Bourg de Batz, near Guérande, with its salt marshes. The war was to stop my painting for years.

The event that upset me the most between 1935 and 1939 was my mother's death, which happened after I got back to Paris from Le Grau du Roi. For many years, my poor mother had been suffering from leukemia, the disease that killed her sister Eugenie. She had been receiving X-ray treatments that, by irritating her spleen, caused it to produce white corpuscles but also made her as irritable as her spleen. Her bank stocks had steadily gone down in value so she had had to give up her comfortable apartment on boulevard Montmorency with its view of the park and take refuge in one of the cheap modern buildings of the rue de l'Assomption, where she lived with Agafia, her only maid and friend. The one positive element in this sad and lonely life—my cousins, her nephews, hardly ever visited her—was that, for the first time, she had been able to make a friend outside the family. She met an Alsation widow, Madame Schmidt, a lady of her age, very rich. They saw a lot of each other and, for the holidays, would go together to Alsace, my mother as a paying guest. After my mother's death, I continued to see Madame Schmidt whenever I was in Paris, in memory of my mother; I would invite her to tea at Rumpelmayer's.

During her last days, my mother, who knew she was dying, was very courageous. I was with her the whole time. I sent many cables to my brother in the United States, but received no answer, which grieved the dying woman who wanted to see him once more. The physical change in her frightened me: Her beautiful face was becoming so ugly that I hardly knew her. We had always loved each other but, as at my stepfather's death, a quasi-physical paralysis prevented us from expressing tenderness. At one point, after I had written something at the desk, I put her Waterman pen in my pocket; my mother noticed it. "Put it back," she ordered. "I am not dead yet." My cousins were away, Genia gave no sign of life. I was alone with Agafia and my mother when she died. "You have been a good son," she said as she kissed me—we were both crying. "As for Eugene, I disown him!"

Right after this scene, my mother told me to run to the bank and withdraw her money, her whole fortune, some fifty thousand francs. Later, I sold the Empire furniture through Madame Savastina, an antique dealer, and my mother's few jewels, for which Anatole scolded me, saying I had hurried and sold too cheaply. But I wanted to get rid of everything as quickly as possible. Genia refused his share of the few tens of thousands of francs that remained; I gave it to Agafia, who moved to a room in the apartment of some Russians near Auteuil. Since I was seldom in Paris, I saw little of her. She died a few years later, suffering from rheumatism and seeing devils everywhere.

After Granville · 1935–1939

My mother's service, as had my stepfather's before, took place at the Russian Church on the rue Daru, the cremation, at Père Lachaise, and the interment, which is to say, the deposit of the ashes, in the family vault at the Montparnasse cemetery. My mother had been obsessed with the fear of being buried alive and had asked to be incinerated, which put me through a horrible moment. First I had to wait, sitting alone, before the ovens, for my poor mother to be consumed by the fire—in a huge empty room as icy as a mausoleum. Then the red-hot oven was opened and I had to see a few incandescent bones, the sight of which shocked me and filled me with horror. Finally came the miniature coffin that, by some macabre magic, now contained my poor mother, or rather, all that was left of her. And for a long time, her absence from this world struck me as a monstrous, intolerable injustice. I have always wondered why my brother didn't come for our mother's death, or at least send a cable. Why did he refuse his little inheritance? What happened in his youth to make him behave this way?

Chapter 9

Raymonde

1937–1939

IT WAS ONE EVENING at Léon's that Raymonde Effron came into my life. She had just driven in from a winter resort with her husband Ivan, who was Léon's cousin, and both, though tired, were full of life. I had not met them before. They lived in the north near Lille. From the first moment, Raymonde attracted me strongly. She was my type, very dark, my height, very lithe and cheerful, and twenty-seven, the best of ages. She had black eyes with long, curving lashes, a delicately curved nose and forehead, and exquisite lips. I also loved her sporty and supple walk, rare in those days, and her voice that seemed to caress my name—and she liked saying it. The next day, as I took her to the station in a taxi, I dared to tell her all the attraction I felt for her, and she said she felt the same for me. Soon after that, Léon and I went to spend a weekend with them at their Seclin estate, a visit that ended in a happily victimless car accident. Driven by a chauffeur, the big Buick that was taking Léon, two other guests, and me back to Paris skidded in the rain, turned on itself several times, and, avoiding the border of trees, fell into the ditch with its wheels on top; a ridiculous situation from which we were not able to free ourselves without help.

This visit was followed by others—without Léon. They became more and more frequent and soon became lengthy stays. Everybody was delighted: I, because I was in a new place and often alone with Raymonde; she, because she was no longer alone all the time, and Ivan, because his wife had a companion; for in that little provincial town, a distant suburb of Lille, they led a very solitary life, Raymonde especially, as Ivan was much taken by his business. They lived in an imposing house with a courtyard and garden, in back of which stood the factory. I ended up liking the noise of the machines as I liked everything that surrounded Raymonde and isolated us: the grey lowering sky, the identical, ugly little houses, brick and slate uninterruptedly alternating along the main road, and finally, the perfectly flat plain, without a tree, without a farmhouse, planted with beets and with a few black anthracite pyramids on the horizon. In this inhospitable climate, in this ugly and unpleasant setting, life indoors was all the warmer, all the more charming. On the third floor where Raymonde's six- and seven-year-old sons, Bernard and Philippe, slept, I had been given a big room, a little dark, it's true, but in which I nevertheless worked productively and well. Sometimes in the morning, Raymonde would pay me a visit and, forgetting the time, we would tell each other our life stories. In the evenings, when Ivan was away on a trip and the children asleep, we spent long hours before a wood fire. The passing of time brought us closer and closer, with a voluptuousness all the more powerful for our never speaking of love. And while I did love Raymonde, I felt friendly toward Ivan, who reciprocated my feelings and trusted me totally. It was less dishonorable for Raymonde to deceive her husband because she had never loved him, and though he knew it, Ivan had insisted on marrying her. He had divorced his first wife, with whom he left their many children. Raymonde had finally accepted him in order to escape the poverty in which she had been left when her first husband had deserted her and their two young children. So I manfully attempted to resist the temptation that was obsessing me. But I was sliding down a fatal slope, and it was too late for me to run away; I could no longer do it.

While Raymonde's profile reminded me of Marie Antoinette, the best way to describe Ivan Effron is by comparing him to Léopold II, King of the Belgians. He was a strange man. His trust in me was more than blind, it was stupid. It was incredible that he should have noticed nothing, suspected nothing. Silent and unsociable, he was always absorbed in business. He was a chemist and had inherited from his father, one of Aunt Mania's brothers, a factory in which leather was tanned through a special process. After having fled Russia as a young revolutionary, his father had made some discoveries, and then his fortune, in Spain. He founded the factory in Seclin and lived both there and in Belgium, as he had married a Belgian baroness. The big house was divided into two separate parts, the entire second floor being occupied by offices to which the employees came via the big staircase in the courtyard.

Apart from my work (which always came first), I was now leading the Effrons' life, gifted, or cursed, as I was with the power of assimilation. I saw their Boulogne and Calais friends, went golfing and skiing with them; in fact, I later broke a leg at the Alpe du Éze. While my work was improved by my exile, by my distance from Paris, my career suffered from it. But I didn't really care because of my sales in the United States. Perhaps because of my isolation in the country, my canvases became more and more serene, detached, concentrated, and sensitive to nature.

And since I was leading the Effrons' life, they in turn decided to follow me to the beaches I chose for my summer work: Ambleteuse, near Boulogne, and Pourville, near Dieppe. In both places there were golf courses, and in the first, some friends: Roger Brunet, a lace manufacturer in Calais and the main fishing-boat owner in Boulogne, and André Fourmentin, whom I knew slightly because, several years earlier one of his trawlers, the *Seagull*, had been grounded by a fog near Ambleteuse where I was then staying.

My fall from grace, which had to come sooner or later, took place in Pourville. Once I became Raymonde's lover, my scruples regarding Ivan weakened. After all, I could not fight fate. Our "threesome" made a short but charming trip from Étretat to the Sables d'Or d'Erquy, where Ivan played golf by himself and Raymonde and I went swimming and found isolated spots in the dunes. The following winter, Raymonde was jealous of me, thinking I was having an affair with Nadine, Ivan's sister. Now that we had returned to Seclin, I was, in my turn, becoming more and more jealous of any man who would flirt with Raymonde and take up the precious moments I should have spent alone with her. As soon as Ivan left for the factory in the morning, I would join Raymonde in her—in their—bed and would leave only when she rang the maid for breakfast. I now no longer slept on the third floor, but in a little room next to hers. When we were in Paris together, I would be waiting in the street as early as eight for Ivan's departure; I would then rush past the concierge's door and up to Raymonde's. The first time Ivan came back because he had left some papers behind, I escaped by the back stairs. But when he came home feeling ill, I barely had time to grab my clothes and lock myself in the bathroom, with the excuse that Léon's bathtub was being repaired. How he could have believed this lie, I cannot imagine, and this made me suspect that, perhaps, he knew all but preferred, from motives of discretion, that "it" should take place within the family and not with a stranger. In this suspicion I was wrong, as was later to be proved when Jeaninne, Raymonde's best friend, betrayed our secret. And while Ivan remained blind, his mother, the old baroness in Brussels whom we visited now and again, must have seen the situation more clearly. Raymonde soon preferred me not to show myself at the baroness's and told me to wait for her in the museum. All the office personnel, on the second floor at Seclin, must have found my permanent presence very strange, and the concierge's daughter, who came every morning from her pavilion near the gate, once came upon Raymonde half undressed, hiding behind a closet while I was there.

The following spring, I often borrowed Raymonde's Matford to go and work near Saint Omer in an area of ponds, canals, and little islands where the farmers' lives were spent on water and their plow horses were moved about on boats. One day, I was arrested by two policemen, questioned at the Town

Hall, and brought to Seclin, where Ivan finally convinced the police that I was not a spy. I had been careless enough to be too close to the Belgian border while I "drew the topography of the area" at a time—was it already after Munich?—when war was very close.

It was about this time that Raymonde began to grow away from me. She did not hurry back with me to her apartment when a Polish sculptor who had done her head in Seclin joined us at a café terrace at the Rond-Point; and I was furious. At the Alpe du Éze, from which Ivan brought me back to Paris with a broken ankle, I was only able to sleep with her once. Then in Lucerne she told me that she wanted to be "just a friend," to which I would not consent. We went to Geneva. Ivan, as usual driving his Lincoln at ninety miles an hour, was headed for a chemists' convention, I, to see the exhibition of paintings from the Prado, saved from the Spanish Civil War by being transported on men's backs across the Alps. Since Ivan was busy, Raymonde and I drove along the lake, ate fried fish under the nets of a picturesque little inn, and went for a swim. As Raymonde lay on a little pier, her wedding ring slipped off her finger, fell between the planks, and came to rest on the fine sand at the bottom of the lake. Even though I tried to retrieve it and some other swimmers also helped, at first we all failed. Each time we went for it, we increased the possibility that it would get buried in the sand. So holding one of the pillars with my legs, head first, I went under the water and, stretching my arm, seized the ring and gave it back to Raymonde. Was it a symbolic, if unwilling, gesture? That very evening, in the Lausanne hotel, Raymonde insisted on having separate rooms.

Even though our affair was over, I had not the strength to leave Seclin. For the holidays, Ivan took Raymonde to Saint Tropez without me. My stay in Bourg de Batz, where I was painting the salt marshes, was morbidly sad, for it was clear that the war would be upon us any minute. Finally we all rushed home, and a few days later, together in Lille, the

Effrons and I watched the declaration of war. Normal life had been brought to a halt; my own personal grief melted into the world's catastrophe.

Now, suddenly, people all became extremely busy; feverish activity took over the countryside. In our vicinity, trenches were being dug everywhere. The arrival of the first Scots regiment was greeted with enthusiasm. Ivan gave a great party for the General Staff during which I discovered, by chance, that one of the brilliant officers was an old school friend from Saint Petersburg who had become an English citizen after the Revolution. I now saw much more of Ivan than of Raymonde: She was taking nursing classes and, along with charitable local ladies, organizing hospitals and sending packages to the soldiers at the front. As for me, I passed my truck-driving exam and, since Ivan's drivers had been mobilized, helped make deliveries. I also organized a card file of the seven hundred soldiers who were being sent packages and drove all around to gather wool and bring it to the ladies who were knitting for them. Every package sent to the front had to have at least one woolen item: a scarf, a sweater or socks, as well as some chocolate bars, tobacco or cigarettes, and some canned food. I wrote to some American friends, and Philip Lasell sent me a thousand francs for the Red Cross. All winter was spent this way as the war of anticipation continued. Everyone except Ivan, who was running his factory, was in uniform. André Fourmentin, Roger Brunet, and even people my age were soon to be called up. I could still be friends with Raymonde, but I wasn't able to bear the sight of a certain flying ace who drove around in a luxury racing car and was attractive to her. He had been introduced to her by Ivan. "Here is another letter from your admirer," Ivan would say slyly, as he sorted the morning mail. One day, Raymonde asked me to get the mail from the Post Office; when I saw a letter from the flyer, I tore it up. When, during one of Ivan's trips, she went away to spend the weekend with Jeaninne, her best friend, I at last came to a decision. One evening I packed my suitcase, phoned for a taxi, and said what I thought was a final good-bye to Raymonde. Fate, however, mocked me. I arrived at the station at the very last moment, ran after the train, and, as I jumped up on the running board, I felt myself pulled back to the platform. Two soldiers took me to the military police post in the station where, for hours, my suitcase was searched, my papers and letters all carefully examined—which scared me, because the letters were from Raymonde. A net had been drawn for someone, and I had been caught. I had seemed suspicious because I had arrived at the last moment, wearing a loud camel's-hair coat that Boris had made from one of my mother's old blankets. I was allowed to leave about midnight and, returning to Seclin, I related my misadventure. The next day, Ivan, who knew the military commander of Lille, called him, and I received an apology. That evening, I took the train without any incident and only saw Raymonde twice more in my life: once a month later in the restaurant of the Quai d'Orsay—I was already in uniform—and one other time during the German occupation.

PART III

WORLD WAR II: THE OCCUPATION

Chapter 10

The Barracks
The Debacle
Return to Occupied Paris

1939–1940

WHEN I ARRIVED IN PARIS, I found a city altogether different from the one Parisians had always known: It had an Eastern feeling. Sandbag pyramids covered all the statues, new sandbag walls had risen in front of the facades of many buildings. The sharply reduced traffic paralyzed life. I felt a kind of abdication within myself, the abdication of my personality, as I renounced my past life. Painting, Raymonde, beaches, my career, it was all so far away! There remained only great pain. And a kind of *schadenfreude* overtook me. I wanted to sink into the general disaster like a molecule into the universe. While waiting to be called up, for I knew that I would be, I found myself alone. Friends and acquaintances were dispersed—gone or mobilized: Léon in Nérac, Virgil Thomson, the only one to see me in uniform, getting ready to leave for the United States. And so I decided to say good-bye to my past, to enter my new existence naked. I gave up my flat for a small apartment in Virgil's building, where the concierge, an excellent cook, made me delicious little meals. Then I went out on the town, so when the time came to take the train to Meulun and the barracks, I was penniless.

There I was, a lowly private, first in the 216th Regiment, then in the 212th. My barracks were outside the town on a hill with a view over the countryside. My dormitory housed some thirty soldiers whose beds were lined with headboards against the wall. I found it moving to see the personal touch many of the men used in decorating their little space, their "home." They would put family photos on the wall: their mothers, their wives, and sometimes naked women cut out of the papers. Some had found an old crate that they used as bedside tables; they would adorn them with a few objects, sometimes even a vase containing flowers. At first, I was kept awake nights by the general snoring, some of it really thunderous, but no one wanted to curtail his neighbor's freedom. We were given leggings, old caps, Gras guns left over from the last war, but no cartridges—they were kept in Fontainebleau. So, behind the heavy gates of the barracks courtyard began the life of a prisoner, for there were no Sunday passes. Nor could we get any news of the war, or of the world, since we were allowed out only on maneuvers. Overladen, dying under our heavy coats, our heads bursting under our scalding helmets, we would go for long walks under a burning sun. As we crossed the good town of Meulun, we would sing together, especially a song in northern dialect that the local people did not understand. It was about the male sex organs: "*la bizoute*." I don't quite remember the lines, some of which reminded me of Céline:

> Ah, it's so fine, so fine, so fine, "*la bizoute*,"
> Ah, it's so fine,
> With, with hair
> Under the ro-o-ses . . .

Slang was widely used, and there were some really picturesque images, like "casting some bronze" to mean defecate. And we had to clean up the pyramids of excrement that sometimes reached so high in the latrines that we had to stand up. While there were other fatigue duties that took longer to perform, they were also more pleasant, such as standing guard and peeling potatoes. For exercise, we would go to the shooting range where we were given a few cartridges, or we would run through a forest, spread out in a line of sharpshooters, our bayonets pointed forward as we pursued an imaginary enemy. Old officers, their sabers held high, ran in front of us. Some of our more experienced comrades found these maneuvers ridiculous, and our leaders old-fashioned and just plain dumb. The most privileged men in the barracks—free from all duty and exercise and still practicing their pre-war trades—were the cooks, shoemakers, and barbers—these last even earned a little money. I liked the dry rice so nicely prepared by an Algerian cook that we were given at first; but this was replaced by horrible mush, much enjoyed by the whole regiment. During their free hours, some of the men played volleyball; two or three others, myself included, were learning to fence. But what really poisoned our lives was being cut off from the world, without any word of the war raging in Europe, without word of our own front; we never learned about the fall of Norway. We had the feeling that everything was going wrong in France because everything was going wrong in the barracks. Were we betrayed, sold out, victims of the German Fifth Column, of the Communists, or was it all wildly exaggerated? In any case, if our barracks was anything like the army in general, we knew what to think: Our weapons were antiquated and lacked cartridges, and on the other hand, many planes were stationed in Meulun and never left it. Our nightly expeditions against German paratroopers were complete fiascos. Suddenly awakened, bundled into trucks, we would go off helter-skelter, without maps or drivers who knew the area so that by the time we reached our destination the paratroopers would be gone— unless, of course, we never got there at all! After more than a month of this, we were finally allowed Sunday passes. At the market, by coincidence I ran into Robert, Léon's ex-servant, who was now a married man and the owner of an inn on the banks of the Seine. I would go there every time I could. And then, there was duty in town, like picking up old pieces of metal in all the houses and gardens to be used for making future guns! Then, later, I was on guard at the railroad station, watching the trains go by during the day and kept up all night by the noise and vibration which shook the floor of the switching cabin in which I slept. The soldiers who were convoying guns and trucks up to the front looked unhappy, with their heads down. They received no encouragement from the people on the station platforms, for whom this was not a popular war. There were a few air raids over Paris and some bombs dropped on Meulun. From our trenches, we could see a multitude of little dots shining in the sun, but not a single French plane came to intercept them.

The beginning of the end came with the reversal of the convoys to the front, when they stopped "going up" and started "coming down," which is to say, going toward the Loire. We could hardly believe our eyes: The archives were being evacuated. This evacuation was the prologue to a three-act drama, with intermissions lasting a few hours or perhaps a day or night. The first act opened with sumptuous chauffeur-driven limousines gliding through the countryside slowly and silently, carrying one or two important people, factory owners, magnates, who preferred to leave in comfort well before everyone else. The second act brought a flood of cheap cars, of dirty old jalopies, overloaded with passengers and luggage: It was time for the petty bourgeois, the storekeepers, the salesmen, to get the hell out. And then we watched, bewildered, the tragedy of the third act. First we heard a noise, then it grew louder and all at once on the main highway there appeared a crowd on foot. This was the exodus of the farmers abandoning their land; one would have thought the whole population of northern France was fleeing before the enemy. Big forage wagons pulled by plow horses carried three generations perched on top of these moving mountains of cages, furniture, and assorted possessions. The wagons themselves got swallowed up in the crowd of people on foot. The human lava ran on both sides of the road, exhausted crowds filled the ditches. And on a small country road running parallel to this one, in an effort to get ahead of the masses, were the military convoys, the beaten armies. When this cataclysm came within sight, Meulun too was seized with panic and started emptying out.

Exhausted regiments invaded our barracks, rested, and resumed their march to the south. The usually quiet square in front of us became a mass of pedestrians and autos. Old cars would move forward, stall, pass one another, often driven by old men or adolescents who did not know what they were doing. I saw one car pulling another with no one at the wheel! It seemed that the end of the world was coming because the whole sky in the direction of the German advance was getting as black as ink. Was it an eclipse? It was only later we found out that what we had seen was a smoke screen thrown up by the Germans as they crossed the Seine before Rouen, that the wind was pushing toward us, raining ashes and making us cry black tears. . . .

The military headquarters, the Secret Military Police, the Red Cross were being evacuated; the police had gone on ahead. The hospital personnel took off, abandoning some of the sick; the doors of the prisons and insane asylums were thrown open. Sometimes, in an abandoned house, a locked-up dog would be heard shrieking; the hens in their yards, the rabbits in their cages were left to starve. The only cheerful note in this macabre nightmare was the free flight of the pigeons. On June 13, out of the original twenty-three thousand men of the Meulun garrison, only five hundred, including me, were left to defend the town. With old guns and a few cartridges, we were supposed to delay the march of the most modern, most powerful army in the world. We were being sacrificed. On June 14, at noon, the mines under the Seine bridges were to be detonated. It was now five to twelve; the last fugitives were crossing at a run. My heart was pounding. Suddenly we heard the order freeing us from duty, but would we still have time to get across? Expecting the worst, I had worn light shoes so as to be able to swim; but here I was at last, on the other side, in the courtyard of the Brasserie Gruber, abandoned by its owners. The beer was flowing but there was nothing to eat. Exhausted men were lying down among broken bottles. Having found or stolen some bicycles the previous day, several of my comrades were forming cycling teams. Our sergeant, Desaloux, told us to get to Nemours under our own steam, and, once there, to gather on hill Number 78, Northeast —which, of course we would never be able to find without a map or a compass. Why couldn't it have been the railroad station or the town hall?

Following are the notes I scribbled on bits of paper during our flight. I lit out with my friend Robardelle. We were so happy to be out of the barracks, and away from both our own officers and the Germans, that our mood was good despite the circumstances.

First Day, June 14

Good-bye, prison, freedom, here we come! The road and adventure call us. Feeling fresh and rested, we walk fast, carrying only our military equipment.

Everything seems to happen strangely, we can't believe our eyes. Are we living a dream or a nightmare?

The roads remind me of severed veins from which all the blood of Paris is pouring. Millions of people are fleeing the capital. Overcome by exhaustion, some sleepers lie in incredible positions. Peasant carts pulled by horses in file move slowly forward. Tractors drive strings of carts, and trucks disappear under human clusters. This tightly packed crowd flows as thick as a volcano's lava. Groups of cyclists weave in and out. The pedestrians carry little bags or suitcases; some look as if they are off on holiday, as if they were going to catch a train. Many push perambulators full of luggage, some pull trailers. I pass a courageous young girl pushing her grandfather in a wheelchair. A little boy is holding an aquarium with a goldfish in it. The people sitting in a stalled truck wave to him, in imitation of the Volga boatmen. A deaf-mute accompanies a blind man. A few coquettish girls wearing shorts add a frivolous note to this tragic spectacle of sobbing women, lost children, masterless dogs. French and Belgian soldiers are mixed in with the civilian flood; leftovers of an army in flight, they move forward, exhausted, like sleepwalkers. Some are in rags and barefoot. Some come from very far away, from Dunkirk or Flanders.

My friend Robardelle and I meet three young girls who want to reach Nantes or Dinard, where they have relatives. We push their carts, they share their food with us. Flirt in Fontainebleau forest. We sleep under the stars.

Second Day, June 15

The night is freezing. Huddled together, we shiver with cold. It is best not to tarry too long, the Germans might outflank us. The day breaks, shadows leave the forest, join the road, make up a black mass that begins to flow. I am sliding through a grey dawn at the edge of an impossible world; all is real, nothing is true. How long has this nightmare been going on? These dead horses, these German planes fly very high and force us to scatter into the woods.

The endless forest of Fontainebleau is finally behind us; here we are in the plain over which blood-colored clouds reflect two huge fires on the horizon.

A few kilometers before Nemours, a gigantic jam keeps us in place for hours. I lose Robardelle and find him again by chance. In the meantime, our young girls have disappeared, packed by my friend into the last freight train.

Nemours is at the crossing of two major roads. Whoever had not come through it with me would not be able to imagine the human eddies created by contrary currents breaking in the center of town.

There is no bread, no food. Long lines in front of the baker's. The shops have closed. The owner of a vineyard offers all his wine to the soldiers. All stocks are liquidated so as to leave nothing for the enemy. Pillage? There is fighting on the second floor of a big food store abandoned by all its personnel. Our quickly improvised haversacks fill with soap, chocolate, canned peas. We see some comrades from the barracks and learn from them where we should go: Argent by way of the village of Airville. For a rest, and to be of use, we regulate the traffic. As a reward, we are picked up in a colonel's limousine; we are dropped off some fifteen kilometers closer to Airville; we see its steeple across the fields.

We are struck by the village's strange silence; it is the first we see without inhabitants. Chickens are scratching about in the streets, cattle walk along blind facades. Baaing sheep come to meet us. My companion explains to me that a cow, if no longer milked, must finally die. We meet no one from our company but see, in a farmyard, an unknown military group carving up a sheep. We steal away silently: The memory of prison is still too unpleasant, our freedom too precious. So we go toward another farm, another gate, which we open carefully. No one in front of the stables, the main building, anywhere. Good peasant beds, a pleasure we have not had in months, seduce us. . . . Hardly do we think this thought when the door opens, as if by magic, and a fairy appears. She is a neighboring peasant woman, a Pole, who has had the courage not to abandon her land. She feels sorry for the hard fate of two poor soldiers and takes care of us like a mother. Not only does she take pleasure in preparing a chicken with peas, accompanied by wine and a tureen full of milk, but she's offended when we mention payment.

Exhausted, sated, we sink into a deep sleep.

Third Day, June 16

Violent knocks shake the door and startle us awake. Five A.M. The good woman is worried; the unknown group has left long ago. We dress quickly, drink a bowl of milk, and tenderly kiss our foster mother who is crying with emotion and fear.

A bad sign, the Germans can't be far: The road is empty, the whole area is deep in calm before the storm; there is barely a car or pedestrian. We hurry, after looking back. Will we be petrified like Lot's daughters?

A Citroën passes us. I signal it just in case. And the incredible happens, it stops. A liaison agent, coming back from an exhausting mission, gives me the wheel and goes to sleep; he continues sleeping for almost thirty-six hours uninterruptedly during which I drive the car, often faced by the worst difficulties, at the limit of human endurance. How could there not have been more accidents with all those people who did not know how to drive? Somehow, we were on another plane. The cars are moving along in three files, so close that they touch, waiting for hours to move just a few meters.

All the little towns we pass are alike, a spectacle of pillage and abandonment.

We stop in Bellegarde on the pretty Castle Square. The hotels have become camps, all house shutters are closed, all store doors open. One walks in freely everywhere. The windows of a beauty salon are emptied of their contents; only useless wrecks are left in the garages. There is nothing in the bicycle store, at the butcher's, in the delicatessens. By contrast, the back room of a pharmacy still displays its whole range of poisons; apparently no one was tempted by the samples of these noxious powders. And yet, when could a murderer find a better occasion for committing the perfect crime?

The shoe shop is full of merchandise thrown about on the floor. People come through, stumble on the piles of shoes, and, unable to find a matching pair, leave again.

Everywhere, both inside and outside the houses, chaos reigns.

Before the Church, there is a huge pile of military equipment left behind by some regiment; everything is in there, including large pieces of rotten meat, and the passersby who dig through it chase away huge clouds of green flies.

Some planes dive down and shoot. Instantly the square empties, people panic, rush in opposite directions, bumping into each other, pushing children over.

Then I have a strange vision. From a notions store, a thief comes out, all wrapped in ribbons. Her speed unwinds all these red strings and, mixed with the young woman's long red hair, they give her the appearance of a witch devoured by flames. The beautiful fugitive, as graceful as a Botticelli figure, runs past, brushing against a group of men and women as still as statues. But these living statues are smiling beatifically! A little boy, huddled with me under the porch, whispers that they are lunatics. Then, the planes having left, the little boy and I go over to check a car left there by its owner, which has borne the full blast of the machine gun. Among the broken windows and pierced suitcases, a cage of canaries is intact, and the birds are in full song.

We stop our car a little farther on, in front of an empty villa that we explore, but uneasily, for the owners must have just left. Walking over to the window, I notice that by just a few inches, the wall of a garden separates two different but equally disrupted worlds: a dried-up well and a broken dike. On one side, life has fled, all is silence and desertion; on the other, life roars past like a rising river. Taking advantage of other people's troubles, I appropriate two pairs of darned socks, a towel, and a knife. In the sitting room, a pretty little sailing ship in a bottle seems so tempting I am about to put it in my knapsack when, suddenly, I am shocked by my own gesture and put the bottle back. Already normality has gone. I then come back from the cellar with my arms full of bottles of champagne and good wine, which we later exchange for gasoline.

White rabbits of all sizes are hopping around the garden. We keep seeing them in a stew, like in *The Gold Rush*. We naturally capture the largest but when Robardelle, our chef, takes it off the spit, it is too tough to eat; we have to pursue a smaller one.

The cat, motionless on the wall, is watching us. The dog, that faithful guard, is torn between his duty and his anger at having been betrayed by his masters: He lets himself be caressed and growls at the same time. I save him by undoing his chain.

The human tragedy strikes the animal world too: lost dogs, starving horses, cows sick from not being milked. Chickens and rabbits are forgotten in their cages. Death does not spare a family of orphaned chicks; a soldier rushes in and takes a few. I feel outraged, as outraged as if I had been the owner. Are we not the masters of the place?

Leaving Robardelle to his culinary enterprises and the liaison agent to his sleeping sickness, I walk into the garden, an oasis of peace and coolness. This enclosed orchard with its fruit trees, its blue sky, and its flowers seems like paradise. I sing as I pick strawberries and currants, artfully arrange them in a dish, intermingling them with flowers and fruits. I unfold a lace tablecloth, bring out silver and crystal. Our luncheon on the grass may be madness, but it returns to me a taste for life.

Two hours later, coming out of Bellegarde, we are shot at by planes attacking a military convoy. We must pass this convoy at any cost. It is then, while I am parked on the sidewalk, that a gutter breaks my muffler. I manage to pass the line of trucks but the car moves as if it were limping, it roars loudly and gives out flames. Terrified, we stop every time we can to fill the radiator with water, then, since nothing terrible is happening, we get used to this new state of things.

I try to be clever: To escape the crowd, I take a little side road. I am soon punished, for these little roads can be treacherous, and I promise myself not to try it again. As we arrive back on the road, we are stopped by a line of cars stretching to beyond the horizon. Hours are wasted. People lie down in the grass, pick flowers, get acquainted, and scatter when the planes return. Here are the first graves at the edge of a field: a little mound of earth, a cross, and a few flowers. Robardelle and I sit by the side of a well bearing a big sign: "Water unsafe to drink." A vagabond comes up, reads, and drinks peacefully. "Are you crazy?" my friend explodes. "Can't you see that it's poison?" "I don't give a damn," the other answers quietly. "I'm not from here." Suddenly a burst of laughter shakes the whole group. An old Ford comes out of the motionless lines, crosses the planted fields, and, on the railroad line, moves jerkily forward.

The sun is going down. The movement forward starts again slowly at first, then faster, and ends in a mad race of a few cars through Sully forest.

The Loire becomes an obsession, all these people fleeing and crawling toward it, thinking only of crossing it. The Loire means salvation, just as the Seine did a few days ago. As we come nearer, nerves become taut.

A patrolling group stops us with bad news: The Sully bridge has been destroyed. We must turn back. Will we be luckier elsewhere? The gasoline is running out, the detour will take time, this precious time of which every minute counts.

Discouraged, my friend thinks of walking through the fields to the river and looking for a boatman; I'm against the idea.

The night is already upon us, a dark and moonless night. All their lights out, coming from both directions, the cars appear, like ghosts. Each looks for salvation on this road that runs parallel to the river.

I'm exhausted, I can't react any more, things happen in spite of me. Having found a crossroad, I park the car and go to sleep at the wheel.

Fourth Day, June 17

While the crossing of the Loire is Calvary, its approach can be considered as the most anguishing moment. It takes us twelve hours to go the last twelve kilometers before the crossing.

If you had been able to look down from a high-flying plane, the human currents of this great exodus would have seemed like smaller streams merging into a great river, the difference being that rivers, as they grow, end up in an estuary while the crowd's flow, on the contrary, is squeezed in a funnel ending at the Gien bridge.

At the entrance to many towns, barricades made of overturned trucks, useless for stopping the enemy, terrible for the fleeing crowds, let through only one of the three lines of cars; and then there are eddies and even countercurrents like that group of civilians that, having almost reached the Loire, suddenly turns back toward the Sully bridge, which we know no longer exists.

In the car ahead of us, I can see a newborn baby swinging in a little hammock. Robardelle says there is a corpse in one of the cars following us.

During our many stops, we check the tanks of all the abandoned cars and are able to find a few liters of gasoline. We get another fifteen by exchanging, with the occupants of a military truck, the four bottles of burgundy we have taken with us. The Bellegarde cellar has done us an immeasurable service.

It is four P.M. when we arrive in Gien. At a crossroads, against a background of collapsed houses, a group of superior officers covered with decorations—contrasting with our fear, dust, and flight—direct us down a little street; one would think it was a General Staff directing a battle. The lower town looks the same: Pieces of walls are suspended in emptiness, huge funnels are open where houses once stood. The ruins are smoking.

All faces are grave; we reach the quay and start across the bridge.

Luckily, we have come at a quiet moment. We're told that, yesterday, the bridge was being used as a target by Italian planes; yesterday, a bomb scored a direct hit, sowing death, splashing the parapet with blood. Corpses were all thrown into the water so as not to interrupt the traffic. We can still see the traces of this massacre: a few tarpaulins covering the dead, disemboweled horses, and burnt-out cars. I turn around and take a last look at this apocalyptic vision of Gien, which will never leave my memory.

The river marks the separation between past and present.

But then, suddenly, as we reach the middle of the bridge, through the low cloud ceiling, planes reappear and shoot at us. We're stuck on all sides and, as my friends rush out of the car to find shelter anywhere, I bring my helmeted head down into my shoulders and continue slowly driving forward. We reach the other bank, the road widens, becomes free, my friends jump into the car and I start off at top speed, thinking only of getting as far away from the bridge as possible when all at once a terrifying thought sneaks up on my consciousness and chokes me. This truth is so monstrous I can barely face it, but the facts are there, they speak, they burst: France is dead.

The second miracle of the Marne never took place. There, on the Loire, no one thought of his country; all were too busy saving their skins. The Loire turned out to be just one of many stops on the road to exile.

The country's leaders, the top generals, all had known for some time that it was hopeless. Why then didn't they try to stop the flight from Paris, the ensuing tragedies on the Loire? Why these policeless roads, the hospitalless wounded, the leaderless fragments of an army? And so, right then, soldiers stop saluting their officers.

Argent is full of troops. The liaison agent leaves us. We meet Sergeants Audinet and Landry; they tell us where we are to go: Vierzon.

But as we go past the fence of a park, we are literally snatched up by a commander who, paying no attention to what we tell him, orders us to walk into the estate. We are caught in a trap.

In the meantime, in front of the castle wall, where the beds are sprouting soldiers instead of flowers, I have myself shaved for the first time in several days. Not such a bad profession, the barber's: One of the few that can be practiced in the barracks and the only one that, throughout the exodus, continues to bring in money. The sensation I feel now is simply marvellous: I am coming back to life. This private is actually giving me a very good shave, so much better than a Lille barber who, one day, stretched my cheek by putting his thumb in my mouth. I found his method so startling that I did not stop him. Many years later, a Breton peasant gave me the explanation, saying that years ago in the small villages the barber would ask his client whether he preferred to be shaved with spoon or thumb.

It is soup time and bread is being handed around, the first we have had since Meulun. Two big loaves in our arms, avoiding everyone's attention, we sneak toward the back of the garden looking for a break in the enclosing wall.

And here we are again on the road; our new experience has enriched us by two loaves.

Now we avoid the main roads. We hear fighting in the distance. Toward eight P.M., a loud explosion tells us that the Gien bridge has just been destroyed. Planes are flying about, we see them as we hide under the willows near a little stream, finishing our last tin of sardines; it reminds us of more abundant meals and living in houses.

Luck is with us; it now guides us to an isolated farmhouse where a motorized troop is camping, along with three women and their children picked up along the road. And while the migrating human flocks suffer indescribable miseries, these few favorites of fortune are living in complete luxury. Nothing, it seems, is lacking; the planks disappear under avalanches of tins, bottles, even candy-filled jars. As they are about to sit down to eat, one of the cheerful guests shouts, "Shit! We have no bread!"

It is at that crucial moment that we appear, carrying our loaves. Here it is, the missing bread! It is greeted as a miracle. There is a kind of Indian dance, we are declared Tabu. We become the good-luck charm that the group will not want to lose.

The Bellegarde cellar allowed us to reach the Loire, Argent's bread helps us to get away from it.

Fifth Day, June 18

What luck to be taken in a truck when millions of people are dragging themselves on foot along the roads, to have crossed the Loire when so many of our comrades, who probably haven't been able to do the same, became German prisoners.

We look like a group of beggars with our wrinkled jackets and worn-out, spotted clothes. The barns and the ditches have left their mark on us, as does this dusty truck in which, piled on one another, amid cans of oil, we clumsily open tinned food and, shaken by the bumps, take the corks out of wine bottles.

But while we are dirty and pitiful-looking, all our faces shine with a strange brightness. Each soldier, to my eyes, personifies a type, a hero of the "Great Parade"; their several-days-old beards, their hollow cheeks, tightly clenched jaws, and hair escaping from the helmets have sculpted hard and resolute masks with eyes enlarged by fatigue and as if enlightened by suffering. Whether they look within, or in the far distance, these eyes, in any case, stare at you unseeing: Human, infinitely beautiful, they are martyrs' eyes.

Another spectacle of disorder and misery in Vatan where thousands of people are trapped. Car owners, out of gasoline, cannot go any farther; leaving their autos full of suitcases would mean the loss of probably the only property they have. The poor women are especially pitiful; they no longer think of doing their hair, putting on makeup, cleaning their nails. I speak to one poor soul waiting since yesterday for her husband's return: he had left for just a few minutes. Another had just taken in two sobbing children accompanied by a superb spaniel. Some children are sick with hunger, others, because they have eaten nothing but canned food. Where can one find milk for the babies? The Welcome Centers can offer no more than a bowl of thin soup, a crust of bread, and a few mattresses. There is indeed some meat for sale, but no oil or butter; and, anyway, where would you cook it?

Along the way, we see wounded men lying by the side of a ditch; they are waiting for ambulances that will probably never come. And then we see many more abandoned cars, stripped of everything—wheels, batteries, cushions—in spite of the naive signs: "Please don't touch anything, we'll be back." The bare auto bodies are used as shelters; every time you open a door, you find someone asleep inside.

From time to time, planes still appear, flying low, shooting at I know not what. They provoke some imprudent soldiers who, not caring that they are surrounded by women and children, answer back with carbine salvoes.

Now, over all the big cities we cross, the white flag is flying. These are the "open cities." But isn't all of France, its earth, its sky, open to the enemy? "We'll get them!" had been the war cry; and we have indeed "got them." Never has prophecy come so true; but, unfortunately, in reverse.

Sixth Day, June 19

We are driving toward Bourges when we are stopped by incredible news: The German vanguard would be beyond, not just Bourges, but even La Rochelle and Angers.

Where can we go? Tossing a coin, the driver of our truck heads for Vierzon.

Those that were going toward the Loire had a tragic look; a wind of disaster blew on them, they were under the signs of misery, panic, and death. The road we take as we come out of Vierzon is nothing like that. It is calm, almost cheerful, with an open view on both sides; no more crowds, pedestrians, or tragedies. Clean cars drive about freely. A convoy of armored cars creates a sensation: It disappears under human clusters, it looks as if people are off to the fair. And, from the depths of my truck, I am the amused witness of the beginning of a romance between a handsome officer driving the bus in back of us and a very pretty blonde who has apparently fallen for him. This young and elegant couple might just as well be actors in a Hollywood studio. From time to time, the seducer winks at me with complicity.

Since there is no more General Headquarters in Châteauroux than anywhere else, Doudou, the driver, whose farm is close by, decides to make a detour and take us all to his home.

A son back from the front! We thought to receive a warm welcome from the parents; not at all. The whole family, wife included, is gloomy. Not only are we not offered a glass of wine, but Robardelle and I are obliged to cover the countryside looking for an egg, a bowl of milk. That evening, new disappointment. Gathered in front of the radio, we hear the following communique: "The Armies of the Loire [us], while engaged in valiant combat, are withdrawing in good order near the Loire to previously prepared positions."

Bitter tears roll from our eyes.

Seventh Day, June 20

Can there really be life without danger, a sky without planes, a countryside without fleeing crowds? Is it real, this little corner full of joy, calm, and peace?

Wonderful convalescence in the midst of nature, with no distractions other than water lilies, the wind in the willows, the ringing of the cattle bells, the coupled dragonflies, and the trout swimming a little way down.

Ecstasy of sleeping, eating, exposing our tired bodies to the sun's caress; wonderful morning at the Doudou farm! We would have liked it to last forever!

But at four, we leave again. On the road we come across men looking for the Town Hall, a military authority. While swimming across the Loire, these civilians who are really soldiers have lost everything, even their military papers. Wanting to be within the law, they ask a passing police troop what to do. "Friends," the police answer, "just do like us, try to get back to your homes; there are no more deserters."

Some planes fly over Argenton-sur-Creuse. A young girl, in a panic, starts to sob. From the door of his looted garage, the owner shakes his fist at us. The nerves of the population must be worn to a frazzle. Not content with the priority given soldiers over citizens, one man pushes a poor woman in the line in front of the baker's and showers her with insults. The passive crowd does nothing; so, full of indignation, Robardelle intervenes and chases the brute away.

Since Doudou still doesn't know where to go, he decides to return home to his farm.

And so he drops us, Robardelle and me, in the middle of the road, in a torrential rain. We are still more than a hundred kilometers from Limoges. We then decide to get rid of all extra weight and throw down our old guns, adding them to the bunch already in the ditch. There are even some carbines. These modern toys tempt us, but are useless and too heavy. There is no ammunition.

Our worn-out shoes let the water in, we are soaked to the bone. Still, luck does not desert us. We spend part of the night on the fenders of an American truck, the rest of it inside an armored car. Then begins a new Calvary. We have had nothing to eat or drink, we cannot find a refuge or even a well to quench our thirst, so we sleep by the road in front of a gasoline pump. We have lost everything in the world; only the earth on which we walk is left us.

Eighth Day, June 21

Haltingly, like two sleepwalkers, we walk through the intensely green countryside. This is the Limousin. Twisting roads cross a hilly terrain and make us feel as if we're not moving. No longer are we in areas that can be looted, where we could find abandoned houses, hospitable farms whose inhabitants understand misery and war.

If after a twenty-four-hour trial, we are in this terrible state, what must it be for those soldiers who have been retreating from the north and Belgium? Breughelian hordes, tattered wretches, wearing espadrilles or sometimes barefooted and bleeding, they make their way leaning on sticks, a bag on their shoulders.

Trucks full of people pass us, along with a long file of empty buses bearing the sign: "Madeleine–Bastille." There is no use in signaling these Parisian drivers. One finally stops, even seems to be waiting for us. So, gathering our very last strength, we run, only to see it go off just before we get to it. We must try another method and I tell my friend to dissemble: We now wait for the trucks to slow down on a hill. I manage to get up, then realize that Robardelle, who is heavier, is not able to follow me.

The passengers of an enormous stalled truck are pushing it up a hill: labor of Hercules. Some gypsy athletes are camping in front of their caravans. An adolescent, right out of Picasso's Blue Period, is juggling with three balls. We watch him work for a while. By a river, a few bare-chested men are washing. A little farther, under the bridge, a woman, her back turned to the crowds, is cleaning her private parts. We are asked to hold the leg of a mule being shod. Yesterday, drenched by the rain, we were covered with mud; today, we are exhausted by the tropical heat and the dust makes us look like millers. On a signpost, I read: Paris, 342 kms., Limoges, 34 kms.

In a village, we discover an inn where a refugee butcher is selling meat. We queue up to cook it in a communal frying pan.

Limoges can't be much farther. I'm vaguely hoping I may find my friends Léon and Olivier with the Belgian government.

Everything has an end; we cannot walk any farther and collapse in a ditch.

When I wake up, I can't believe my eyes. Our Sergeant Riom is looking at us, Riom, my comrade from the barracks, my adversary at billiards.

Saved, we are saved! We beg him to take us along even though his truck is more than full. Enough adventures, we are fed up with freedom.

Ninth Day, June 22

We reunite with Marquis, Maquart, Savtchenko, and Delgrandi. Riom lends me a blanket, Cormier his jacket, Brunet a sweater. I ask everyone to contribute toward a shave. I feel rich. I have luggage.

For the first time, I eat well and regularly.

A solid friendship united us during the exodus, but, with the relaxation that follows our final arrival, our relationship sours. Each man thinks of his own problems; many words shock me.

Riom is our providence. Not only did he not abandon his men— a rare occurrence during this rout (Sergeant Delvage boasts of having lost those he disliked)—but he even managed the miracle of feeding them. The debacle had caught him in Châteauroux where he had arrived in a truck with some Italian prisoners. In spite of the intensive bombing of La Souterraine, he managed to salvage some two hundred and fifty liters of gasoline from the bursting tanks. With the money obtained from the sale of the gas to stranded drivers along the road, he was able to buy meat.

The truck is so old that it is a miracle it isn't falling apart. Havard, the makeshift driver, manages quite well; and, from the roof of the cab where I have been given a place, I can look over the countryside at leisure.

The normal life in La Coquille we find as striking as the sight of our troop-filled truck is to the population crowding the sidewalks. They seem to know nothing of recent events, and consternation shows on every face. These good people are as distant from my reality as I am from theirs, and we must all make an effort to accustom ourselves to the sight of open shops and intact windows, decorated with geraniums and untouched by the blackout. The power to buy what I need or want seems strange. Money is all-powerful again. Unfortunately, very few of us have any. I give myself the luxury of a few little cakes and find an infinite pleasure in my first cigarette.

Indeed, we've come a long way. Young girls applaud us as if we were heroes and one of them throws me a rose. I am ashamed of our filth and realize how strange we look.

The change first noticed at La Coquille is now obvious everywhere. The police stand at a crossing outside of Périgueux. They are organizing traffic, separating civilian and military convoys, grouping single men, giving the regiments their orders. We finally know where to find the 212th and that we are to gather at Tartas in the Landes. We will thus no longer drive on blindly.

We also meet a few comrades on bicycles, heavily loaded, and get Guilberteau, sick with jaundice brought on by fear at the Loire, to a hospital. The Post Office in Antone is open and I quickly scrawl a postcard to Anatole in Arcachon to say I am still alive. By a miracle, he actually receives it.

People speak of an armistice.

Tenth Day, June 23

Deep sadness. Even the weather adds to it; there is nothing but rain.

We feel uneasy; we are drenched, wade through the mud to farms, hear the Alsatian refugees speak in the enemy tongue. The sky is sulking and gives a melancholy look to one of the most attractive regions of France, this Dordogne where, years ago, I thought I might be happy. We even make camp right near my old house. How little of the past is left for this gypsy traveling down the roads with his entire fortune in a little knapsack!

Eleventh Day, June 24

Vineyards, oxen tied to the plow, dovecotes on pillars, old villages sheltering under huge roofs covered with wine-red tiles.

The bad roads, soaked by the rain, are making it very difficult for us. The truck skids and becomes mired. The Bergerac bridge is closed to traffic by vans placed across it so we have to cross the Dordogne at Moyleydier and from there, through wild forests, go toward Issigeac.

I have never seen a more picturesque farm than that of Fulgeyrat. The stable that the farmers give us for the night is as big as a theater whose semi-circular shape it has. The cows, their heads coming through round openings, seem to be watching a show and looking from their boxes at an orchestra of sleepers.

Twelfth Day, June 25

We are in a state of shock. What is happening to France resembles an amputation; the anesthetic is gone now, we feel shrunken and ill.

We go from farm to farm, from stable to hen-house. We sleep in the straw, we sleep in the hay; our idleness weighs on us.

The Germans now occupy all the coasts to a depth of fifty kilometers, which means we can no longer go to Tartas. This is a hard blow [coup dur] and, ironically, we hear it in a little town with a predestined name, Coudures. Our regiment is lost again; for we are now, and intend to stay, in the nonoccupied zone.

Mont-de-Marsan has lost nothing of its pre-war activity. Luxurious hotels, elegant women, flower shops, bookstores, I even see some Libby's tins in a marvelous delicatessen where a huge ham rivets my attention.

The day after we pass through it, Saint Sever is occupied by the enemy.

We are survivors whose lot is becoming unendurable. All around us, life is still normal. But from being the elite of the rout, we have suddenly become paupers and at the same time are everywhere tantalized; we are starving in the midst of plenty. We have used up all our extra gas and can no longer buy food. Our only way out is to find, at any cost, our vanished regiments.

As for housing, it hardly looks better. Like a cloud of locusts, refugees are everywhere. The lower part of the Landes is flooded. Even our old truck is out of breath and shows signs of fatigue. The brakes have given up. They finally go as we roll downhill.

Thirteenth Day, June 26

You go to sleep by lantern light, are soothed by the breathing of oxen, and awakened by the clucking of a hen who has laid an egg in your coat.

By day we wash in a pond, fish for gudgeons, look for mushrooms, waste hours in the grass by the water.

This camping would be charming under other circumstances, if we were not so unhappy and worried.

Some men help the peasants gather the hay, others never sober up. Robardelle and Marquis, who is from the Cantal, can't bear it anymore. They go home to wait for demobilization.

Fourteenth Day, June 27

We find that the remains of the 212th regiment are to be taken over by the fourth company of the 216th. Our good Sergeant Riom has safely delivered his cargo. After the hamlet of Urgons, Puyol-Cazalet becomes our harbor.

A few more single men come and join us so we think the bulk of the regiment must follow. This doesn't happen, no one else comes, we are just ninety.

The demobilization is as hard to find as the regiment. The general disorder is blamed. We're told it will proceed according to age, or locality, or profession. . . . It is only on August 4 that we will be permitted to go to Geaune, then to Air-sur-l'Adour, and, from there, we will be sent on to Paris.

The separation of the two zones, the destruction of all the bridges, the lack of trains, all create an obstacle just as effective as the ocean surrounding a small island. Three weeks later, a few lucky people get two or three messages from Rennes, from Nantes, finally from Paris. But it is only a glimmer in the fog. We have the horrible feeling of being buried alive. The debacle has created impossible situations: Half of France is looking for the other half; families are lost at home; and the French are prisoners in their own land.

It is exile.

Puyol-Cazalet is composed of a few scattered farms on a hill from which, every morning, as far as the eye can see, we look over a surprising, harmoniously undulating landscape. Every morning too we witness a phantasmagoric and infinitely varied mirage: the snowy peaks of the Pyrénées floating above a layer of clouds.

Seventeenth Day, June 30

For the first time today, a Sunday Mass is celebrated. Delgrandi, our tenor, sings. The regimental postman, Michaud, plays the violin, and little toads hidden under the altar accompany them with their high voices.

All pray that the soldiers may find their homes, that the country may be saved:

"Saint Joan of Arc, throw the enemy out of France."

I took every chance I could to get away from that hole of a village. Remembering that Virgil Thomson was supposed to be visiting a rich American near Oléron Saintes Maries, I walked forty kilometers, only to learn that he had left the day before for the United States. I barely saw the hostess, but found myself, dirty and rumpled as I was, surrounded by elegant young Parisians, some of whom I knew. They were pleasantly passing the time, chatting and arranging flowers in the reception rooms. Any hope I had of staying there for a few days was quickly dispelled by the mayor who, learning of my clandestine presence, ordered me to leave his town because I was a nondemobilized soldier.

A little later, I borrowed a bicycle and went off for the day on a visit to a friend who was temporarily working on a neighborhood farm; I preferred working, being well fed, and living with a family to the morbid idleness of Puyol-Cazalet. I got there during the hay-making and joined the group of men laboring, bare-chested, under a burning sun. Suddenly, an unusually violent rainstorm started to pour down such quantities of water that the workers, who wanted to finish taking in the harvest no matter what, stripped naked, sheltering their trousers in the haystacks. They looked like devils, with their white bodies and their pitchforks moving about against a dead-black sky. It was already very late when, after the storm and an abundant dinner, I began to think of going back. The night was very dark; suddenly, as I was rolling down a hill, I felt myself going in to water up to my knees. The whole valley was flooded: no more roads, ditches, or fields; the only landmark was the line of telephone poles.

The winter that followed my return to Paris and my demobilization was like a long, a very long dark tunnel. Paris was covered with swastikas. Nazi troops paraded down the Champs Élysées at noon. The city no longer belonged to the Parisians; one never saw a French uniform on the streets. We lived in unheated, unlighted apartments. On the streets at night, after lights-out, one would bump into passersby visible only by the glow of their cigarettes. Except for the lucky few, everyone was always hungry, and the German soldiers gorged at our expense. There was nothing left to eat in the restaurants but carrots and turnips. Several times, nonetheless, I was invited to gigantic meals by the Dadaist poet Georges Hugnet, a friend of Virgil's, enthroned like a lord in his blackmarket restaurant among his mistresses, who grew prettier and prettier. He had lived modestly, just like me, but suddenly he was spending a fortune every day. And even though I had never liked him much—like most of Virgil's, Léon's and my brother's friends—I was infinitely grateful to him for those few superb meals in the midst of famine.

Léon, as I said, was in Nérac, and on his way to the United States. I took possession of his apartment, which would have been confiscated by the Germans, who were seizing all Jewish property unless the owner could prove that three generations of his family had been baptized. Thus my brother lost his apartment, full of all his things. My occupation of Léon's apartment did not stop the Germans from coming in one day and taking away all his rare books and manuscripts in a truck. The Vichy French themselves had been more merciful. But Vichy never stopped raising its demands. Whether you were in France or not, you had to pay all kinds of taxes, and the manager of our building, the dreadful Dr. Pfuhl, kept pitilessly demanding payment of the maintenance on Léon's apartment. So I had to sell some of his belongings: The piano went first; then I pawned the silver and sold the lyre-shaped console, for which Léon never forgave me. But I never touched his paintings.

The money went for the apartment and my own expenses, for I could receive nothing from the United States. Only one person could have lent me money and that was Ivan Effron. He was in the Free French zone but kept up a clandestine correspondence with his agent in Paris, whom I often went to see. But there was never any answer from Ivan to my requests, a mystery I was only able to solve much later when I learned that Jeaninne had told him all about my liaison with Raymonde. I received financial help only once during that grim winter: The Quaker Marvel gave Kristians Tony and me a thousand francs each from our New York friends. All the Jews were in great danger, whether or not they wore the compulsory yellow star. After months of uncertainty, Jean Bertrand, Raoul Leven (Camondo's illegitimate son), and I asked a German painter we knew what we should do. He advised me to keep a very low profile. Léon's Pétainist friend Jacques de Pressac once brought me a young Breton called Brustmitch; he was pro-German and knew Otto Abetz. I was happy to sublet him and his fiancee half the apartment, safe in the knowledge that now it would not be seized. I was paid for several months in advance and never saw them again.

A part of this sad winter was already past when I ran into

an old acquaintance at the Deux Magots: Maryse Robinet d'Uris, who had been married to the son of Joseph Kessel, the writer, and was already divorced. She still wore a Red Cross uniform, had served in an ambulance at the front under bombardment, and, like me, was patriotic, anti-German, anti-Vichy. Now absolutely without financial means, she was starving and froze every night in the garage where trucks were kept. I felt sorry for her and gave her the maid's room on the eighth floor once occupied by Robert, the servant. I took her out to restaurants and she kept me company at Léon's. One night, I went up to her little room to sleep with her, but she refused, saying she was rewarding me with her whole-hearted friendship. The word "reward" put me to shame: I had never thought of claiming one, and so I never propositioned her again although I was shocked by her lack of generosity. After some time, I had her come downstairs to the guest bedroom. Several people, including Nadine—but not I—had complained of receiving mysterious bites in this room, much to Léon's indignation. This time, when Maryse, too, complained, we took away the fringe and the material draped around the bed and uncovered a thick black line that went all around it: a cemetery of hundreds of thousands of bedbugs. I had to have the room sealed and fumigated.

I left Paris only to visit Robert's inn on the Seine. Soon, however, I had to stop these visits because German officers were always there, and our former servant, egged on by his wife, was getting to be more and more pro-Nazi. Then I was invited by Lorna Lindsley, a friend of Virgil's, for a short trip to northern Brittany, where she was to join her young lover in Saint Brieuc. I gave her a small painting in exchange. I didn't especially like her, but just knowing a few people seemed so precious in now-empty Paris. Lorna was a Communist, very ardent, and an adventuress, a hippie, who had liberated herself by scandalizing her family, whose pet hate she had now become. But she was rich and could do anything: sail around Cape Horn, tame wild horses, run here and there, shoot wild beasts in Africa. While visiting Lorna in Paris could be quite pleasant, our northern trip turned out to be a disaster. The spectacle of that weird-looking couple, Lorna and her lover, would shock the good people in the countryside who would stop with open mouths and stare at them: he, young, small, and slight, trotting next to the old stick, thin as a skeleton, dry as parchment, who marched forward with long strides, draped in a cape, a wide-brimmed felt hat descending on her hooked nose. They made as grotesque a sight as Don Quixote and Sancho Panza. I always stayed a few steps back staring at the ground. Nor was this limited to innocent walks and the picking of mushrooms eaten on the recommendation of the village doctor. Wherever the Germans had forbidden people to look and take photographs, Lorna felt compelled to do exactly that, putting us in danger of being arrested as spies. In all the little ports, all the little estuaries, she was interested in the barges and pontoons that the enemy was gathering for the invasion of England. As soon as we went to a beach, the *Feldgrau* would come and ask for our papers. Moreover, we were surrounded by Germans everywhere; all the hotels, for instance, were full of vacationing officers. For me the contrast was especially striking at Les Sables d'Or d'Erquy. There, in the past, I had played around with Raymonde; now, on the door of the Town Hall, I read the names of ten patriots the Germans were going to shoot. Thus, this trip turned out to be neither pleasant nor relaxing for me.

In the spring, I received a letter from my friends, the Fougeroux, asking me to spend the summer with them in Esnandes, near La Rochelle. I accepted with joy and left Maryse in charge of Léon's apartment.

Chapter 11

The Fougeroux Family and Esnandes The Atlantic Wall

1941–1944

I WAS DELIGHTED to join the Fougeroux, whom I hadn't seen in several years. When I left that most depressing Paris, which was occupied by the enemy and where I was now in constant danger of being arrested, I felt I was flying to paradise. I was going to stay with a family I liked and who had adopted me. I was going to see "my" village again and that magnificent dune country where I had painted mussel banks with such fervor.

The Fougeroux, a large family, were cheerful, handsome, close-knit, and happy. One could not have imagined them in a different setting, or away from one another. They would have lost their sheen like shells taken out of the sea. The eldest of the three daughters must have been twelve and the youngest son five when I first met them.

With the whole world full of fire and blood, and individual freedom gone, how can I without shame confess the well-being I felt when I lost myself in this tiny universe? I thought I was Fabrizio del Dongo, Esnandes was my "Farnese tower," and the four Fougeroux women, the embodiment of Clelia. A prisoner of that paradise, I never felt lonely; my ivory tower was resonant with the songs and laughter of the young girls mixed with their mother's good humor. In this amiable atmosphere my taste for life returned. Not only did I help with the work in the house and garden but I taught art and sports to the children. And while I was paying very little for my food (Aunt Mania sent me money every month), I would often give the boys shirts and socks, both things no longer to be found.

The little kids worshiped me, the "flowering young girls" courted me, and the parents esteemed me—a great compliment.

The father, Frank, two years older than I, had been gassed and severely disabled in World War I and thus had had to give up his trade as a cabinetmaker. Since his family allowance and his invalid's pension weren't enough to feed his household, he became a gardener, growing first Parma violets and then strawberries. Since if it were known that he was working he would have lost his invalid's pension, his gardening, as well as their license to operate a café-restaurant, was in his wife Eglantine's name. The café did badly. Frank complained about competition, jealousies, a bad location, the lack of tourists; these ideas were in no way shared by his wife, who taxed her silly husband with Communist talk.

Frank Wilfred Fougeroux was small, thin, nervous, never relaxed, always on the boil. He had the body of a jockey while his head was just like that of God the Father on the north portal of Chartres cathedral. A very hard worker, extremely handy, he made a striking contrast to the beautiful, plump, and placid Eglantine, who reminded me of the majestic Roman peasant women I had seen years ago. The brains and head of the family, she lacked neither ambition nor personality, while Frank felt quite at ease in the restricted life of a low-wage earner. Eglantine wanted a better education for her sons and a higher social level for herself. She was not afraid of starting new and sometimes hazardous enterprises, and she had firm expectations of inheritances that she never received. She was generous, strong, full of authority, charm, and contradictions, feminine, illogical, practical yet lacking perseverance, simple, naive, imaginative, and a fatalist. Nothing, except her hatred for the Germans, could upset or alter her good humor. One day, she arrived late for her train and saw it pulling out of the station. "Too bad for the train," she said.

Since I myself was so in love with the family, how could I have suspected that the parents were unpopular in the village? Local public opinion held it against them that they were foreigners—they had been born in the next village; that they were bourgeois—leading a very private existence behind the high wall of their property right in the middle of the village while the other villagers never closed doors or windows and pursued their lives in front of the entire world. This criticism, naturally, didn't apply to the Fougeroux children, born and bred in Esnandes, who were present at dances, attended school, and shopped in the stores.

Eglantine, the mother-hen, was only happy when she could keep her whole family under her wing. So all the rooms on the second floor were empty except for three. In the smallest were two beds for the three girls; in the fine big room next door were the parents and both boys; I was in the third one at the end of the landing. The doors remained open and, once in bed, the family members would visit one another; conversation flew from room to room until, finally, the family fell asleep. An outsider seemed to upset the clan; but they couldn't do without one another and needed no distractions. The village and its life were their theater. The last one to arrive home always brought some kind of sensational news with him. Leaving out no detail, he would imitate the person, the accent, seasoning his story with many Esnandois swearwords. I would see the whole procession go up to bed at night and come back down in the morning. Before getting into bed, they would all line up in front of the toilet. They were draped in oversize nightgowns that were mirrored in the waxed wood floors. Nothing could have been more chaste than the whiteness of these thick shrouds. One would have thought they were angels and, though wingless, they reminded me of Chaplin's film, *The Kid*. In the morning, though, I would see solid flesh-and-bone creatures, barely awake, their hair tousled, hastily dressed and still smelling of their warm beds, come down in a file. Once they got to the kitchen sink, the women undid the tops of their dresses, the men folded down their collars, and all used the same soapy corner of a washcloth behind the ears. "When I'm rich," Eglantine would say, "I'll have a bathtub to wash in on Sunday and a car to go to the theater." If the inhabitants of Esnandes were no cleaner than any other peasants, their feet, by contrast, were thoroughly washed every night.

I belonged to the Fougeroux clan and had become a new man. The village had no secrets from me. I knew the farms, the paths, the inhabitants, who was who's cousin, or bastard, down to the private life of the good priest who was not scared of preaching against the Germans. Everything was familiar to me: dialect, tax map, even the complex topography of the marshes.

The seasons repeated their cycles of rural labors. I grew strawberries, hoed the vegetable garden, picked mushrooms and lettuce in the fields, caught snails in the bushes, brought back headless squid from the beach, gleaned before the harvest, which was allowed during the Occupation, and took advantage of moonless nights to steal broccoli on the Moindreau hill. After fruitless attempts at getting wood for heating, we first took down a barn, and then the four-century-old oaks in the yard. Then we turned the disfigured front yard into an orchard. Like a new Le Nôtre, I traced paths, planted pear trees, and arranged flowerbeds. Only a part of the "castle" was furnished and inhabited: It was actually no more than a noble-looking house. A short tower near the backyard and the typically Charentais white stucco main porch with its coat of arms broken during the Revolution were the only traces of the past. I was never tired of admiring the facade, dotted with pink and rust wild grape, pierced with French windows; it was now given back to the sun after its long imprisonment in the oaks' shadow.

In addition to loving the Fougeroux, their house and country, I was fascinated by the melancholy grandeur of the vast deserted spaces, as flat and green as a billiard table. The salt meadows were full of cows, the sky and the bay vibrated with flights of birds, and each low tide uncovered mussel shoals. In these maritime vineyards covered with black clusters worked the *boucholeurs* ("growers"), sliding their sleigh-boats along the mud. It was a separate and fantastic world, existing nowhere else. While years before I had painted this world enthusiastically, I no longer had the heart to do so during the Occupation; anyway, I could get neither paints nor canvas.

A hard-to-cross demarcation line split France in two equally occupied halves, the northern by the Germans, the southern by the pro-German Vichy government. And even that half, the so-called Free France, had seen its shores amputated to a depth of fifty kilometers. The Germans decided to fortify these areas, declared them to be military zones, expelled anyone who did not actually live in them, and started to recruit workers among the population. The organization thus created was named after the Labor Minister of the Reich, Todt, the originator of this dreadful slavery. I already had visions of myself being sent back to Paris when the mayor of Esnandes put me down on the town register as a resident. But when the Germans demanded workers to build the Atlantic wall, the poor mayor had to call me up among the very first since I was unmarried and not essential to the life of his village. I felt like a plague victim, rejected by the rest of humanity, dishonored, soiled forever—no matter that my collaboration was forced. On December 1, 1942, the rural constable Dorna handed me my call-up papers; on the second, I went to La Rochelle to register with the recruiting office where, greatly to my relief, I was allowed to choose Esnandes, a future center of major fortifications. On the third, at five-fifteen A.M., I arrived at the mustering point. I had become a number, 39556, according to the *Ausweis*, the German pass, now more important than any identity papers.

Once again, as a Todt worker, I kept a daily account, a document of the occupation, some of which follows as I recorded it:

Night, mud, cold, a few silhouettes around a fire. . . .

I arrive at the mustering point, enter an abandoned village court-yard. It is dirty, sad, open to the winds, and depressing to look at; this is the place where my life will be spent!

In the middle of the courtyard, a dozen men are warming them-selves around a fire. I come closer to the group and join them, holding my painful hands up to the warmth of the flames. We exchange a few words and I look more carefully at the faces that the flickering of the fire alternately lights and darkens.

How beautiful these faces are, though dirty and badly shaven. Would they have been as attractive under ordinary conditions? The hour gives them a feeling of mystery, and the gravity of the moment transforms them into masks remote from all earthly vicissi-tudes; only the eyes stay alive and human.

The sky pales; more and more voices are heard. An imperceptible link is forming between my neighbors and me. All of a sudden, I realize that these men around me are my new family, my com-rades of tomorrow, for we are all in the same jam.

The circle widens, now a crowd is stamping its feet in the mud. I dimly see people of all ages and origins, real and phony workers, draftees and others who by volunteering hope to escape being sent to Germany. The fire is dying. The ramshackle buildings around the yard, the trees, the roofs, the broken-down wall that separates us from the marshes, even the bay in the far distance, all shapes take on consistency and become visible.

Suddenly, a bell rings three times in the old church, a quarter to six, tolling our death-knell. I have ceased to be a free man. From now on, every morning, seven days a week, I must be present when my number is called. The wind sends a torrent of soot flying from the smithy now being lit. A grey day rises on Esnandes and this miserable yard lost between earth and sky. . . .

The draftees who live in the village are allowed to go home for lunch and at night, which is a saving for the French construction companies who have also been forced into this job by the Germans. The people who live nearby arrive each morning on their bicycles. As for the others, who have come from afar, they must still count themselves lucky to be in France and not in a German concentra-tion camp or factory under bombardment.

I now barely see the Fougeroux. Up with the hens while the household sleeps, I shave in the dark for lack of candles or elec-tricity—this last is constantly being cut off. And at night, dinner over, I sink into a brutish sleep. Stupefied by work and exhaustion,

I have no time left to feel sorry for myself. Still, after a week, I am convalescing and feeling that life can be good.

As soon as one feels better, of course, and gets used to things, one becomes more demanding. Those who go home for lunch find the half hour they are allowed too short; and a lot of men complain about the monthly wage, which seems unfair. Why are some draftees paid two or three times as much as others? The wage reflects a salary plus a family indemnity for those who have had to leave relatives behind. And as for the salary, the professional workers get the maximum, the others the minimum. The differential family allowance has been based by the Germans on the relative cost of living in the more expensive cities or in the cheaper countryside. Thus, the draftee from Paris or Lyon, for instance, is paid the maximum, the one from a small town of less than five thousand, absolutely nothing. I am in the lowest class, that is, minimum salary and no family allowance: twenty-three hundred francs a month after taxes and insurance. Since I had not been making a living before, this amount actually allows me to survive without Aunt Mania's financial help.

Everything I see around me is surprising, for I have never been on a construction site. My lack of experience places me at the very bottom of the work hierarchy. Everyone gives me orders, and I am stuck with the lowest jobs. Cleaning the yard, loading and unloading the trucks, bringing the planks to the man in charge of the saw, such are my occupations. I am part of the sawmill—carpentry–structural section run by the Spanish worker Rachadel, who is surrounded by a clan of his compatriots. The whining of the mechanical saw pierces my ears, I am constantly banging and pinching my fingers, the sawdust coming through my shirt irritates my sweaty skin, the twelve-hour workday seems endless. Stupefied, exhausted, exiled, I envy the working-class aristocracy, perfectly at ease and merely continuing to practice its trade.

I am most surprised by the cynical attitude of the workingmen. How can adults cheat like schoolboys? And yet, it is this very lack of dignity that helps to create the resistance. As soon as I understand this, I imitate my new comrades. Aside from the executives and a few specialized workers, everyone is cheating the French companies, which in their turn cheat the Germans. Stacks of wood conceal us, shadowy areas make us invisible, and behind these screens laziness flourishes and chattiness rules. Never before had I realized, even in the regiment, that a man's volubility can surpass that of a feminine chatterbox. And as long as we are all slaves of the enemy, our savvy at goofing off is part of the resistance. Since no rest is allowed, we spare our strength by working in slow motion and by stopping when we feel like it, but without sitting down or putting away our tools. Whoever sees a foreman coming closer gives the alarm by whispering "twenty-two," a secret code word originated by convicts. These magic syllables immediately produce a miraculous effect: We hammer laboriously, attentively measure a plank of wood, and are so absorbed by our work that the pleased foreman walks away. We are even more pleased than he; work stops and chatter starts again.

And then comes a day when a little incident greatly improves my position at work. Since I am the only one who speaks German and since our director, Séjourné, can't communicate with the Nazi officers, he calls on me to interpret. Then he comes to use me regularly in this new capacity. These work stoppages are real holidays for me, especially when he sends me to La Rochelle in his Citroën. There I pick up German engineers whom I take walking through the fields at Esnandes; on their orders, I stick stakes into the ground to mark the place of a future *blockhaus*. A young colonel even wants to take me on as an interpreter-chauffeur but I decline his offer: I prefer being the lowest among French workers to having a high career with the enemy.

Every day the countryside changes; it is becoming a giant ant-heap. My peaceful village of mussel growers, with its courtyards full of faggots and stakes, had been spared a German presence until now. The closest garrisons did not go beyond Nieul. The only sign of the enemy one could see was far away in the marshes where two giant cranes were digging a canal that was to be part of the La Rochelle redoubt. Esnandes was picked to be one of the three hinges of this redoubt because of its three natural defenses: the marsh, the cliff, and the muddy coast. But its life had not been upset until two months ago when three French engineers appeared, followed by a woman. For several weeks, they came every morning and had lunch at the Chocolat restaurant. Then one day lightning struck. The main street was loud with foreign voices, the thunder of trucks, and hammering. Houses and stables were commandeered to be transformed into offices, workshops, dormitories, canteens, and warehouses. There is now no family that does not house a Todt worker. Chocolat and Gauget, the two rival hotel-keepers, who never had anyone take their board, are coining gold by selling clandestinely bought wine to a large clientele. In the spring our work is to grow less intense; then we will be allowed to rest on Sundays. Séjourné is even to organize soccer matches. But dances, that favorite local pastime, will always be forbidden for fear of incidents with the German soldiers.

Since the embankments—i.e., the preparation of the ground for the building of fortifications—are not yet completed, all the workmen, whatever their specialty, are sent to dig the excavations. There, I learn about the shovel and pickax, tools I have used before without realizing how perfectly they are shaped. Still, in spite of my great facility for sports, I am not able to handle a shovel as well as a peasant.

When the Germans drafted us, they did not give us any clothes. We wear our oldest things and look like a horde of brigands; we are actually lucky we don't have to wear a uniform or swastika armband. Our group presents a striking contrast to the dazzling Nazi General Staff we see when Rommel himself comes to inspect the work.

At dawn, the village sleeps. Its shutters are closed, its eyelids down. Dressed in haste, I run toward the main street to join my team as it passes. Except for a few roosters' hoarse cries, the silence is only broken by the sound of my steps in the little street. And yet, I feel the presence of others; I know that other men, still as sleepy as I, are hurrying to present themselves to this damned master. The sky, paling on the horizon, announces a new day of slavery. But now from far off I hear a sound like a murmur; it gets louder and louder and becomes the muted thunder of a marching crowd. Already I can hear voices and footsteps, and suddenly, the human stream catches me up and carries me along with it. I move forward as if borne by a flood, surrounded by shadows whose voices I try to identify. Within a few minutes, the wave has broken on the village and melted away into the night. Six o'clock rings at the fortified Church as we pass it and we move into the marshes. The ground is frozen hard and the moon crescent shines like a diamond.

Cliff of Villedoux! From your summit, we see the day being born and dying. How long will our "eternity" last? As we get to the rock, some say, "Quick, bring on the evening!" And once the evening has come, "And all this has to start again tomorrow!"

The mists thin out, the birds glide, the cattle graze in the salt marshes. Sometimes we see the silhouette of an eel fisherman coming out of a ditch. Behind us, on the wide plateau, a peasant talks to his paired oxen, calling them by double names as is the local custom: "Cavalier-Parfait, Commis-Voyageur, Ruban-Bleu" ("Perfect Horseman," "Traveling Salesman," "Blue Ribbon"). The gulls follow the plow, changing the earthen furrow into foam. Having lost my freedom, I take pleasure in seeing a free world.

It is still night when we arrive on the cliff swept by the north wind. The cold chases us into the excavation but there the humidity is such that, without orders, we start digging frenziedly. A poor, shivering Algerian, his head covered with his thin coat, implores the sun, in the name of Muhammed, to hurry. After a wait that seems endless, the red disk appears on the horizon, then rises. With the warmth, for which we beg as if it were bread and which now penetrates us, we come back to life and put down our tools; the miracle has come! The shower of sunlight spreads down our line and lights us up. Our rags become precious materials and the steel in our hoes shines like diamonds. The magic of a moment, quickly dispelled in the full light of day, restores all things to their usual appearance.

How can I break the chain of which I am the link? Twelve hours' hard labor exhausts me. I neither have the habit of it, nor the strength for it, nor the youthful energy. And in this I am far from alone. What is difficult for some is, by the cruelty of fate, mere child's play to others. Intellectuals, waiters, barbers are exhausted, while heavy laborers—carpenters, bricklayers, and peasants—have never had it so easy. Five specialized workers dig the excavation with drills; the earth is then lifted shovelful by shovelful, and the stones are handed along from one to another in a chain that ends at the little trucks. But two lucky guys get to play around, effortlessly lifting grassy sod from the meadow to be used for covering the future bunkers. Having noticed them, I await the arrival of our overseer, Stomboli, and ask for permission to join them. I receive it.

The days have become so short, night falls so early, that work stops well before six, the official quitting time, and the draftees can go home. But while the carpenters, metalworkers, and welders who were sent back to the mill from the cliff can take advantage of this, the rest of us are the victims of our distance: exhausted as we are by evening, we have a choice between walking four kilometers or waiting around for trucks that arrive only irregularly and that, once loaded, won't stop to pick up pedestrians.

Through a bit of luck, I am transferred to the mill, which I was once so happy to leave for the cliff. Now I am happy to return for shelter from the winter weather. Some joker had broken my pickax and I was sent to the village for a new one. I took my time on the way, visited the Fougeroux, finally got to the sawmill, and, since there were no pickaxes there, awaited Stomboli's arrival. All this meant rest instead of work. And when the overseer arrived, he told me to take back my old place at the mill.

After my plain good luck, nothing less than a miracle! From a beast of burden, I have suddenly become an important person. Since they are starting to deliver building supplies for the *blockhaus*, Séjourné has now appointed me interpreter-delivery man. I work as a foreman. Without, however, getting any increase in pay.

I will now spend my time on the roads, sitting on the high seats of the old trucks or drays along with the driver, shaking in a sort of St. Vitus dance. But what do I care about the shudderings and the creakings of these old jalopies, so long as I can be away from the building site! I drive around in every direction, become more and more familiar with the suburbs of La Rochelle and the villages around it. This moving about near the old Huguenot capital has for me now all the attractions of faraway travel, and I collect my impressions the way I did in Paris or Rome. Every day, my trucks go through Le Moindreau, the highest hill of the region, from which one has an endless view. To the south stand the towers of La Rochelle, to the north, when the sky is exceptionally clear, I can see the steeple of Luçon; the Île de Ré is to the west and to the east are the fallow lands, with whole colonies of birds which give this landscape the appearance of the world's very end.

Each time I can feel the pleasure of entering the old capital all over again, so white, bristling with masts, towers, and steeples. Under the arcades, the crowd becomes more dense as we get closer to the covered market. From my high seat, I admire the eighteenth-century facades adorned with gargoyles; I see again the shady little hotels on the harbor where, since all the other hotels had been commandeered by the Germans, I would take Geneviève in secret; I wave to the widow Lecordier, standing by the door of her rope shop and hail a few acquaintances on the Quai Duperré.

The invasion of Russia is in the air and our trips help to confirm it. The railway station is full of German soldiers already in transit. Others are trying to ski on the lawns of the park. The village garrisons fade away and are replaced by adolescents, old men, and cripples. The city is full of rumors. It is said that some Gaullist flyers, considered traitors by Vichy, had to jump out of their planes during the last flight over La Pallice and preferred death to falling into the hands of torturers. The graves of English flyers are mysteriously adorned with flowers during the night, much to the fury of the occupiers. People talk of English prisoners chained up as in the Middle Ages. True or false, these rumors confirm the public's turning to the Allies, and demonstrate that France can be saved. So our trips to La Rochelle put us in a good mood and we joke as we pass a villa with the incredible name of Les Cénobites Tranquilles.

The commandeered Lying-in Hospital of La Rochelle has become the headquarters of a German organization called Porta, which is in charge of building the Atlantic wall in Charente. It is from the offices of Porta that we receive our orders; it is from the hospital that, armed with duly signed chits, I go off to look for supplies. When he sees me, Chief Engineer Koubitsky smiles, and the employees of the factories, barracks, and warehouses, who work in overheated offices, are delighted to have the same person to deal with regularly, and a person moreover, with whom they can communicate. My routine has turned me into an expert, and my daily contact with the Germans so completely removes my awe of them that one day, in front of my delighted team, I bawl out a disrespectful rookie. Getting assigned to my team is considered privileged duty because since no one keeps track of our time, we are able to take long breaks, sometimes lasting all day, with the help of the truck drivers who are paid by the day.

Of all the supply depots, we prefer the freight station of Angoulin because of its remoteness. There we load steel rails, small beams, T-shaped steel bars, and especially wood; planks of all sizes and thicknesses of which our sawmill is in great need and which are in the greatest supply here. The Algerians, their heads covered with blankets (the first time I saw them, from afar, I thought they were headless giants), unload the convoys of railroad cars. It is painful to see their degraded condition, suffering as much from the cold as from the bad treatment meted out to them by the Germans.

It is forbidden for the truck teams to stop on the way and have a drink, but nothing, not even the fear of a heavy fine, can keep us out of the bars. Deprived of his daily ration since the occupation, no worker can resist the temptation of a glass of red wine, even if a small one costs fifteen francs. These innocent revels depend on me and the drivers. We hide our trucks in the side streets and hope for the best.

The drivers drafted by the Todt Organization are members of a privileged caste. Since trade has stopped and supplies are gone, the shops are empty; the only chance of finding what one needs is either barter or the unfairly maligned black market. And that is where the drivers come in; they hold every trump. Only they have authorization to move around. Their pockets jammed with passes, they alone receive gasoline every morning. They alone are sure of being paid both their salaries and fees for renting their trucks to the Germans—those old wrecks that would otherwise have long been ordered off the road and could not have stayed on the road anyway for lack of spare parts, gas, tires. Among all the French, only drivers and Todt overseers have access to the German warehouses, full of supplies taken from everywhere by the Occupation; only they, for instance, are in touch with the ill-fed watchmen, ready to do anything for a little food. In exchange for some farmers' eggs, butter, milk, or chicken, watchmen can supply drivers with boots, tools, coal, or gasoline. Even the age of these middlemen's trucks is an advantage, for among all the legitimate breakdowns, it is impossible to distinguish a phony one. Breakdowns thus become the excuse for any detour or lateness and provide the drivers with time they can call their own. Even we, unhurried though we are, are sometimes put out when, without warning, one of them stops by his house, his garage, or some farm and keeps us waiting for hours.

Three kinds of theft among the many engaged in by drivers are considered capital crimes. The Germans don't fool around about cement, gasoline, or, especially, tires. One day we notice that Bertrand, a notorious black marketeer, has vanished.

The first time that I enter the fortified camp of La Pallice, I feel sick. The rain is pouring down. After passing Laurières and some evacuated working-class housing projects, our trucks come to a no-man's-land with mine fields, trenches, barbed wire, artillery chambers, underground shelters, and D.C.A. (anti-aircraft guns). On the runway, Nazi planes take off and land. In front of the harbor wall, we have to show our *Ausweis* to the Pétainist militia in their black uniforms—whom we hate, if anything, more than the Germans.

Here we are in Vulcan's smithy, at the foot of the modern Babel, this famous submarine base whose three hundred cubic meters of reinforced concrete have shortened the port by a third, or ten acres. Between the base and the sea, a second block is being built, but it is not quite as large: It is to protect the lock linking the front and back harbors. Along the quays several torpedo ships and one of the famous pocket cruisers are docked. Two submarines are on their way out, their crews saluting.

The painting of the base leaves me puzzled. I can't understand why they use those sharp colors, these black, white, and ochre stripes that look like gigantic cubist frescoes. How repulsive this colored mass looks; the cyclopean proportions frighten me, they remind me of the pyramids, transform us into groups of slaves and reduce human beings to the size of ants.

This is the food situation in Esnandes, a village like many others in occupied France: A few kilos of a meat as hard as rubber, when it isn't scraps, fat, or cartilage, are the monthly ration of an Esnandais; they can be had in the Tonneau delicatessen for tickets, at an exorbitant price and after having queued the whole day.

Our baker, Jamain, like all his colleagues in the area, has received strict orders about the baking of bread. The flour must be 90 percent bran, a third water, and the bread is to be sold only when stale, the day after baking, to discourage consumption. This indigestable food, called "dog's bread," makes you break out in a rash, "bread scurvy."

As for potatoes, they are requisitioned during the harvest on Villedoux plateau by German soldiers who fill bags bearing the inscription "Imported from Germany"; these bags are destined for the Germans themselves. A few weeks later, the mayor gives each person twelve kilos of inferior, half-rotted potatoes. They do not come from our fields but the inscription is the same. This allows the Germans and collaborators to extoll the Reich's generosity, "feeding," as Dr. Goebbels said in a speech on October 8, "a continent which does not deserve it."

One day I receive some incredible news from a man on leave from La Pallice: There was to be a canteen selling meat to the workers on the base who were going on leave. This meat would be of first quality, available without tickets, and dirt cheap. So being alone with my driver one day at La Pallice, I easily convince him to make a detour to see the mysterious canteen. The sentry on duty outside does not even move. As soon as we walk into the dining room, crowded with workers, my eyes pop: My informant has not exaggerated. A magic carpet has, in fact, taken us to a land of milk and honey, where there is an embarrassment of riches. We wolf down several lamb dishes followed by some veal. The abundance, the quality, and the low price thrill us: twelve francs for a portion of meat with vegetables, thiry-five francs for a liter of red wine. It is only after the huge meal is over that, happily sated, I remember the Fougeroux. I have an inspiration: I buy seven more portions and hide them, with the dishes, under the seat in the truck. I can already see myself walking into the kitchen and, like a magician, offering my friends the kind of food that has not been available for years.

The waitresses do not notice the disappearance of the plates. Before leaving this oasis, I go to the kitchen to meet the chef, who immediately wants to sell me half a lamb for forty-five francs, which, unfortunately, I don't have.

Henceforth each time I am near La Pallice, I come to visit this canteen until the day when, finding it closed, I am told that the butcher has been jailed as a black marketeer.

Since we now have all the supplies we need, there are no more deliveries. I have nothing to do, and the weather is bad. Rochadel no longer dares to give me orders. Helplessly, not knowing how to kill time, I begin to envy those who are working.

In order to escape this suffocating feeling, I install myself on the little wall and look in the distance. The embankment of the anti-tank canal now hides part of the marshes and forces some of the bird flocks to make huge detours. Since I have now lost my freedom, the remembered charm of these watery plains only depresses me. Far away, where the seaweed advances into the mud, lies a forgotten wreck. Its angled mast is reflected on the wet ground from which the sea is withdrawing. This boat, suspended between sea and sky, becomes for me a symbol of Liberation. It puts me in mind of other boats, of ships, of an Armada that will bring liberating armies to our coasts. For I trust in Churchill's word, like three-quarters of the people here, and believe that "the Allies will land before the leaves fall off."*

My only distraction during this empty period is to steal bits of plank, leftovers lying under the worktables. In spite of the order forbidding it, I fill my knapsack with them every noon and evening.

* They did, but the following year.

Then I think of stealing three small beams apparently forgotten for months in a corner of the yard. Selecting a good moment, I throw them over the little wall into the marshes so that the Fougeroux boys can take them home in their wheelbarrows at night; but they come home without having found them. How surprised I am the next day when I see them back where I had first picked them up!

What a pleasure it is to leave the sawmill once more and accompany my friend Loulou Texier, a clever young cabinetmaker, to Villedoux cliff. At my request, he is taking me on as a helper for the installation of platforms for the cement mixers. I am impatient to see my old comrades and return to my old haunt. But what a difference has come over the place since I left. It is impossible to recognize the once-lonely plateau of Villedoux. Where the plow once opened its furrow, I see shacks, canteens, roads, railroad tracks, telephone poles. Yet after a winter spent in the sawmill, how pleasant to breathe the sea wind! Spring is coming. The birds fly in harmonious curves, field mice run between the planks, and, in the marshes, partridges sit about confidently, since the Germans forbid hunting.

Because of a new draft we are now two hundred and forty strong: all single men and childless husbands. The site now employs all the men it can get hold of. At the bottom of the cliff, on the side of the road, the steelworkers have set themselves up and the bending of steel rods begins.

In La Rochelle, the Feldgendarmes (military police), always in twos, wearing giant helmets, with a moon-shaped metal plaque hanging around their necks, all speaking perfect French, often quite without accent, control the traffic and give the drivers tickets; and it is a real hail of tickets since the cars are falling apart, working poorly or not at all since nothing can be replaced and the number of circulation permits is growing all the time.

I witnessed a curious scene this morning. Stopped and ticketed by the first Feldgendarmes on the quays because his lights don't work, my driver, who is used to these unavoidable fines, pays without a wince and we start again, only to be stopped some two hundred meters further, and here we go again. Now the headlights are working but not the brake lights in the rear. The gendarmes expect to be paid but this time my driver, sure of being right, refuses to pay the same fine twice, takes out of his pocket the receipt from his previous fine, written on yellow paper bearing today's date. Suddenly we are in the midst of a grotesque and highly unpleasant scene. Forgetting their dignity, and even their impeccable French, the "Huns" begin to shriek as only they can do, accuse us of cheating, and demand the driver show them a receipt on *green* paper, the color of the day.

Stunned, my driver is at first unable to speak, then he rebels, starts swearing, jumps down from his seat and insists on taking the policemen to their colleagues to settle this scandalous business. The incident is closed, however, by the threat of force and we can do nothing but get out of there as fast as possible.

Which of these groups of policemen was stealing from the Reich?

A hay cart is moving slowly along the quay, its horses at a walk, its driver, a German soldier, half asleep on his seat. From the opposite direction comes a woman pushing one of those picturesque conveyances built with anything handy.* As they pass, two bales of pressed straw fall silently from the top of the big cart. Faster than lightning, the woman grabs one of the bales, puts it on her wagon, crosses the canal bridge at a run, and disappears in the labyrinth of little streets behind the Quai Valin. The whole thing takes only a few seconds. The hay cart, whose driver is unaware of what has just happened, goes on its way under the amused glances of passersby. The second bale is still there, the center of attention for the growing crowd. Who will dare brave the hundred-eyed Argus probably hiding in the port? Finally a cyclist gets off his bicycle and, with the crowd's tacit approval, slowly moves towards the bale. But precious time has been lost, the cyclist is old, and suddenly realizes he has no way of carrying this huge object. So discouraged, exhausted by the risk he's just taken, he sits down on the sidewalk and puts his head in his hands. He has just lost an unanticipated golden opportunity, either to sell this bale or to exchange it for something.

A few soldiers finally appear, the entire incident having taken only a minute or two. One of them runs to warn the driver of the cart. Whereupon Judas, in the person of a beggar known to the whole town, makes his appearance. This despicable being, not

---

* A tireless bicycle would pull a box mounted on two wheels often taken from a child's toy. Both vehicles had to carry registration plates and rear lights.

even expecting a reward, tells the soldier about the theft and points insistently in the direction taken by the woman.

Luckily, it is too late to find her and the silent crowd disperses, abandoning the traitor, who is left behind, rubbing his hands.

Cited as a witness in a theft allegedly committed by a Spanish worker named Hervas, I am summoned by the German military tribunal in La Baule. It is an unpleasant job to go such a distance. There are hardly any trains; the ones there are stop at every station; the carriages are overcrowded; the hotels are commandeered, and the restaurants impossibly expensive, offering strangers only carrots and turnips. So when I come across the accused worker in the La Rochelle station, in handcuffs, with a policeman in full uniform, I find it more prudent to join them. As long as we're all going to the same place, I might as well force the Germans to see to all the difficult details. The trip is indeed long and unpleasant. Despite the crowding on the train, as soon as the policeman comes in our compartment empties. This isolation, however, is far from a blessing since Hervas won't open his mouth and the policeman, no doubt believing himself a member of a superior race, doesn't deign to speak either. Just before we reach Nantes, we are joined by a fourth person, the supervisor who is Hervas's accuser.

We get off the train in Nantes after midnight. The place is in total darkness. In the moonlight, not seeing two paces ahead of us, we grope about, walking single file like Breughel's blind men. Since I know the city, I lead with the German's hand on my shoulder and the Spaniard's hand on his. What a sight, a prisoner following his jailer! For Hervas, having given his word he wouldn't run away, has been freed from handcuffs. One wonders what the poor man could have done even if he had run away, in an unknown country without friends, money, food tickets, or identification papers. For both of us, at the moment, the German is the person we are most attached to, the only one capable of taking care of our most urgent needs: food and rest. But all the doors that open to our knock close again; we are entitled only to the hotels commandeered by the Wehrmacht and they are all full. Thanks to the persistence of the German, we end up in Nantes's most elegant hotel where, locked in a luxurious bedroom, I have to share a double bed with Hervas.

The few days spent on this trip will remain, for me, the darkest of the Occupation. Here I am in the enemy camp, among the Germans. I am oppressed by the noisy cheerfulness of the still-victorious soldiers, by the presence of French women serving in the messes, by the portraits of Hitler on the walls, by the endlessly repeated strains of the "Merry Widow." The farther I get from Esnandes, the more I fear I am going to my end. I have been a fool to give up my safety to help save someone I barely know. During the hearings, my Jewish name will certainly be called; I can already see myself in a German concentration camp. These moments of panic are followed by cooler reasoning, and I make fun of my apprehensions. To chase away the black thoughts and kill time, I imagine I am a spy on a secret mission. I watch everything around me, knowing this to be a unique occasion.

Leaving the La Rochelle region, which has been spared by the war, coming out of my hole, I discover a France that is mutilated, bled white, and in its death throes. My trip is becoming a pilgrimage during which I kneel at the grave of a very dear past and say my good-byes. Whether it be Nantes, that martyred city, the victim of two deadly and mysterious bomb attacks, Saint Nazaire in ruins, or the resort of La Baule, transformed now into a fortress, where we arrive the next evening, everything is in a state of lamentable desolation. La Baule has succumbed to the epidemic now ravaging all the coasts. Like anthrax, or the pustules of a gangrenous body, the hideous lines of defense gnaw away at the beach when the tide is low. The ocean walk has become a dead-end corridor. Toward the town, all the streets ending on the boardwalk are blocked with cement walls painted to look like facades; alternating with real houses, they make a defensive line several kilometers long. On the ocean side, the barbed wire blocks access to a beach full of metal triangles stuck in the sand to stop the landing. On the deserted boardwalk, a few idle German soldiers shoot into the sea.

We have to cool our heels for two days before being called by the court.

But everything ends, our turn comes, and we are introduced into the sitting room of a sumptuous villa. The first thing I notice is a long table covered with a swastika flag behind which sit several dazzlingly outfitted naval officers. Others are called first, then it is our turn. The supervisor makes his accusation, and I answer him, speaking in French. But since the interpreter translates badly, I annoyedly switch to German, which amazes the judges and predisposes them in our favor. My alibi, anyway, is positive: When the theft took place, the accused was dining with me at the home of his fiancee's father, the mailman Perrot (he it was who had begged me to be a witness). The plaintiff begins to contradict himself, and the tribunal acquits Hervas—who has already suffered four horrible months of prison—thanks me for my help, and pays me for the workdays I have missed.

There is no joy on the Spaniard's face. He doesn't even thank me as we set off with the policeman on our unpleasant return trip.

A tragic week that begins with the fatal fall of Catebras, the chief metalworker. Neatly dressed before going on leave, he is coming to say good-bye to his fellow workers. He slips and falls into the excavation, which is full of metal spikes. We take him out unconscious, with his head open, and bring him to La Rochelle where, to our indignation, the Saint-Louis Hospital at first refuses to admit him.

We have barely gotten over this loss when a tragedy strikes the workmen: The Germans are drafting men born between 1898 and 1901 and sending them to work in the bombed-out factories of the Reich. Leaving their identity cards at the office, many young men disappear, go in hiding somewhere. All through France, a hunt for human game is opened.

From the window of the Forestier mill, now a cement dump, I can see the blue sky above the village roofs. Easter is coming, the swallows are here, the hawthorn is in bloom—so are the apple trees, and the peasants compare them to the Church on Communion Day. In the streets, the children ring the "Stabat Mater" with their "*racassous*," "rattles" that they shake in evocation of the old story of the bells going to Rome.

After a hard winter, there is joy in the coming of better days.

We have been around the countryside so much that we are now familiar with the fortifications of the La Rochelle redoubt. They are feeble obstacles to a landing, we think. Then we realize suddenly, with surprise, that everything looks to the land, not the sea.

The redoubt is shaped in a wide semicircle with La Rochelle and La Pallice in the center, the base leaning on the sea and the outside perimeter going through the following villages: Villedoux, Andilly, Donpiere, Saint Rogatoon, La Jarne, and La Jarrie. The line of fortifications is neither visible nor continuous, unlike the Great Wall of China. Only an expert eye would be alerted to certain signs that there are hidden defenses. I deplore the disappearance of the fine poplars that once grew along the Maran canal; the Germans have taken them down to make for greater shooting visibility. But it is starting in Donpiere, where the plains begin, that the country has been the most ravaged. There the farmers live surrounded by minefields, barbed wire, and anti-tank stakes. The redoubt is simply a phony landscape rife with traps. All is dangerous, nothing is what it seems. The artillery chambers and their guns are hidden; the *blockhauses*, which will shield garrisons, are buried; only the airpipe emerges aboveground, like the periscope of a diving submarine. Fortified farms, some in the open country, some hidden in woods, are full of troops. Anti-tank obstacles, metal rails stuck into the ground, cement walls and steel doors brought here from the Maginot line restrict to a single narrow passage the entrances to the villages. A staggered system of machine-gun nests commands several of the roads. Everywhere you can see the red spots of the fez: Teams of Algerians are digging ditches for telephone wires that will link all the strategic points of the area. The lines of younger grass and the bumps on the roads indicate their course. While each defense emplacement in itself seems insignificant, the ensemble is impressive. We are flies caught in a spider's web. If our muddy coast, unsuitable to an invasion, is in this state, what must it be elsewhere! Remembering La Baule, I try not to think of it.

Starry night, spotlights, trestles: Is a movie company shooting exteriors in front of our fortified church? No, the reality is more prosaic; we are casting our first *blockhaus*.

Klieg lights show up the scene in which I have a walk-on part. Since being drafted, I'd always wondered what casting was like; the very word intrigued me. And however banal the event may be, it is not without grandeur; I can imagine hell looking very much like it. Wrapped in poisonous vapors, the damned labor without cease. The cement dust powders our bodies with a phony snow, makes our faces into plaster masks, gives our eyes a strange beauty; they are shiny, wide-open, as if lined with kohl. A visionary looks at the world, a soul in torment speaks through it. This sabbath soils the church and tombs: The Germans have come up with the diabolical idea of burying the *blockhaus* in the graveyard among the dead so as to protect it from bombardment. And since the cemetery was too small, part of its wall has been torn down and rebuilt. Divided into night and day shifts, all workers take part in the casting, which lasts for about forty-five hours.

Months have passed since the ground was first broken; with the help of many other workers, excavators have prepared a hole; the cement workers have cast a floor on the bottom, the carpenters have put together a frame built of separate pieces at the sawmill; the metalworkers have filled this frame with metal rods going up, across, sideways. Then, for the casting, a temporary platform has been put up above this whole ensemble; on it are motors, electrical lines, transformers, concrete mixers, tracks, and a water reservoir.

Once the casting starts, it cannot be interrupted. The concrete mixers will continuously make cement from the mixture of gravel, cement powder, and water. Little carts pour it down funnels into the platform. The mix goes down to the bottom of the frame, is shaped by it and hardens to become concrete—actually, because of the steel rods, reinforced concrete.

The rest is just routine. Like a sculptor breaking the mold to reveal his statue, a few workers will free the *blockhaus* of its temporary structures, fill the spaces between its walls and the edge of the excavation, cover it with earth, erase any trace of its existence with plants. Only the airpipe and the concealed door are left.

The cement bags weigh fifty kilos; since their arrival by truck never stops, the workers must carry them to the cement mixers at a run so as to keep time. For we are casting too fast, putting in too much water. It is sabotage. We are moved mostly by patriotism, but that does not preclude our self-interest. Since the Germans are paying a fixed price for the *blockhaus*, Séjourné trades or barters with the extra cement bags, thus helping local masons who are short of materials; as for the workers, they get to rest for a few hours. It is, however, a dangerous game, for German cars come all too often, bringing officers, engineers, and inspectors who select samples of our mixture directly from the carts and take them away in their test tubes to have them analyzed. To obviate this danger, we have a permanent watchman who stands on the water reservoir, the highest point on the site, so as to give the alarm; the cement makers then immediately thicken their mixture.

Unfortunately, the accident happens at the break of day when everyone is exhausted. The watchman had gone to sleep and, suddenly, those damned Germans, as if springing from the ground, are already at the site and going toward a cart that will supply them with obvious proof of our treachery. No miracle can save us now! And sure enough, we hear wild shouts, the Germans are shrieking, literally tearing their hair, and mean to throw us all in jail. Were it not so grave, the scene would be comical. Stomboli sends a cyclist into Esnandes to wake Séjourné, who drives up hurriedly in his Citroën and talks fast, insisting that the French method of softer casting has its advantages, saying it is only an accident anyway, and finally managing to avert the disaster.

The casting at the cemetery is followed by two others at the Villedoux cliff, with diverse results. For the first, I have to work beyond my strength, for the other, I am lucky enough to sleep instead of being there.

Two splendid starry nights allow Allied planes to fly over us. As soon as we hear their roar, we put out all fires and disperse into the bushes.

Since these raids come so often, Séjourné decides to have one of us stay in Esnandes as a night watchman, in the dormitory linked by phone to the customs office, which in turn is in permanent contact with La Rochelle. In case of an alert, I am to jump on a bicycle and pedal to the cliff at top speed.

But nothing happens, and I spend my two nights sleeping the sleep of innocence.

The arrival of two new people starts an era of change. While the coming of the first is greeted favorably by everyone, the second causes universal displeasure and finally costs me my job as an interpreter.

The first of the two, Miard, comes from Paris to replace Rochadel, who is a mere workingman. As a result great improvements are brought to us carpenters. Now, finally, we feel we are in good hands, that we are at the same level as the other trades. Miard's open and human spirit and his deep technological skill make him both the workers' friend and the executives' favorite; he will be listened to and obeyed. He stops the awful burden of Sunday work imposed on us by the Germans. He raises the carpenters' salaries so they equal those of the other workers. From 6.50 francs an hour, I go up to 7.60 and finally to 8.40. While Miard is purposefully blind to our laziness, as soon as his responsibility is in question he demands real effort.

Opposite the Café Gauget, replacing our miraculous canteen, which has been taken over by the Germans, a German bar-general store opens its doors and displays in its windows the famous "*ersatz*" as well as some products stolen from France. A few housewives are seduced at first by objects of immediate necessity but they quickly give up when, to their fury, they find their purchases unusable. The pleasure of once more buying goods that had vanished at the beginning of the Occupation is only too brief: They are all fakes, ghosts, insults, caricatures worthy of a new kind of waxworks. Sewing thread, string, candy, combs, all break, unable to resist pressure or humidity. Soap, absolutely devoid of fat, foams no more than a stone. Razor blades scratch. Eglantine Fougeroux breaks several combs and finally gives up having one for the entire family. She washes her new *ersatz* blouse and never sees it again: It has melted away. The housewives ignore the bras but give in to nylon stockings: disastrous purchases. The bar-general store will soon be empty of women. And as for the men, they never once go in. Can you imagine a peasant or a fisherman perching himself on a high stool in front of the bar to sip a liqueur instead of drinking his red wine standing up before the zinc-covered bar of his cafe?

Moreover, since the canteen has been taken over by the Germans, hygiene and chemical food have replaced our good stews. Everyone is upset by it. The house used as a canteen wasn't overclean: It simply looked like many others in the village. This wasn't to the Germans' taste. All was changed from top to bottom. The inside was painted white, two sinks were added, the chimney widened so it would draw better, fly catchers hung from the ceiling, the pipes outside cemented in, the garbage and toilets relegated to the backyard. And, crowning all these modernizations, a new cabin appeared in the middle of the courtyard with an enormous, brand-new boiler inside, decorated with levers and manometers. This standard Todt machine chews up the standard Todt stew, a tasteless mixture of mashed potatoes, chopped-up vegetables, and a trace of meat; our palates can never get used to this daily pap.

The presence of the occupier is felt more and more; it weighs on us even when we stay home. In the main street, German soldiers pass, walking in step, singing war songs. And we hear other songs coming from the school where, first thing every morning, the children begin with the hymn to Pétain:

> "Marshal, we are with you,
> With you, O kind savior of France . . ."

And during class:

"No more slackness,
No more laziness,
No more frowning faces . . ."

In other words, no sulking against the generous occupier! We must be happy with the Occupation, Laval keeps insisting in his speeches; and on June 22, he proclaims: "France cannot remain passive and indifferent before the immense sacrifices consented by Germany to build a Europe in which we will belong. French workers, it is for your country that, in great numbers, you will go and work in Germany."

Here is a spelling text of Roger Fougeroux, age six, which I copy here without his spelling mistakes:

"I am the shoemaker
I know there are frivolous people
like the rich in the cities
Who wear shoes made of leather.
It's unhealthy, it's ugly,
It makes for misshapen feet. . . ."

Even before the Todt Organization took over, sports had been imposed in the village. To everyone's indignation, Esnandes received the order to make a sports field in the big space behind the town hall. "Son of a whore!" Eglantine would say. "That beautiful field Favart has to give up! To think we've lived long enough to see this nonsense of which nothing will be left when we get rid of the Huns. The young will go back to dancing and my rascal [Coco] will forget his ball [soccer]. Now he's killing himself on Sunday instead of resting and uses up his shoes when we have nothing to put on our feet."

Thus the good Eglantine, as the practical woman she was, in her indignation only expressed what everyone thought. The German-mandated female basketball team brings another revolution with it: the wearing of shorts. In this new outfit, the local girls walk around proudly, showing off their milky white, short and pudgy legs; it is as remarkable an emancipation as that of the Turkish women when they gave up the veil. Still, among children swimming is most successful. This is not due to German propaganda, but to a little accident during the digging of the anti-tank canal when a section caved in and created a small beach. Since almost no one in

France, not even sailors and fishermen, knew how to swim, the progress made by the village children under my tutorship is amazing. The beach has even become a goal of the parents' Sunday walks so they can see their children having fun. And even a few young couples, wearing their nightshirts or old-fashioned bathing suits, are now bold enough to go into the water.

My popularity is at its crest, my career at its summit: Village and workers, all need me. The accelerated deliveries make me dizzy, between the truck and my bed, not a moment's leisure. I barely have time for lunch at the Fougeroux: I am always being interrupted by people asking for help, peasants, mussel growers, the teacher, even the mayor himself. All bring offerings: a chicken, some grain, eggs, all need my help with the German customs men who know neither French law nor the usage of the sea. The customs men have given our boats a new anchorage, and it is dangerous. They are suing mussel growers whose boats bear Communist names when, by law, it is forbidden to change them. I am happy—my role as a lawyer-interpreter is lively, creative, and varied, and I have the pleasure of serving the public good.

As for the deliveries, they are beginning to interest me. My contact with the watchmen gives me vast possibilities of exploitation. Still, it costs my pride dearly when I make my first request to the enemy, even if it is only a few sticks of wood so Eglantine can do her cooking. But I become used to it and think of it no more. Often the watchmen ask me for farm products or, simply, I take something on the sly without asking for permission.

How far I have come since my beginnings at the sawmill when I would secretly bring home a small bag with a few end pieces of planks and feel as if I had done a heroic act. Today, a watchman gives me five enormous beams without asking for anything in return just because they have a few small defects. My wood stock, hidden in the Fougeroux shack, already weighs more than five tons! It is therefore not theft I worry about, but how to hide what I have appropriated. It is a difficult problem, a hide-and-seek game with Séjourné, who would naturally suppose, if he found me out, that I'm stealing from his own stores and, anyway, would forbid me to continue setting a bad example.

So, every day, I have the same constantly changing problem depending on the direction from which we enter the village: Where shall I put my wood before we reach the sawmill? The Fougeroux house gives on to a small street. A stop there or a detour to it would look suspicious, and a bad hiding place has already made me lose some wood, taken away by invisible witnesses.

When we get to the place I have chosen, the truck slows down and, helped by my team, I slide the wood into a ditch or throw it behind a hedge. When we come back with the five beams, we stop in the little street and, from the top of our load, are able to throw them over the boundary wall. Once they almost fell on the Fougeroux who were weeding in just that section of their garden.

I continue increasing my usefulness as a go-between. The Dutch in charge of the coal at La Pallice, for instance, are starving because they are being punished by the Germans for the Resistance in Holland; so I convince Séjourné to give me three loaves of bread, which I exchange for three tons of coal, including three bags for the Fougeroux.

Among the big sheds in the village, one belonging to the Fougeroux was requisitioned, much to the detriment of the angora rabbits that were raised there. It is now one of the four cement warehouses. The coming and going of the trucks is bad for the orchard; every time the cheap paper bags are loaded or unloaded, in spite of all the care, some burst, giving out a grey powder that burns everything it touches and is itself spoiled by its contact with the air. To calm the furious Fougeroux, Stomboli has authorized Frank to pick up this precious waste. But this compensation hardly seems enough when the Todt Organization pays nothing for the use of the shed. At first, we kicked open a few bags to get their contents, but since no foreman keeps an inventory of the bags when they arrive or leave, we think it better to hide some intact bags in the back kitchen and do not realize how dangerous this is. Why are we so stupid when we can just help ourselves in the shed? In the dark of night, when the village is asleep, we "oblige" a bricklayer, "recompense" a first cousin, help out a neighbor, and they bring us in their wheelbarrows covered, peasant-fashion, with a tarpaulin, unseen, unheard, a bag of wheat, potatoes, or eggs. Learning from example, we cast a new floor in the washroom and another basin at the back of the garden.

Paradoxically, the Occupation and the presence of the Todt Organization does bring certain great advantages to the villages of Marsilly, Charron, and especially Esnandes. That is, the universal food shortage in France gives an unprecedented impetus to the growing of mussels. The trucks of the neighboring regions come down to the harbor to load them. The poor mussel growers who, in peacetime, couldn't make a living, now export their maritime harvest by the ton, already bring in next year's production, and pocket thousand-franc notes at every tide. The prices go up and, unlike the peasants who hide their profits in a wool stocking, the mussel growers, aware that soon the devalued currency will be worth nothing, immediately invest it in their clean little houses. Their humble interiors are now modernized: imitation wood in the staircase, model kitchens, electricity scheduled to be connected after the war. The two rival hotels, Gauget and Chocolat, are enlarged. After years of idleness for lack of cement, one can again see the builders on their scaffoldings; they have all the cement they need. They use ours for repairs and, for bigger jobs, the bags Séjourné has sold or exchanged with the big mussel growers.

All the workers who have access to the sawmill warehouse secretly take whatever the villagers need, thus pillaging the Germans. Electric wire, motor belts, boots, gas, oil, grease, and tools are moved to the farms. Some Todt workers become a farmer's friend and his wife or daughter's lover. Two marriages have taken place during the winter. Two or three mama's sons are protected by Séjourné because he needs their help. None of the workers is offended by this. It is the case, for instance, of Pierrot Duprat, who arrives an hour late every morning from Charron but brings Miard a liter of red wine. The case of Guy Narquet is more edifying: His father finds, and will continue to find, cows and oxen for Séjourné's clandestine slaughterhouse. The son thus only appears on the site a few days a month so he can be said to work. We sometimes meet him on the road, pushing his herd before him.

Only once have I found Séjourné to be an ingrate. The Germans in Angoulin made a memorable error when they forgot to check out two truckloads of wood, thus enabling me to make our director a ten-thousand-franc gift. He advised me never to mention this, but forgot, alas, to buy my team a round of drinks.

A few weeks ago, my thumb was almost cut off; this morning, someone's clumsiness causes a chain saw to explode and two of my fingers receive deep cuts; I am sent home. The nice doctor from Bechavel comes and gives me an anti-tetanus injection; I am to spend three days away from the mill.

Delicious hours in spite of my pain, slow and calm days of sweet isolation, I even feel I have gone back centuries to the time when peasants led primitive and self-sufficient lives. In a France worn down to the core, pillaged by resident Landsknecht, each housewife becomes a heroine of improvisation. Each home is an Ark of Noah traveling through the flood. Here is a glance at the daily activities of the Fougeroux, a family of market gardeners, handicapped compared to the peasants but much more at ease than city dwellers.

Eglantine does her wash with wood ash. The eldest girl, the pretty Christiane, darns the "potatoes," the holes worn the previous day in the old socks without which men would hurt their feet inside their wooden clogs. Since one can buy neither socks nor wool, Christiane has to unravel the most worn-out ones, and the coming together of the different colors produces surprising polychrome effects. The sweet Geneviève churns butter, a delicate task that can succeed or fail, go fast or take forever. To get a churn, it was first necessary to find a model in the neighborhood, learn how to use it, then borrow it so that Fougeroux, an ex-cabinetmaker and a very handy man, can copy it. As for the youngest, Gisèle the merry, who is just one big burst of laughter, she combs the wool and turns the spinning wheel that, after an endless quest, we found in an attic in Marsilly.

Here is the evening. Fougeroux comes in from the garden followed by his shadow, Frank II, or Coco, and they, after having washed their feet, join the women in the little room used as a dining room, which buzzes like a hive. The father cuts heel pieces, Coco prepares traps where the wild ducks "will come at night to neighbor themselves." The Germans have requisitioned all the coffee grinders to stop the villagers from making flour, but that doesn't prevent Eglantine from making us pancakes. To the sound of voices and hammer blows are now added the trills of a saxophone that Gisèle is practicing and the garbled radio broadcast. The B.B.C. speaker announces: "This is London. You are now hearing [or not] our third news bulletin." And all that cacophony in no way bothers Gégé, who is doing homework. He asks me for help in solving his problem: "A retailer buys 20 chickens and 15 ducks for 500 francs, then 10 chickens and 18 ducks for 444 francs; what are the prices of a chicken and a duck?"

We feel the pleasant warmth of the nest, the whole family is snuggled down in its lair. In spite of the daily headaches, our primitive life and the father's obsession for pre-war dishes (a common phenomenon), morale is high. No one complains, and yet heaven knows the wait for the Liberation is heavy. All those who are not collaborators are feeling slowly stifled like the crew of a sunken submarine holding onto the hope of being saved. The sense of time is wiped out; the past seems short because of its monotony. No change, no new event interrupts the succession of days. Months and years are too much alike. We are hungry without appetite. Mussels and "mojettes" (white kidney beans) follow mojettes and mussels—and we're lucky to have them! We've brought the beans from the Vendée, avoiding the French police on the way: That area has been the least affected by the Occupation and wealthy peasant weddings still last several days, the way they did before the war. "Vary your dishes, don't tire the stomach, and especially eat heartily," an old cookbook advises, while Professors Tonon and Perret, in a speech delivered at the Academy of Medicine, recommend eating rat; it is excellent, they say, almost better than rabbit or pork. "Why are you complaining," a paper asks with surprise, "when you have such a free choice: lucern-grass, leaving the stalks for your rabbits, peanut cattle-cake (no, Madame, it is not only for animals), soja (a complete food), and substitutes (or asses' success,* as the peasants say)?"

We hear that the flag of famine flies over Bordeaux and that cabbage, thyme, and parsley tickets are handed out. In La Rochelle, fat people and dogs have disappeared. The number of tuberculosis victims is rising; Roger, like all other French children, never sees candy. Except for barter, shops have nothing to offer. Lacking sugar, people look for beehives or honey. After much effort, Eglantine found sugar beet seeds. Once harvested and boiled, this vegetable gives her a barely sweet blackish liquid; the residue helps keep our animals alive. Pingouin and Fauvette, the two German shepherds that we haven't the heart to kill, are reduced to skeletons. Finally, thanks to my unexpected meeting with an old friend, André Fourmentin, a shipowner from Boulogne, now a refugee with his trawlers in La Rochelle, we are able to save them. André introduces me to the Dahl fishery, where I'll be able to buy bags of fish flour. We'll give it to the dogs mixed with sour milk and the beet residue. This strange mixture keeps them perpetually thirsty. The lack of grain gives the poor hens constipation. The eggs, as Eglantine says, "stay in their behinds," or they lay tiny, shell-less eggs.

For lack of tobacco, people smoke leaves and grass. Each extolls his choice, his mixture, his drying method. As for me, I have never been sick, but I have known some severe cases of extreme intoxication. When I have nothing left to put in my pipe, I strip a young tree in the garden, cut the leaves into thin pieces,

---

* A pun in French.

and dry them in the sun or on the stove. The monthly tobacco ration is down to two packs of Gauloises or one pack of tobacco per person of either sex. Since no housewife smokes, the men take advantage of it. You cannot imagine the bad quality of the tobacco and the waste products we find in it. A few tobacco plants, grown secretly in a distant corner of the garden, are also smoked too green.

Life under the Occupation is a cunning fight starting anew every day. It is a great achievement to cook without gas, wood, coal, charcoal, or electricity and to light the stove without matches, paper, or a lighter. For this last, even if you could find a drop of gasoline, you could get neither flint nor tinder. How often, as I go down a side street, do I hear an old man's trembling voice begging me to light his fire! Many people live without light. Electricity is down to twenty kilowatts a month with, however, a little extra for women in childbirth. The other day, in the widow Lecordier's rope shop, a woman in mourning came to beg for a candle so she could sit up by her dead husband.

The newspapers are reduced to such a small format that it is impossible to take them seriously, especially with all the lies they print. We still buy them because we need paper, for the toilet, for instance. Not only is there no toilet paper, but all paper, including school notebooks, is sparingly handed out. Because of its scarcity, the teacher, instead of giving extra work to a punished pupil, slaps his face, which the student also prefers. I even wonder how school-children can manage to write with ink like water, blotters that don't blot, and scratchy pens.

Everything has been going from bad to worse for the poor French, and now nature gets into the act. Drought is grilling vegetable gardens, no more vegetables in the markets. In the streets of La Rochelle, in scenes reminiscent of the Middle Ages, water-sellers ring their bells. In the country, anti-Christ is evoked more and more often. The war will end, the peasants say, when the wheat rots; they pass from hand to hand a printed prophecy made by Saint Odile in the eighth century that actually mentions a Germania wanting to conquer the world but, in just retribution, is to be punished "ex omnibus partibus."

With the harvest about to take place, the peasants have an urgent need of pre-war string as bales cannot be tied with *ersatz*, which resists neither pressure nor humidity. To obtain such string, he would give an empire," which is to say, wood or two hams. There, too, André Fourmentin comes to the rescue. Every time the trawlers come in he gives me cod and soap made secretly out at sea. He now hands me a royal present: four balls of good string. The Fougeroux, who are grateful, will supply him with strawberries and will exchange the string for two hams. These, the wood accumulated in the shack, and our cement are the master cards in this game of survival.

On the second day after my hand is hurt, I go with Gégé on what used to be my favorite walk, to the port and the grottoes. The two words give the wrong idea of the reality. We call grottoes the shacks where the mussel growers (*boucholeurs*) put away their implements; the port is where the plates are anchored near Saint Clement's Cape. The place is wild and picturesque and only comes to life with the tides, that is to say, the arrival and departure of the *boucholeurs*. Besides the cliff, one sees a few small trees, faggots, stakes, and rods leaning against the shacks, ponds in the middle of the stones on the beach to wash the mussels, a pavement stone half in the mud and, in the distance, mussel reservoirs on a series of piles. This landscape with its mussel vineyards is unique in the world.

As we come out of Esnandes, the road goes straight between the watery plain and a reddish cliff, partly covered with ivy and very Courbetlike. Seaweed, rushes, yellow flowers advance on the dry mud, which becomes wet when washed by the movement of the tides. The sea, the sky, the sandy shore of the Vendée in the distance blend today in an opaque radiation. It is a laguna where everything is reflected, nothing moves, nothing has a shadow, and where only two or three details, mysteriously lit, can be clearly seen.

All along the way, multitudes of birds wheel over us; I feel as if I am going into a winged universe, vibrating with flight. On the horizons, the flocks look like plasms, transparent scarves sometimes shaken by an invisible hand when a bird of prey comes among them. As we go closer, here and there, the red pelt of the marshes wrinkles; it is the result of the mass rising of groups of starlings. Colonies of seagulls, those snowdrops of the shore, trace a harmonious curve where the wave expires. Sparrow hawks stand motionless in the air. And behind the cliff, like lava thrust up from a volcano, the crows come up.

We go, little Gégé and I, to fetch two *mannequins* ("baskets") of mussels, which Eglantine sells with her vegetables once a week in the covered market of La Rochelle. The little boy gets between the cat's shafts and plays at being the horse. We run, for, in the distance, we already see the *boucholeurs* with their boat-sleighs sliding before them.

And suddenly, debarkation fever is in the air. We make a dash against time to get there before the tide, coming in with the speed of a galloping horse. In a few minutes, the last *boucholeurs* have come in, the mussels have been washed, put into baskets, loaded on trucks, and the beach is empty again as the last men leave on bicycles, in trucks, or on foot.

The hostilities started by Séjourné with a view to making life impossible for the new German head of the canteen claim me as their first victim. In spite of Miard's protests, the director takes me away from the sawmill and I lose my job as interpreter.

The cause of my exile was the closeness of the canteen and the mill. Since the sawmill yard had all the supplies needed and I was doing nothing, the German asked me to go with him to fetch food in Rochefort. I refused. Then he asked me to make two signs, which I thought I'd better do: one for the dining room, the other for his new infirmary. When I told Séjourné the next day, he immediately sent me away from the mill, furious that the German had used one of his workers without his permission. He did offer me a job as his secretary, which would have meant spending the whole summer indoors and, finally, when I refused, he made me a part of Tonton's flying team.

But who is Tonton, and what is his flying team, called the Woodpigeons?

Recently arrived from Paris, Tonton, a pleasant man, was not trusted at first because the unpopular Stomboli was his uncle. He invented the flying team, a stroke of genius comparable to Columbus and the egg. Tonton, over sixty, with no trade, trying to be useful, suggested using a light truck as a permanent liaison between all the different sites; this innovation was to spare the director time and unnecessary expense. Until then, the trucks rented by the day to bring in the supplies were too busy to help where needed, too heavy to go through muddy fields or up a slippery hill. But we always needed to move from one site to the other—something had been forgotten, someone had to be fetched. As soon as the light truck is put at the disposal of the overseers, its usefulness becomes so obvious that Séjourné wants to have a second one. But the two teams are not to get along, the new one being unable to forgive the Woodpigeons their seniority and popularity.

For we are some team! I am more than a little proud of sharing in its name both for strength and laziness. It is made up of the cream of the crop, strong, handsome men with knapsacks full of treasures. Under a perfect sky, these toughs go around bare-chested, singing together, and bringing all the girls to their door-ways. No more deliveries for me, no more waiting in the grim saw-mill yard, no more contact with the hated enemy. For the first time, I feel free, young, careless in the company of these attractive adolescents and, like them, I am ready for all kinds of mischief. I barely have to lift a finger; it is like holiday at work.

There are eight of us, including Tonton and me. Two cousins, the Narquet of Nantilly (one of them, Guy, the son of the cattle dealer, has bags full of meat), the miller Forestier of Saint Michel en l'Herm (bags full of white bread), Etanchot, the fisherman from Fouras (fish), Gaudin the barber, son of the best restauranteur in La Rochelle (meat and delicatessen), and Boucher, son of a Fetilly butcher (meat). Wine keeps pouring out and every one feeds Tonton and me, the poor relations. We enjoy taking turns driving the truck. Its owner is happy to give us the wheel so he can sleep; some of us are inexperienced drivers, others experts. When we get to a site, we start with friendly stone fights, then lie down in the grass. Tonton never reproaches us with anything; that is how he holds us. Seeing that none of the cheerful young men is ready to work, the poor old man, bending sometimes under too heavy a burden, starts in courageously; then we feel ashamed, everyone pitches in, and, in no time, the job is done.

Everywhere, I continue to get wood; this special vice leaves me defenseless before many temptations! The difference is that now I can indulge openly thanks to a trick: the "bench." Since the back of the truck does not have any seats, at each site I take a few planks on which the team can sit while in transit. These, however, at a place chosen by me, are thrown from the moving vehicle into a ditch or on the other side of a hedge. It is an amusing sport since it must be done so that Tonton, sitting next to the driver in the cab, will know nothing. But when, instead of going through the small side streets, our truck, backfiring away, comes down the main street, the only place where I can unload, if I do not want to waste the trip, is the empty lot between the Cooperative and the Bidot carpentry shop. It thus happens in full sight of harmless passersby, but with the risk of being noticed by an overseer. My friend Bidot, wounded in the war, a builder of flat boats despite his atrophied arm, helps me hide my wood out of hatred for the Germans.

But, suddenly one day, everything starts to go wrong with my wood. My comrades get fed up with my game. They prefer to give the wood to their friends. But since they aren't careful enough, all becomes known. An inquiry gets nowhere; still, I have to give Tonton my word that I won't do it again. And since he is the only man I respect, my wood supply is finally cut off.

What a contrast between Séjourné and Stomboli!

Séjourné, the director, is a Parisian engineer, tall, pot-bellied, with flabby flesh, bent back, rounded arms, and cauliflower ears. He is a typical intellectual who has neglected his body from childhood. His shirt is dirty, his badly knotted tie hangs crooked. Stomboli, the head overseer, on the other hand, is small, squat, neat, closely shaven, cologned, and carefully dressed. Wearing a hunter's outfit, adorned with gaiters, this ex-boxer is a perfect fop. His jaw reminds one of an English bulldog and his weasellike eyes make you feel uneasy. Stomboli can neither read nor write. A mysterious war friendship links the two men who live in the same house in the village with the young and pretty Madame Séjourné, Stomboli's supposed mistress.

The overseer was always very nice to me. I used to be grateful and did not slander him like the others. Later, though, our relationship was to be spoiled by a memorable game of billiards.

We were of even strength and sometimes played together but I always lost until the day when I caught him cheating. Instead of taking it lightly, I decided it was my turn to win and cheated as well, adding points to the score. How great was my surprise when, the game over, the loser accused me of cheating before the whole café! I kept silent, my face red, not daring to tell the truth.

On the shifting sands of the Occupation, all this work gives me temporary safety, which is menaced anew each time our identity cards are demanded by the office. That means a new recruiting wave for the bombed-out factories of the Reich. The Germans have by now learned from recent desertions and hide their game so well that this time none of us suspects anything until it is too late: One evening, at the end of the day's work, soldiers come by truckloads to surround and take the men born in 1924 and 1925. A few friends escape the roundup, however. Bourgeron vanishes, Forestier goes into the hospital for appendicitis; as for Duprat, it suddenly turns out, according to his card, that he was born in 1923! Only the next day are the terrified families notified and allowed to come and say good-bye to their children, bringing them some clothes and money.

Throughout France, a great cry of indignation rings out. The roundup takes place the day before the Allied landings in Sicily and just before the Führer's last speech, in which he says: "If I were fighting adversaries worthy of me who knew how to fight a war, I'd know where they'd land—but since they're all just imbeciles. . . ."

This last bleeding of manpower has had disastrous effects; discipline is now gone. Work stops, which is not surprising since we have hardly fifty workers out of two hundred and forty left; it is doubtful whether the contracts can now be fulfilled. Séjourné protests in La Rochelle and refuses all future responsibility. He manages to save five young men *in extremis* by putting them down as cement makers and pretending their help is essential.

Empty places on the teams, mourning in the village and at work, this memorable twelfth of July has shattered morale. We don't think we'll last much longer in Esnandes.

Defying the decree punishing with death any man who does not turn over all his firearms to the authorities, many Esnandais, obeying their centuries-old instinct for cheating and avarice, prefer to risk their lives rather than give up their old hunting guns and have hidden or buried them. Six men, however, including Fougeroux, have been informed against and subjected to a thorough search: Nothing is found. Everyone promptly suspects a certain mussel grower but it is only after the Occupation that a light can be thrown on this affair, thanks to the anonymous letter carefully preserved in the Town Hall's archives. To everyone's consternation, the accuser is none other than young Goubert, the son of the new mayor and Christiane's fiancé. I suspect his parents had influenced this handsome, sickly, and irresponsible young man with their pro-German attitude. While his sister was flirting with a German customs man, who boarded with them, the brother would enjoy trying on his uniform, then having himself photographed and even showing these photos to friends. Everyone in the village knew Mayor Goubert's political views, of course, and that he preferred Pétain and the "New Order" to the Allies, for fear of the Communists. His wife went so far in her taste for Germans that, along with some of the most influential women in the village, she offered them sheaves of flowers when they ran away from Esnandes by commandeering or stealing a number of cars.

There is no more work at the site. Tonton and I wander about like two lost souls. Jean and his truck are gone; the reign of Jojo, the little hunchback, begins.

Jojo, the son of rich farmers near the Loire, his pockets stuffed with money, is the driver of a van of Séjourné's that is spending its time in a garage while Jojo is spending his in the bar paying for rounds of drink, something to make him popular among the Esnandais. One forgets the deformity of his body, struck as one is by the extraordinary beauty of his face; little blond curls, one rebellious lick, vertical folds crossing an archangel's forehead, long, curving eyelashes, and, especially, eyes of a turquoise-blue and a disarming candor. But their look seems broken, turned inward, blind. Does this Quasimodo blame the world for his imperfection? For one feels uneasy at the sight of this fallen angel, this prince of darkness whose soul is black, whose heart bursts with envy. Jojo hates all his co-workers.

When the work stops, Séjourné's van is suddenly repaired and Jojo goes off alone, without bothering to take Tonton or me, on mysterious and personal errands for Séjourné, some Esnandais, and himself.

In spite of my refusal, Séjourné forces me to replace the warehouse keeper, who is going on a holiday: "This is a key job, you must let no one in, including myself. This is an order," he tells me; which doesn't stop him from defying his own command the very next day by coming in despite my protests, followed by an escort. Then I learn that the head mechanic has always held a second key to the doors.

The warehouse is next to the smithy and opposite the sawmill. I already know that anyone can get in. I had been the first to look there for electric wire, inner tubes for bicycle tires, and other desirable articles.

My new job starts with an inner conflict: Whom will I betray? For, with the best will in the world, I cannot be neutral. While Séjourné has my word, my comrades expect me to return past favors: Tradition demands it. Is it for me to change old customs and become a Fafner watching over German treasure?

All these problems, however, are soon resolved. Through the little door, I am always being asked for supplies, the places and even names of which I sometimes don't know; I then have to let people in. Since I cannot pour certain liquids without help, I invite the demander into my sanctuary. And since there are no signed chits, how can I know whether the supplies I give out are going to a work site or to a farm? So why follow instructions if all control is impossible anyway? This doesn't stop me, though, from feeling uneasy and guilty.

What a grim stay in that dark, dank cave where I live in the company of mice! It is a chore that brings me nothing but unpleasantness since Séjourné later holds me responsible for all things having disappeared before, during, and after my tenure.

I am now the watchman perched on top of the water tank and must give warning of the Germans' arrival. Suspended between earth and sky, I endure tortures. On an icy night swept by the north wind, I am so lightly dressed that, frozen and half fainting, I count the seconds.

Peace in the sky, murder on earth. While groups of stars shine in the firmament, projectors carve a violently lit rectangle on the cliff: a purgatory. It is a Dantesque vision, with the damned leading a death dance. My plunging view shows them to me, emerging from clouds of cement that choke their throats and make them cough. Their eyes are wide open, their faces coated with such a thick white layer that when, exhausted by his effort, one of these wretches wipes his forehead, a dark mark remains; it looks like blood, like a wound.

The fever of the first castings has completely subsided; no one cares, not even the Germans, who don't bother to show up. Since our team is not numerous enough, that of the Grands Travaux de Marseille, equally decimated, comes from Villedoux to help us.

In the morning, a human rag, I have barely the strength to drag myself home where I'll stay in bed for two weeks, trembling with fever.

The submarine base of La Pallice is being bombed more and more often. Already during our last visit, we had barely arrived back when we saw, from Villedoux cliff, a violent bombardment. The destruction from the last Allied raid is such that our help is urgently requested. This is understandable, considering the extreme importance of the base, the shortage of workers, and the fact that our work is run by the Christiani and Nielsen Company who, together with the Grands Travaux de Marseille and Grün and Bielfinger of Hamburg, make up the Porta consortium.

When, cured, I come back to the sawmill, I am sent off to La Pallice where my comrades have been clearing for two weeks. While this work was only supposed to last for a few weeks, it drags on into three long months. Our *Ausweis* are stamped with *"Kriegsmarinewerf"* ("War Navy Work site"), which allows us into the port. And every morning at a quarter to five, two buses come to take us to the little station in the La Pallice suburbs where we catch a workingman's train.

My first view of La Pallice harbor is grim: All has been powdered into dust except reinforced concrete constructions—the shelters, the lock, and the base itself made invulnerable by more than twenty feet of concrete covered with sand. As for the buildings all around, nothing is left but ruins. Before the war, I had liked ruins because they added a historical interest to the landscape, made it more picturesque and romantic. The patina, the stones covered with moss and ivy pleased me. But now, in the midst of the rubbish, I am seized with horror as I realize that the beauty of the past is the calamity of the present. All these ruins around me are hideous wounds, our own wounds, our blood, our suffering, our stumps, our cemeteries.

How, I wonder, can human beings live in this hell without going mad? Isn't the very indifference I am beginning to feel a sign of my decrepitude? We walk among sheds burst open, exploded beams, headless cranes, pieces of wall defying all ways of balance. It is all senseless, formless! We go about in a labyrinth of never-seen amalgamations, of monstrous couplings, of hideous entanglements! This boat I see pushed into a *bouée* could have been invented by the diabolical mind of Hieronymous Bosch! Huge boilers in dreadful clusters hang from impossibly weak scaffolds; forests of burnt iron have come up to replace factories; blocks of stone, like tartar on a shell, cover the open roofs; surrealist doors open on emptiness. . . .

In this hallucination, in this jungle of iron, stone, and wood, paths have been cleared for the human ant heap.

At the heart of the pirate's nest, we lead a difficult life; forced to conform to the Germans' discipline, we hear only their detestable language and see only the hated enemy. Now we realize how much we have lost. Yesterday, we lived in France, in Esnandes, at home. Today, the drawbridge once crossed, the heavy iron gates once closed upon us, we are sequestered in a German prison; we are in exile. The lock crushes us with its huge size, the defensive balloons look like elephants, and, on the water, we see the warlike activity of the submarines coming in or going out on a cruise with their crews saluting.

Sad days in which men are twisted in the childbirth of a new order. The war that in Esnandes seemed so distant has suddenly come closer. We are now exposed to frequent bombings and go down into shelters when we hear the alert sounding. The twelve hours spent among the Germans, added to two hours in the often-late buses, leave us no time for ourselves. Having left Esnandes at the break of dawn, we return at nightfall.

The submarine returning from a cruise crosses first the front, then the back port, linked by the lock that the cement screen is supposed to protect; it then arrives before one of a dozen huge doors apparently belonging to a mammoth garage. This is the base. One of these steel curtains is raised, lets the submarine through, then comes down. The ship is now safe in a box half full of water. This box, which is also a dry dock, can hold one large or two small submarines.

One day, unable to resist temptation, I sneak around the base. First, with a friend, I walk down the main street, part quay, part boulevard, part waiting room. On our left, the bows of the subs are lined up; I can count up to six. On our right are several stories of workshops, offices, electric plants, and even a hotel, we are told, for grounded crews.

In the intense activity, no one pays any attention to my friend or me. A deafening din fills this temple of war, for the sound, unable to get out, echoes everywhere. Workers and trucks go about, the hammers bang on the subs' hulls, the welding torches give out machine-gun-like bursts, and, louder than everything, the stentorian voice of a huge loudspeaker keeps pouring out that same "Merry Widow Waltz" so dear to German hearts.

A painter is required to copy three signs; a few minutes later, armed with supplies, I am installed in an empty room. A window separates me from my comrades, who are working under the rain. Through the broken pane, I hear the pulsing of the site, that dreadful noise made by the drills' crackle, the humming of the human hive, the squeaking of the carts to which are added the moaning of the cranes, the clattering of the chains, and the strident whistle calls.

The Babylonian scaffoldings make me think of Piranese, especially the rising perspective of a temporary wood stair leading to the top of the lock screen. Since my window is almost at ground level, the workers going up shrink rapidly and disappear suddenly into the sky.

The little building with the Porta offices in which I now find myself has miraculously escaped destruction. A thin cardboard wall separates me from German engineers whose voices I can hear. Sometimes at noon my nostrils smell the delicious odor of roast pork. Alone from morning till night. I see only the watchman, Muhammed, an Algerian.

Solitude and idleness are more depressing here than at the saw-mill. There, at least, I had the view over the marshes and could move about, even visit the Fougeroux. My instinct still tells me to hold on. When my nerves are on edge, and in order to stretch my legs, I go looking for my three daily cigarettes that nonsmoking men resell. They cost me the pretty sum of eighteen francs, or two hours of work, and, while I offer myself this luxury, I cannot go beyond it.

My three signs reading "*Grün und Bielfinger*" have long since been finished. But since no one comes to ask for them, I start others to have something to do, trying to work against time and to make them perfect. I even manage to get other signs from some workshops to paint anew and, all day, I stultify myself copying words like: "Workshop," "No Smoking," "Entrance Forbidden."

Having found out I am a painter, Chief Engineer Battenfeld decides to have me do his portrait. He starts by asking what I will charge, I naturally say nothing, he then invites me to lunch alone with him and even goes so far as to promise I will be freed from the Todt Organization because of my age.

I start with a life-size charcoal drawing depicting him in full military glory: Nazi uniform, armband, helmet, and decorations; he is very pleased with it at the end of the first session. But things are, alas, soon spoiled. Messengers keep interrupting our meetings to request his presence elsewhere and I spend my time waiting for my model. Little by little, I stop seeing him until, on the third day, he comes accompanied by a young and pretty woman. The couple look at the portrait for a long time and keep on whispering. I suppose their reaction is not very favorable since Battenfeld disappears for good. And yet, there he is in his office behind the wall. I hear him speaking and giving orders, even whistling, when he is alone, always the same tune—much to my surprise, it is that popular song of World War I: "It's a long way to Tipperary,/It's a long way to go. . . ." Who is he? A German or a disguised Englishman, a spy? There are whispers that the base was sabotaged by a British agent who has since been shot.

As Battenfeld's painter, I enjoy complete immunity. No German can give me orders. My wait for an invisible patron puts me in a privileged position.

The sirens of the ships are so many invitations to the open spaces, invitations to travel that start me dreaming. Their strident cries bring me to the quays where, for lack of freedom, I pace back and forth like a caged lion.

Existence becomes a burden, routine weighs heavy. For years now, my painter's eye hasn't had the joy of seeing color, strong, lively, varied color. All has become grey or khaki, uniformly alike, all is hidden, all tries to go unnoticed. Like the prisoner in his cell looking for a little bit of sky, I search for something red or yellow or purple, and when I finally discover a rusty *bouée* covered with emerald seaweed, and then a tug with a smokestack where you can still see the original color, my eyes fill with tears.

Last week, the Esnandes work site was closed. Where will we go tomorrow? While the present is dark, the future can easily be worse. Wouldn't it be more prudent to hold on to the neighborhood of my village by volunteering either for La Pallice or for the Grands Travaux de Marseille working in Villedoux?

My wish is granted, the miracle has happened. As of November 24, 1943, I will never again see La Pallice or the Todt Organization. An enormous abscess on my spine nails me to my bed like a butterfly pinned inside its box. But physical pain is nothing compared to the joy of my resurrection! My convalescene will take five weeks during which, gradually, I will become, once more, a human being.

In the meantime, Séjourné and company leave Esnandes for the Île d'Oléron; I find this out only when I go out again for the first time and see no trace of the Todt Organization. My memory of them now seems like a nightmare. The village and I become again what we were before. An insurmountable disgust for Todt, for slavery, for the Germans fills me. Encouraged by the mess that prevails, I am told in the registry office at La Rochelle that once my hospital visits are over, my insurance no longer valid, I can hide at the Fougeroux and become a deserter.

Chapter 12

Return to Liberated Paris

1944—1946

A FEW MONTHS LATER, with the entire male population of Esnandes I was again mobilized, but this time by the Wehrmacht, to dig trenches. In fact, paradoxical though it may seem, I felt relieved. I no longer had to hide, I was a deserter no longer. Two mornings a week were mere child's play. The old soldiers who watched over us, Poles, Czechs, or Lithuanians, would sit down when we arrived and pay no attention to us. For several weeks, I lazed near an abandoned farm by the sea called "Breaking Waves" from which, in the distance, one could see the roof of Georges Simenon's villa.

Since mussel growers were feeding the Charentes population and lost a lot of money every time they missed a tide, they were authorized to send replacements to whom they left their knapsacks and pay. I made it my job to be one of these replacements and, from a chore, it became a way of exploiting the Germans. Since I spoke the language, it was up to me to write the names—some twenty—in the register. The Germans checked only the names, not even the number of men drafted for the day. This indifference permitted me to write my name next to that of the man I replaced, so that I could receive two or three times the pay at the end of the month. I had a setback, however, when a mussel grower whom I was supposed to be replacing saw me in Esnandes one day when I had returned early. He never again required my services, nor did the other growers.

The few Germans who occupied the blockhouse were old and nice to us, while we were distant and cold. They couldn't understand why we weren't on their side, especially since they had won. It was in their house that I had the most beautiful present of my life: on July 10, 1943, the Allies landed in Sicily. After the few trenches were dug, the Germans asked me to decorate the white walls of their rooms, which I did for a few weeks with the help of Cossar, the carpenter. I painted a Churchill tank, a French cruiser, an American plane, and a gun.

In the meantime, the war to liberate France was coming closer. Royan was taken, but had been so badly damaged that, in order not to destroy one town after the other, the front between the partisans and the Germans stopped between Charron and Esnandes. The planes, diving, burned up the railroad stations, bombed out trains and tracks; the guns roared and, at night, in the marshes, we could see tracer bullets. For weeks some farmers were unable to get their cows in the marshes. One day the Germans in Esnandes got drunk at Chocolat's and became nice, realizing their time was short. All the customs men ran away, stealing or requisitioning the mussel growers' cars. But, as nothing happened, these same Germans became arrogant again. Soon, however, we began to run out of food; Esnandes was part of the besieged, fortified camp of La Rochelle, and it was in the Germans' interest to let go all those who wanted to: pregnant women, old people, children, sick people, and foreigners. They would give a pass and eight hundred francs per person for traveling expenses. This arrangement was ratified by the Germans as well as the Free French Forces. For several days, I debated with my conscience about where my duty was: to stay with the Fougeroux or to return to the recently liberated Paris and think of my future. Finally, I joined Gisèle and Gégé, whom their parents were sending to stay with Christiane, now Madame Menantaud, in Jonzac. In the La Rochelle station, we saw our first train with French officers in uniform, a sight we hadn't seen since 1940. There were stretchers with wounded men, prisoners were exchanged, there were nurses with old and sick people, pregnant women, and children; then the train started while hundreds of handkerchiefs were waved. It was a moving moment of separation between those who were recovering their freedom and the rest, prisoners with an uncertain future. Two kilometers farther, the train stopped, the Germans got off, partisans hiding under the embankment got on, checked passes and arrested a few collaborationist women, whose hair they cut off. I was finally in Free France. Soon, in Niort, Gégé and Gisèle changed trains. It normally took seven hours to go from La Rochelle to Paris; now it took three days, with the compulsory detour to Limoges. There, among thousands of travelers, at night in the station I came across Jean Ozenne, who was going from Paris to Royan, where his family home had been destroyed. It is impossible to imagine what the railroad system looked like then, sabotaged by the French to stop reinforcements from reaching Normandy. The tracks were torn off, twisted, intertwined, the stations and switching cabins in ruins, there were hardly any carriages. One would sometimes have to walk for several kilometers with one's suitcases. When we got to the flooded Loire, since all bridges were destroyed, we were transferred in boats.

Where did I spend my first night in Paris? I cannot say. Not in Léon's apartment, anyway. It had been sublet long ago. Madame Bouché, owner of a well-known gallery in Montparnasse, who was interested in my work, asked Jean Lurçat, who was away, if she could put me up in his studio at the Villa Seurat. She even suggested I join Lurçat in Cahors, where he was the director of the evacuated Gobelins tapestry workshops but I refused, having little taste or talent for the decorative arts. I thus spent my nights in the second floor of the painter's villa—the first was separate and sublet—and my days with Anatole's son, André Schaikevich, and Aunt Varia, his mother. They were penniless and living in a tiny basement that one reached by going down the stairs of the courtyard of a private house. This in no way stopped them from dispensing a typically Russian hospitality, greeting all comers and discussing ballet and dancers far into the night. Besides Larionov, Gontcharova, and other Russians, I often saw André's younger half-sister, the classical dancer Nina Tikanova, accompanied by a man named Stalinsky.

André and I were linked by a deep friendship in spite of our age difference—he was eight years younger than I. I had seen little of him in Russia, or in Paris where he had arrived very late, after his grandfather's death. While André was a typical Schaikevich, a man distinguished by his origins, his manners, and his looks, so Nina Tikanova, the child of a notorious Bolshevik, was simple, charming, open, and 100 percent Russian. An intimacy close to incest soon joined these two loving orphans. What a miracle that André should still be alive in spite of his advanced tuberculosis, and Nina also, though she kills herself with work.

My stay at the Villa Seurat was, alas, very short. The winter that year was particularly harsh. It was freezing cold, it often snowed, and houses had not been repaired for a long time. One night, at three in the morning, a water pipe burst: It was an inundation. The water started pouring down the staircase. Nothing could stop the flood, the phone wasn't working, the people downstairs were away. When I found the water valve in the garden, it was frozen solid. In the empty street, desperately, I looked for a policeman, a fireman, found no one. So, unable to do anything, since all was lost anyway, I went home, settled down on my couch, which had become an island, and, exhausted by emotion, fell asleep. At dawn, I ran to Madame Bouché to ask for help. As for Lurçat, I don't think he ever forgave me the catastrophe. That very evening, André talked his concierge into allowing me to spend the nights secretly in the room of a maid, who was away. That is how I started living in the Hôtel de Broglie, 80, rue de l'Université, and also to paint in André's basement with a little miserable light coming through the airhole. I sat on a big table, which filled up the room, my canvas leaning on the back of a chair, with André and his mother chatting next to me or behind the partition where their mattresses were. I exchanged a painting for a raincoat made in Stalinsky's rubber factory, shared with my family the food and warm clothes that, thanks to Virgil Thomson, I received from New York. And finally, money orders came, the product of numerous canvases sold by Julien Levy during the war. Summer was coming. I went off to paint in Brittany.

Carnac was a beach used by middle-class people, surrounded by fields, lines of dolmens, marshes, and salt marshes. To go to La Trinité, I would walk along the wild coast, cross sand banks and a little estuary with water up to my shoulders. The Quiberon retrenched camp had just been liberated; numerous French corpses were found in the fort. There were still barbed wires, mine fields and *blockhauses* that were too hard to demolish. American troops occupied the Hôtel Cumulus, German prisoners were building roads, and noisy groups of Resistance fighters (and who then hadn't been one?) would invade the hotel, coming by car for lunch.

I chose the Hôtel Atlantique for its view, its distance from the main beach, its old-fashioned look, and its pleasant owner, who soon became my friend. Old Madame Diamedo adopted me. She was an elegant, small Breton woman, all dressed in black, a World War I widow who had remarried and was bringing up the three children of her son, who had been killed in a bicycle accident: Marguerite, beautiful and wild at twelve, and the younger and inseparable Paulette and Jean-Pierre. I paid for my pension with a few paintings, ate in the kitchen with the family, felt everywhere at home before the season, painting on any floor, in any room. Every morning, a *sinagot* anchored before the hotel to deliver fish. And since meat was still difficult to get, we had an indigestion of shellfish. As for scenes to paint, they were not lacking, either in Carnac, in the Inner Sea, in the islands, or along the coast, which I explored on a bicycle. It was a memorable and very productive summer.

Return to Liberated Paris · 1944–1946

The second winter in Paris was very different from the first; life had gone back to normal. Eating a whole ham at Sherry Mangan's, being given a razor, cigars, soap by Philip Claflin, an American officer, no longer seemed like magic. Virgil Thomson, reinstalled in his Quai Voltaire apartment, would invite me for meals at Larue's with Mary Garden and Maurice Grosser. At his cocktail parties, I sometimes saw Arp, Janet Flanner, and many American women. One of these bought one of my paintings of the Île de Seine. I had a show in one of the best Right Bank galleries where Balthus, Dali, Bérard, etc., also showed. I even arranged a double contract with the owners, Renou and Pierre Colle on the one hand, and Julien Levy on the other, dividing my whole production between the two for a certain sum. For I wanted still to show in Paris, where I was known and respected, as well as New York, where my work was selling better and better.

Vera and Gregory Schaikevich returned from their temporary exile in Lyon, Claudia and Anatole from Arcachon. Anatole saw Nina Tikanova dance and, full of enthusiasm, thought he had discovered a new star; he had her audition, inviting Lifar and some famous critics. Unfortunately it was a failure, after which Nina, discouraged, gave up her career, and opened a dance school, which did extremely well.

André and his mother were luckily able to emerge from their basement into the light of day and occupied three maid's rooms in the same house, living now under the roof. With the sky, the chimneys, the top of the courtyard's three facades, the flowers, plants, and pots on their windows, some antique furniture, paintings, engravings, and books, a maid now—the Italian Josephine—working across the narrow passage in the tiny kitchen, life for these two formerly handicapped beings became a dream and the apartment itself a cozy nest with which they fell in love.

A little later, I, too, left my hiding place, became their neighbor on the same floor and saw their windows from mine. The kitchen of an apartment below became vacant and I was allowed to make it into a studio apartment. I had a huge brick fireplace torn down, put in a tiny bathroom, had a closet and shelves built by a carpenter of genius, since there wasn't a single straight angle in the room, but had to use the antique toilet outside in the passage. Next to me lived the composer Joseph Cosma and opposite a lush blonde who was the mistress of a member of Parliament. I finally had my own place, was independent, and yet lived with my family.

I went back to Carnac the next summer. My canvases were better now: large sizes, more spontaneous execution. Of all my excursions, the most memorable was that to the tiny Île Molène, so-called after a nocturnal butterfly. A lot of friends and acquaintances came to see me there during the season: Lorna Lindsley with Stalinsky, Sherry Mangan with a horrible woman, Jean Bertrand with a little street-Arab who later stole his silver, Olivier Picard, Nina. All the men were jealous of a courturier who arrived with a magnificent black woman. I saw the first bikinis.

Back in Paris, I was taken up with my request for an American visa; the formalities took months. The Consulate was always crowded, and I felt I was trying to scale impassable walls. While I easily obtained affidavits from Julien Levy and my brother, who guaranteed my upkeep for three months in the United States, I had much more trouble with my French documents: Each depended on another and so on ad infinitum. I felt lost until the day Virgil Thomson accompanied me, introduced me to a young woman employee, and convinced her to take care of me. It wasn't that I was dying to see the New World; on the contrary, I had roots in France and was reluctant to leave. I was doing it out of duty, for my career, to meet my clients, consolidate and expand my gains.

When I was finally given a visa on the Russian quota, I had a new difficulty, that of finding a ship. Too many people were leaving for the small number of cargo ships, each of which took only ten passengers. Several maritime agencies had been trying unsuccessfully for several weeks when, one day, I ran into Vittorio Rieti on the place de l'Opéra; and I believe it was he who helped me. I left for Brest, found it totally destroyed, with only a few pieces of wall still standing. I took passage on a Liberty ship with eleven other passengers crowded in the stern cabin. It took us thirteen days to reach New York, and there my new life was to begin.

Index

Index

Index

Index

Index

Index

Index

Vichy government, 213, 221

Viot, Jacques, 137, 138, 140

Virchbalovo, Russia, 41

Vuillard, Jean Edouard, 106, 108, 110, 111

Wadsworth Atheneum, 175

Walter, Serge, 96, 164

Warroquier (painter), 122

Weinberg, Jim, 17, 23

Wescott, Glenway, 135

Wheeler, Monroe, 135

Wiener, Nora, 144

Wiener (pianist), 131

Wiesbaden, Germany, 27–30

Wilde, Oscar, 63

Windham, Dick, 138

Wishnegradsky (banker), 50, 64

Wohmlich, Charlotte (Madi), 7, 11, 16, 19, 22, 25, 29, 35, 47, 48, 97

Wood, Christopher, 131

World War I, 73–76, 86

World War II, 191–268

Wtorowa, Vera, 144

Yudenich, General, 93

Zack, Leon, 125

Zaharoff, Sir Basil, 93, 101, 135

Zavalevich (tutor), 73–74

Zborowski (art dealer), 107, 127

Zola, Émile, 64

Zuleika, Princess, 80, 86